20-10-24

– VOLUME TWO –

WE WERE EAGLES

THE EIGHTH AIR FORCE AT WAR

– VOLUME TWO –

WE WERE EAGLES

THE EIGHTH AIR FORCE AT WAR

DECEMBER 1943 TO MAY 1944

MARTIN W. BOWMAN

AMBERLEY

First published 2014

Amberley Publishing
The Hill, Stroud
Gloucestershire, GL5 4EP

www.amberley-books.com

British Library Cataloguing in Publication Data.
A catalogue record for this book is available from the British Library.

ISBN 978 1 4456 3366 4 (hardback)
ISBN 978 1 4456 3378 7 (ebook)

Typeset in 11pt on 13pt Sabon.
Typesetting and Origination by Amberley Publishing.
Printed in the UK.

CONTENTS

CHAPTER 1

The Day Before Christmas 1943

I was still caught up in the adventure of war and could equate many things with stories I had read. As a kid I was an avid reader of anything on WWI and the flying aces. By now most of us had at least one mission in so we had been initiated in combat and entitled to a little swagger. Although not quartered in a battle-scarred French chateau we did have a bomb damaged roof in the shower building, a combat crew club and within a couple of miles there were two pubs. One was 'The Red Fox' and the other 'The Black Swan' wherein the Packer Crew had a Christmas dinner including roast pheasant and champagne, vintage 1913.

Even closer was an estate converted billet for twenty-three bonnie Land Army girls, all of whom are spoken for. We met them the second night at the Nissen hut next to the road. Several of the girls were cycling to their quarters. We chatted a moment and they continued onto their billet. I yelled after them or I should say after this blonde beauty, "We'll meet ya at the choich at seven thoity" in my best New Yorkese.

They showed up and I began a romantic interlude with Jeannie with the light blonde hair. The girls worked in the surrounding fields and used to wave as we taxied out to the runways. They confided that they knew when we were going on a mission by either the early takeoff or the length of runway it took to get off the ground.

What a war ... mission in the morning ... dating in the evening ... bed and blankets at night, that was our theme song. The only danger at night was a bike and bitters sortie to the local pub.

'December', W. J. 'Red' Komarek

'The day before Christmas and all was not quiet in the ETO,' Tech Sergeant Larry 'Goldie' Goldstein wrote cryptically in his Quonset hut at Knettishall. On Pearl Harbor day the nineteen-year-old trainee draughtsman with the US Coast and Geodetic Survey was lying on his bed at home in Brooklyn listening to a radio broadcast of a football game when the broadcast was interrupted by a news flash that the Japanese had bombed Pearl Harbor. Within two weeks his draft number was called. Just before entering the Army he met Rose Mandel, his first real serious romance and the girl that he wanted to be waiting for him when his service was over. They only had about six months of dating before he entered the Air Corps. Now he was the radio operator on Lieutenant Belford J. 'BJ' Keirsted's crew in the 563rd Bomb Squadron at far flung Knettishall in Suffolk. Keirsted was a strong, quiet man from Uniontown, Pennsylvania, a tough coal town. He had a dark, brooding look about him. He and his sister Dorothy had toured the country before the war as the ballroom dance team of 'Jan and Janis' (Belford and Dorothy apparently lacked pizzazz). He and co-pilot 'Ace' Conklin prodded the rest of the crew to achieve perfection and at the same time were also working hard to sharpen their skills. Cliff Conklin was a Jock from New Paltz, New York State. He had been a business student. When Conklin was assigned to Keirsted's crew he was crestfallen. He thought, 'I don't want to be with this crew – we've got a ballroom dancer for a pilot!' but Keirsted proved he had more on the ball than a set of twinkletoes. Quiet, reserved, he exuded a calm authority that was universally respected and admired. When they met their first ground crew chief and their own plane was assigned, 'BJ' asked him how many crews he had. He said 'you are my third, the other two went down'. 'BJ's' answer to him was, 'we will make it, you can mark it down'. We were not as sure as he was, but his self-confidence rubbed off on the rest of the crew.

'Goldie' had volunteered for flying status in Salt Lake City at a replacement depot. He was hustled off to aerial gunnery school even before he had a chance to rethink his decision but 'Goldie' and his GI friends were impressed with the glamour of flying and all that went with it, the silver wings of a gunner, the promotions and the flight pay. But all that was about to change. 'We kind of came up the hard way,' he recalled. Later, in combat his attitude was, 'If you got hit, you were hit. If you didn't, you made it. I could never see any point worrying about it.' E. V. 'Pete' Lewelling, the other waist gunner, was a good ol' boy from Zolfo Springs, Florida. The tail gunner, Bob Miller, was a lunk from Chicago, Illinois, and a loner. Howard 'Howie' Palmer, engineer, was from New Hampshire. He also was an ex-student and hailed from Boston. The ball turret gunner, Tech Sergeant Willie Suggs, came from South Carolina. Kent 'Cap' Keith, the bombardier, was a sheep rancher from near Ekalaka, Montana. Phil Brejensky, navigator, was also Jewish and from Brooklyn too. In training Kent Keith had given him the nickname 'Bloodhound' joking that there was a dog on his Montana ranch that could find his way home better than Brejensky. Jack Kings, waist gunner, from Huntington, West Virginia had never met anyone Jewish before. As a kid he fished for food. It was something to eat besides rice and beans. In the depths of the Great Depression his family was too poor to afford new shoes so they stuffed cardboard soles in the old ones.

The crew soon fell into routine flying practice, practice and more practice. It seemed that the 388th command demanded precision tight formation flying and we flew on many days. Tight formation flying brought more guns to bear and increased overall protection. Enemy fighters seldom hit good formation flying outfits.

A period of bad weather had prevented any missions being flown of late, but they resumed in earnest on Christmas Eve when the Fortress groups were despatched on a milk run to the Pas de Calais, where mysterious concrete ski ramps had been erected. Crews speculated what the concrete sites were, but British intelligence had discovered that they were launching sites for pilotless V-1 flying bombs, packed with explosive and aimed at London and its environs. It seemed that 'every plane in Britain was up' on Friday 24 December. Some 722 B-17s and B-24s were dispatched and they were escorted by 40 P-38s, 459 P-47s and 42 P-51s (from the IX Fighter Command). The 447th Bomb Group at Rattlesden, which was commanded by Colonel Hunter Harris Jr, a native of Athens, Georgia, who earned a degree from West Point in 1932, made its debut this day, as the twenty-sixth heavy bomb group to join the Eighth.

This was the day for which they had been intensely training. For those not awake (probably few of those scheduled for the mission), there was a wake-up call at 0730 hours. At each hut the CQ opened the outer door and then the light trap door, his flashlight beam piercing the dark as he went from bunk to bunk to rouse the men scheduled for the mission. It was hard to get out of their sacks. It was cold, a clammy cold, and dark. The occupants of each hut were given one bucket of coke a week for heating. One bucket just did not provide much heat. The clubs were kept warm but most of the fliers did not use these facilities a great deal. They were either flying or in their sacks or getting ready to get into them. After a trip to the latrine to take care of personal morning necessities, the men made their way back to the cold huts to finish dressing. Briefing was scheduled for 0900 hours. As they walked to the mess hall, there was, as there had been all night, a steady drone of engine noise as the ground crews made the final touch-ups to the engines to be sure they were at peak performance. There was one big difference at breakfast – fresh eggs – the first time since they had arrived in Great Britain. Combat crews were the only ones served fresh eggs, and only on the day of a mission. Up to this time they were served powdered eggs. The brown English bread did make very good toast. After breakfast, the crews made their way to the briefing room. There was a guard on the door and everyone was checked off as they entered the briefing room. With all crew members (210 men) in place, they were called to attention as Colonel Harris came into the room. There was a map of the operating area in Europe covered with a black cloth. An intelligence officer stepped up to the stage and removed the cloth. A black tape marked the route they were to fly. The extent of known flak range was shown as cloud-shaped areas on the map. Their route skirted these areas where possible. Their target was Noball No. 50 near Drionville, France, just across the English Channel. They were told the ramps were aimed at London and Southampton.

The crews were briefed about the weather, current, in route, at the target and at the base on return. The B-17s were to be loaded with GP bombs. The planned mission altitude was 18,300 feet. The 447th was assigned to fly the low group of the Fourth Combat Wing. The 385th would fly wing lead and the 94th was in the high group. The Wing would be the last wing in the 3rd Bomb Division to depart the coast. Twenty-one B-17s were scheduled to be airborne, but only eighteen were dispatched on the mission (the others were spares). Colonel Hunter Harris would lead the mission, flying with Captain Smith's crew in *Butch II*. Major Lloyd W. Sheppard would lead the high squadron in 42-31128 with Lieutenant William W. Brown's crew. Major George Y. Jumper would lead the low squadron in 42-31207 with Lieutenant Wayne B. Larson's crew.[1]

After the general briefing, the navigators and bombardiers met in separate rooms for their specialised briefing. The pilots and co-pilots remained in the main briefing room for their specialised instructions. The gunners departed to the equipment rooms to get suited up for the mission. When they were ready, they went on out to the airplanes to install the guns. When the pilot, co-pilot, navigator and bombardier arrived at their airplane, the gunners had all of the guns in place; the ground crew had the plane ready to go. They had worked most of the night to be sure that the plane was ready. The gunners were standing in a group, nervously talking.[2]

Larry Goldstein recalls:

We were called out rather late in the morning, indicating that it would be a rather short hop. We were briefed on a very interesting target. It was enemy installations on the French coast near Abbeville. The installations were supposed to be 'rocket guns'. At briefing we were told that there would be no flak. We were also told that three planes would have two external 500lb bombs besides the regular 10 500-pounders on board. Those external bombs would be armed before take-off. When we went out to the plane we were suddenly aware that we had drawn the short straw. It gave us a rather uncomfortable feeling to be aboard that aircraft. Flight Control ordered the three aircraft to take off first. Normally, our ground crews were blasé about the Group take-offs, but not today. Everybody was on the flight line to watch this odd occasion. We were number two plane to take off and as we started our roll down the runway we kept our fingers crossed. The '17 being the great aircraft it was lifted off okay and the sweat was over for the time being. Now all we had to do was face the flak and fighters.

On a flare signal from the tower at Rattlesden, Colonel Hunter Harris taxied out on the perimeter track followed by the other twenty B-17s and made his way to the head of runway 240. At 1130 hours British Double Daylight Saving Time, Harris started his takeoff, followed thirty seconds later by the second aircraft and then the rest of the 447th, taking off at thirty-second intervals. The planes took a heading to the west, flying a rectangular pattern 10 miles by 2 as they climbed. This rectangle was anchored by the Buncher beacon at the field. Colonel Harris' Fortress intermittently fired a two-colour flare to aid in assembly. When the group assembly was complete, the formation set course for a second Buncher beacon to make wing formation. The Fourth Wing headed for a Splasher beacon on the coast to take its place in the string of wings that made up the Third Division. The wings were spaced two minutes apart.[3]

Larry Goldstein continues:

The bomb run was made at 12,500 feet, which meant no oxygen. The target was hit right on the head and was completely demolished. The lead navigator took a wrong route home and we were almost knocked out of the sky going over the town of Dieppe. The guns opened up on us and were really on the ball as far as tracking us goes. We had quite a few holes but nothing serious. Good fighter cover but no enemy aircraft.

At Seething, Crew 64 led a twelve-ship section, as Alvin Skaggs recalls.

The target of the 448th was Labroge, where we were to locate and bomb any
launching site we could locate. As we searched the area for a target, it became
very obvious that too many different formations were assigned to too small an
area. It became quite hairy as formations of aircraft, with bomb bay doors open,
crossed over and under other formations. We were all relieved when Lieutenant
Elbert F. Lozes the bombardier said, "Bombs away, let's go home." This was an
easy mission for our second one but it had its heavy moments.

Ice Cold Katy in the 447th Bomb Group was flown by Lieutenant Bill Greenwell,
twenty-two, from Norfolk, Virginia, pilot of Crew 21 in the 709th Squadron, who
wrote an enthralling account of the first mission.

Ice Cold Katy and her green untried crew were one B-17 among the graceful
Flying Fortresses. *Katy* was a clone of the others except for some painted
markings and the name. But she was very special and different to those ten
excited men inside because their future rode with her and hers with them. The
men were quite different in age, background, education and experience, but all
were keenly aware of their interdependence. *Katy* was the right wingman of the
high squadron leader so I comfortably watched the lead plane out of my left
side window, much like looking at the side view mirror in an automobile. Glare
from the bright high altitude sun was an annoyance so I wore dark glasses to
protect my eyes. In fact, the crew was covered with clothes and equipment
such as flak vest, parachute harness, Mae West life jackets and sheepskin flight
suits.

The French countryside, coming in from the English Channel, was a beautiful
panorama of green and brown foliage pierced by occasional white chalk rises
and rolling fields chequer boarded by hedgerows. No sign of hostile force or
weapons of destruction were visible, only an occasional village dissected by a
meandering road. "Surely this wasn't a target for heavy bombers," I thought. But
it was a target because the Germans were constructing launching ramps for 'Buzz
Bombs' somewhere in that beautiful countryside. These were weapons that they
intended to use on London, England. Briefing officers described the launching
ramps as looking like a 'snow ski' lying on its side in the foliage.

The lead bomber located the target and turned toward it. *Katy* and the other
bombers followed in a winter sky as clear and blue as the terrain was green. *Katy's*

crew followed the usual routine. Every few minutes I called on the intercom for a crew report: "Pilot to crew. Check in." (Responses started with the tail gunner.)

"Tail gunner OK." (Bill Wilson, seventeen, from Independence, Missouri)

"Left waist gunner OK." (Ed Leighty, twenty-eight, from Baltimore, Maryland)

"Right waist gunner OK." (Al Cordisco, twenty, from Bristol, Pennsylvania)

"Ball turret gunner OK." (Harry Weintz, twenty-two, from Philadelphia, Pennsylvania)

"Radio OK." (James Moran, thirty-five, Chicago, Illinois)

"Top turret OK." (Jack Toomy, twenty-five, from Parkerburg, West Virginia)

"Bombardier OK." (Don Wilson, nineteen, from Pittsburgh, Pennsylvania)

"Navigator OK." (Randy Carle, twenty-six, from Essex Falls, New Jersey)

"Co-pilot OK." (Dinny Fotinakes, twenty-six, from East Moline, Illinois)

"Pilot OK."

The bomber formation began another turn and the bombardier called on the intercom: "We're at the IP turning on the bomb-run. Bomb bay doors open."

"Roger. Pilot to crew, OK ... Keep the intercom clear unless you see fighters, flak or trouble. Report only important things – no chit chat."

The lead bombardier aimed his bombsight and the autopilot turned his plane in response. The other planes followed in close formation attempting to get a tight bomb pattern on the target. Each plane in the formation would drop its bombs when they saw the bombs fall out of the lead's bomb-bay. Only the leader used the bombsight.

No anti-aircraft fire (flak) was coming up from the target area as the bombers reached the drop point and released the bombs. *Katy* (and others) rose upon release of the burden and the bombardier called out.

"Bombs away."

"Bomb-bay clear," confirmed the radio operator, who could see in the bomb-bay.

"Bomb-bay doors closing," continued the bombardier as he moved the door control to the closed position and the formation turned away from the target.

"Fighters at nine o'clock!" yelled the left waist gunner. (Think of the plane as a clock with the nose as twelve and tail as six.)

"Can you identify them?"

"Ball turret to pilot. That ain't no fighter. That's flak – Oh, shit, I just saw gun flashes in those woods." (The Germans held their anti-aircraft fire until the bomb release to avoid helping the bombers find their well concealed target. After the drop they had no reason to hold back.)

Katy's crew stiffened like a patient waiting for a Tetanus shot but continued their routine, only to be jolted by a deafening explosion and violent lurch to the right. Angry black bursts of flak appeared above the number three engine. The bursts were shaped like black boxing gloves thrust through a ring of black oily smoke. The blast raked *Katy* with jagged metal and concussion. She lurched to the right and fell out of formation, shaking from the blow. Crew members in back of the plane scrambled back to their positions and snapped on their chest pack parachutes, checking themselves for wounds. The bombardier and navigator were blown back into the flight deck companionway and lay in a scrambled heap of equipment and humanity, with blood on their suits. The nose bubble was shattered and pierced and there were holes in the plane's metal skin. Up in the cockpit, shattered Plexiglas was everywhere. The right side window (beside the co-pilot's head) was shattered and punctured; Dinny slumped in the centre aisle, restrained by his seat belt, equipment askew, sprinkled with Plexiglas fragments. My skylight had a big hole right above my head. I was slumped over the controls, flak helmet down over my face and a small dent on the right side of it.

The intercom soon became jammed with frantic calls from the green crew.

"What in hell was that?"

"…have damage in … parachutes? Should we … Are we out of cont…?"

"Clear the godammed intercom you bastards," screamed the authoritative voice of Jack Toomey, the crew chief.

"The pilot and co-pilot are out cold!"

"Oh shit. Who's flying the plane?" another voice called.

"…Said clear the intercom! Top turret to pilot! You guys OK?"

"Should we bail out?" interceded another voice but there was no response from the cockpit.

"I'm coming forward! Hang on sir!" Jack called as *Katy* continued to bank right.

Concussion and blow to the helmet stunned me and my co-pilot and practically knocked Dinny out of his seat.

Finally they both stirred! Pushing the helmet back slowly and recovering his senses, Bill regained control of the plane and increased power to rejoin the formation. He rubbed his head under the inner helmet and looked for blood. There was none. Then he noticed the chit-chat on the intercom and pressed his mike button.

"Pilot to crew, we've taken a flak burst. Cut the chatter and check in," I said weakly.

"Tail gunner OK. Glad somebody's flying this thing."

"Left waist, we've got a mess back here. Right side's full of holes, but we're OK."

"Right waist OK."

"Ball turret OK."

"Radio OK."

"Top turret OK but you guys don't look too good, sir." (He was standing right between the two pilots.)

"Navigator to pilot. Bombardier's been hit in the leg. He's wounded and bleeding. Don't know how bad it is yet, over."

"Roger," I responded and looked over at my co-pilot, who had not checked in. Then I called into the intercom.

"Dinny, you OK?"

"Think so," the disoriented co-pilot responded. He was brushing Plexiglas from his flight suit and feeling himself for wounds or blood. I smiled slightly, realising that I was doing the same thing.

Jack was checking both of us and helping get our equipment back in order. "Sir, you're hurt," he said. "There's a dent in your helmet..."

"Just a bump on my head. That damn helmet ... thought I was blind when it slid down over my eyes. Don't sweat me Jack, I'm OK. Go down and help Don. He's got a leg wound. I gotta get *Katy* back in the formation."

"Roger."

I was very concerned about Don Wilson because a serious wound in the high altitude cold could cause deadly shock. Should I forget the protective formation and drop down to a warmer altitude? I pulled back into the bomber formation while others worked over the bombardier's leg.

After several minutes the navigator called on the intercom. "Navigator to pilot, over."

"This is the pilot, go ahead."

"Looks like his leg was cut by a piece of Plexiglas rather than flak. We've bandaged it and the bleeding's stopped. May need a couple of stitches but it's not really bad, over."

"Roger, navigator, am still gonna get the medics to meet us when we land."

We were well on the way home, at first shocked by the experience, then jubilant about surviving the first mission. *Katy* was the only plane with serious battle damage and the first in the 447th to take enemy fire or have a wounded crewman. Coming off an emotional high, the crew was excited, happy, jovial, talkative, even proud of our battle damaged plane and anxious to show off the results of real combat.

Don insisted that his wound wasn't bad enough to report. Of course it was (no matter how slight), because he was the first man in the group to be wounded.

I dropped *Katy* out of the formation and called the base. "Hello Sinew. This is Hotshot 'C' Charlie approaching the base. I have wounded aboard. Request landing instruction, over."

"Hotshot 'C' Charlie; you're cleared for immediate landing on runway two-four-zero."

Jack fired a 'Red, Red' flare (indicating wounded aboard). *Katy* touched down and we noticed an ambulance at the end of the runway. We knew the procedure. The ambulance would follow us down the runway until we turned off and stopped. Then the medics would take Don off the plane. I slowed *Katy* and turned off and the protesting bombardier was gently but firmly carried away by medics, determined to follow through with their procedure even if the wound was slight. After all, it was the first (and only) combat casualty for the new Group.

We taxied back toward *Katy*'s pad on a taxiway lined with spectators looking at the first plane to return from a real mission with battle damage. I was pleased when the onlookers pointed to the shattered Plexiglas nose and flak holes, slowing even more so that they could examine *Katy* more carefully. I turned into a key-hole shaped parking space, spun the big plane around and shut off the engines. Then we joined the crowd that was examining the damaged right side.

"You sure made a mess of my plane," said Don Nafus the ground crew chief, as he approached. Don was a nineteen-year-old youngster from Cody, Wyoming.

"I made a mess of YOUR airplane Sergeant Nafus? One Jerry AA shell did that, just one. It damn near blew our heads off."

"Good God. I never realised they were so powerful."

"Bet your ass and that was a near miss. Whatya think a direct hit would do? That was light flak from two-four gun batteries…"

"And you got over two hundred holes in *Katy* and a wounded crew member. How would it be over Berlin for half-an-hour with 600 guns?" interrupted Don Nafus.

"I'm not hep on finding out right now, Don."

At the crew debriefing, Jack Toomey and Bill Greenwell raised hell about the breakdown in intercom discipline, until Don Wilson showed up with a big band-aid on his leg.

I looked him over and, with a sigh of relief, asked, "You gonna get a Purple Heart, Don?"

"They said I would, but ... Hey, this is Christmas Eve! Did you guys know it's Christmas Eve?"

One ship bombed Noball Target #32, the secondary target. Bill Greenwell made his landing at 1632 hours, with the other seventeen aircraft landing by squadrons: lead, high and low in order. As the landing squadron flew down the downwind leg, the squadron lead peeled off to the left followed shortly by the second airplane and so on until all six airplanes had landed. After all airplanes were on the ground, trucks began to pick up the crews to take them to the briefing room for de-briefing. After the crews had a shot of whiskey, a sandwich, some coffee or hot chocolate, all, except the whiskey, served by the Red Cross ladies, they talked to an intelligence officer to report as much as possible the events of the mission. The strike photos showed that the result of the 447th's efforts was rated 'good'. Upon completion of the debriefing, the crews went to the locker room to get out of their flight clothes. The navigators, bombardiers and the gunners then went to the armament shop to clean their guns. By the time these duties were complete, it was time for the evening mess. After supper the weary crew members made their way to quarters and collapsed on their bunks and talked about the events of the day.[4]

Altogether, 670 bombers dropped a total of 1,744.6 tons of bombs on twenty-three Noball targets without loss. Two B-24s crashed landed after they had collided on the mission. Eighty five bombers suffered minor damage and four crew members were injured. Four P-47s crash landed at their bases upon return. There was no encounter with Luftwaffe fighters.

VIII Bomber Command was stood down from Christmas Day until 30 December, when 658 heavies, escorted by P-38s and P-47s, bombed oil plants at Ludwigshafen near the German-Swiss border.

Wallace Patterson returned to Seething from another twenty-four-hour pass in Norwich. He wrote:

When we got back to camp today, we found out that the boys had raided France and started the plastering of the rocket gun installations we have heard so much of lately. The boys said it was a real milk run: no flak, no fighters and 12,000 feet, which meant no oxygen masks and fairly warm air. They bombed in elements of six ships and the only damage was to a ship that got in trouble near England and eight of the crew bailed out and the pilot and co-pilot landed her safely. This is Xmas Eve. We have the first whisky in the history of the club and lots of beer. We are in the new club, which is very comfortable and we have a new radio. All the boys are singing and playing Black Jack. We aren't going to raid tomorrow and there are rumours of a turkey dinner.

The rumours were true. We got up late and dinner was at 12.30. There were hard candies, a free package of Camels and oranges; then roast turkey with dressing and cranberry sauce and for dessert apple pie and real cheese. After lunch we were going into town to try to go to the Red Cross party, but we were notified of an alert, so couldn't go. In the afternoon Bill and I rode our bikes into Bungay, but everything had just closed and there was hardly a soul in the streets. We got back in time for me to pick up my wine ration. I got a quart each of sherry and port for me and Rod gave me his as he never uses the stuff. After supper we were notified that the alert was off; so into town we piled, only to find the pubs jammed and all the shows and the dance closed. We sweated out the bus home very disgusted.

Bill McCullah was in a homesick, pensive mood on Christmas Day and he wanted to be alone. Not interested in the sumptuous Christmas dinner prepared at the combat mess, he caught the shuttle to Norwich. Getting off the bus, he read a poster touting a British–American get-together at the cathedral. Having no plans for the day, he walked to the cathedral and climbed a centuries-old staircase leading to the second floor. He was awed by the deep wear undulations made by thousands of souls who had climbed the steps before him. At the top of the stair, he entered a room with a large window, overlooking a broad expanse of lawn. Present were about twenty Americans with four elderly British gentlemen and two ladies. A small group gathered around a piano, singing carols. Two of the male hosts prepared crepes Suzettes, a finicky procedure and the first he had ever had. They sought to make them welcome. Amiable, jovial, hospitable, they did their best to entertain them but his heart was not in it. The crepes were delicious. That cold, damp day was a day of recollection where he thought of family and home. He vividly recalled staring out the window, wondering if he would ever again see home. He had flown one mission and had barely begun. Thousands of miles from home, that English Christmas was the loneliest day of his life. In the cathedral he thought long and hard about his chances for survival. The suddenness of the attack on the Fortresses en route to Osnabrück hung with him. What was worse, their Liberators were prone to blow up, far worse than

Fortresses! On that single mission he learned that if you wanted to live, time was your enemy.

'You had no time to piddle, putter or procrastinate. You must make a decision and move!'

McCullah avowed that if ever his plane were hit hard then he was 'outta there! No questions asked'. Once arrived at this decision, his anxiety was greatly relieved. He informed 1st Lieutenant Helander, who smiled when he told him. Next day McCullah went out to a B-24 and practiced turret exit. After five simulated quick exit sessions he was satisfied. He had it down to minimum effort with minimum time expended. His final act was crouching near the nose-wheel door, his hand on the red emergency release handle that would pull the nose-wheel door retaining pins dumping him into space. He relaxed and then forgot about it.

Saul Kupferman, in the 306th Bomb Group, recalls:

At Christmas 1943 British people near our base at Thurleigh invited individual GIs to go along to their homes for the day. A Donald Nicoll went all out and accepted two of us (myself and Kenny Norris, a member of my crew) to share the holiday with his family. Don and his wife Dorothy were in their forties and they had a little six-year old daughter Cynthia. We knew all about how the English folks were rationed and the shortages so we were prepared to go easy on eating and drinking. They couldn't have done more to make us feel at home. I took along a box of chocolates, which was obviously a special treat. They made it last for several days, rationing themselves to one each per day. I don't think 'Cindy' had ever seen chocolates before. After dinner I played darts with the father, who was a prison guard. On that first visit I remember the Morrison table shelter in the dining room and the threadbare towels which they couldn't replace because of the rationing. This was the start of a lifetime friendship and during the rest of my time in England I accepted the Nicolls' invitation to use their spare bedroom whenever I had passes. It was an escape from the military life and the home life atmosphere they provided I feel sure helped me to survive.

Thursday 30 December dawned with the roar of engines and twenty-five B-24s of the 448th began to taxi into position for take-off from Seething to hit the IG Farbenindustrie chemical factory at Ludwigshafen, a very long flight, about 1,100 miles. 1st Lieutenant Thomas Keene's Crew 55 in the 714th Squadron would fly their first mission. S/Sgt Brona D. 'Bo' Bottoms, of Newby, Texas, the twenty-one-year old assistant engineer and right waist gunner, recalls:

Lieutenant Keene told us in Herrington, Kansas, that he was going to carry us over to England, make our tour and bring us back. He was a great guy. Lieutenant James R. Bettcher the co-pilot was always smiling. 1st Lieutenant Smith or 'Relief Tube Smitty' as we called him was a darn good navigator. 2nd Lieutenant Edwin G. Moran of Detroit, the bombardier, was a regular GI. Grover 'Bing' Bingham was an old worn out honest to goodness engineer. William Demetrupoulis or 'Demo the Greek' was the radio operator and boy what a kid. Fred 'Kreeper' Krepser, the kid from Galveston was ball and nose gunner. George 'Sandy' Sansburn was the tail gunner. Charley 'Pappy' Blanton, of Fairmont, South Carolina, a good man, was left waist gunner.

We took off at 0830 and gained altitude over England and hit the French coast at 17,000 feet. I was so tense that I had turned the thermostat on my heated suit up as far as it would go, as the temperature was like 40 below. About 30 minutes after crossing the coast we were attacked by Fw 190s. They knocked one of our B-24s out and it had to turn around and go back. They made an attack on our plane but God was with us and we got through it. By that time I was burning up. My heated suit was extremely hot so I adjusted it back to a normal setting. We also saw flak over southern France and to our target. On the way out four Me 109s attacked our formation and got one B-24, *Consolidated Mess*. I watched it as six crew members bailed out before it burst into flames and disappeared. Gee, it was terrible. It was a long trip; 8 hours and 40 minutes. It was hell.

Staff Sergeant Francis X. Sheehan, right waist gunner on Lieutenant Alvin Skaggs' crew also saw *Consolidated Mess* go down.

Lieutenant Thomas Foster's crew #61 was flying our right wing in a very tight formation. Suddenly, a Me 109 appeared in a head-on attack with tracers streaming at our left side over and under our ship. Shells began to rake the front and top of Foster's plane. The Plexiglas on the top turret shattered and Staff Sergeant James Brant slumped over, fatally injured. At the same time, bullets tore through the pilot's compartment, apparently killing the pilot. It appeared that the co-pilot, Lieutenant Francis Rogers, took over the control and moved out of formation. The whole centre section above the bomb bay was aflame. We could still see crewmen in the waist position as the ship began to fade away from the formation. Several men managed to bail out only seconds before a terrific explosion caused their plane to completely disintegrate. It all happened so fast that no one had a chance to get off more than a few shots at the Me 109 as it dropped down and away. What was to be an uneventful mission turned into a tragedy, as we lost some very good friends. Suddenly, we realised that war is not only hell but dangerous as well. The German fighter pilot had our ship in his sight that day and his intention was to knock down the lead plane. Only God knows how such a sustained burst of fire could have passed over and under our ship and not have hit it. Our fellow comrades of Crew #61 paid the supreme price for glory.

At Seething that afternoon Wallace Patterson, whose crew were on stand down, patched a flat tyre on his bicycle and at four went to sweat out the landings. 'We could tell the way the boys landed that they were plenty beat up,' he wrote. 'Several crews saw Foster go down in flames and apparently three parachutes were seen dropping from his ship, which we had flown on a couple of practices.[5] Lieutenant Ray Gelling, flying *Sad Sack*, crash-landed in Germany and Lieutenant Abraham Kittredge fell out of formation after two engines were shot out.[6] Two more landed in Kent.'

There was no such happy outcome for the crew of *Stubborn Jean* in the 401st, who failed to return to Deenethorpe from the mission to Ludwigshafen. 2nd Lieutenant Traian Neag and his crew were thought to have been brought down by flak about twenty minutes from the target. Before the crew bailed out, the co-pilot, 2nd Lieutenant John B. England, shook hands with his pilot, said 'Good luck' and went to the forward escape hatch, which had been opened by the navigator, Elmer S. Santos, who went out first followed by England. Okey De Raimo, the bombardier, followed them out of the hatch. Neag and Howard P. Monzingo, the engineer, jumped out of the bomb bay and they were followed by Martin M. Hill, the right waist gunner, Benjamin Daskiewicz, left waist, and William C. Bardon, the radio operator. Bert Purwin, the ball turret gunner, and James E. Farrell, the tail gunner, escaped via the waist. Either England's or Bardon's parachute failed to open or they were killed on the ground but both men failed to show up when the other eight crew members were rounded up by the Germans and taken into captivity.

Staff Sergeant John W. Butler in the *Travelling Circus* flew his thirteenth mission that day, as left waist gunner in J .J. Collins' crew.

We took off at 0840. The weather was nice and clear and the visibility was very good. The temperature was only minus thirty-six. When we came in over the French coast, the navigator noticed smoke up in the nose but we didn't pay any attention to it. We were then at 22,000 feet. The smoke started to come back into the waist. We had the engineer going crazy trying to find the base of the fire. It gave you a funny feeling to know you had a fire on board but couldn't find it. I thought I would spend the New Year in France. We were 110 miles inside enemy territory when we had to abort. A lone plane was a really nice target for the Jerry pilots. They loved to meet up with you, as you made an easy victim. As we turned around we met up with a B-17 that was also aborting too so we flew formation back with them. When we crossed the coast of France we ran into some flak. Two bandits followed us for a way but they didn't attack us. We made it back to our base OK.

So too, 'BJ' Keirsted's crew at Knettishall, but his radio operator lost a very close friend, as 'Goldie' Goldstein recalled:

Men living together as closely as we did made us feel almost like family. To lose a friend and to actually see it happen was devastating to my crewmates and me. I had been with Tech Sergeant Daniel Letter since Gunnery School at Wendover, Utah, and all through phase training and into combat. Letter was the radio operator in 2nd Lieutenant A. W. Carlson's crew in *Satan's Sister*. On the bomb run the 388th ran into severe prop-wash from the Group ahead, causing the formation to bounce around. As a result, *Joho's Joker* slid in front of *Satan's Sister*, causing it to go out of control. As I looked up and out of my radio hatch I saw Letter's plane in the high group swing back and forth several times. Suddenly, it was on a wing and flipped over. It broke in half in the middle of the radio room, fell down and back. When my crew realised that this was a crew we had trained closely with, we immediately had a weak feeling in our stomachs. I have never lost a close friend before and it was not easy to take. Our morale was at its lowest point, especially when we returned to our barracks and saw their empty beds. We did not know whether they had survived the parachute jump, or had been killed [Letter, Carlson and four others on *Satan's Sister* were killed]. We did not have time to mourn their loss because our own survival was on our minds. It was about this time that I realised that this was a dangerous game I was a part of. Was the glory of being a combat crewman worth it? I never knew if I was a brave man, I had never been tested. Our crew never once discussed the possibility of our chances for survival, but I am sure that we all thought the same thing. When we first began flying together our goal was to not take chances and to put our faith in our pilots. 'BJ' kept repeating that we will make it and on one occasion when I saw another plane get hit and go down, I watched for the parachutes to open, I immediately felt sorry for them but just as quickly I found myself saying, better them then us. Self-survival can play mean tricks with the mind.

Kenneth L. Zeiger, left waist gunner on *The Squirming Squaw* in the 447th, flown by William H. Johnson, had an experience on this mission that he would never forget:

We were on our first mission to a chemical plant at Ludwishafen, considered an important target. It was protected heavily by flak and some fighters. During all this time to the target, my oxygen mask was gradually freezing even though I was squeezing it to break the ice crystals. When we were attacked by enemy fighters I was not squeezing the mask and it froze up enough so I could not get enough oxygen. I finally did not respond to oxygen check. After I did not respond to the third check, Lieutenant Johnson asked Elbert Williams, right waist gunner to check on me. When he tapped me on the shoulder, I swung and would have knocked him out the open window had there not been a gun in the middle of the opening. The problem had progressed by now to the point that I was fighting for oxygen and my life. It took two or three to hold me while they tried to hold my mask on my face as they broke the ice out of the mask. All during this I had gone through all colors: red, purple and now turning sort of black. When Johnson got this report, he pulled out of formation and dove from 23 or 24,000 feet down to 10 or 12,000 feet. In doing this he could have faced court martial or some penalty. When a person has a black colour, he is usually considered dead. Johnson would never tell me what, if any, discipline we got for leaving the formation. His philosophy was, I quote, "One for all and all for one." It took a hell of a lot to make this quick decision. He may have been thinking of this decision before.[7]

Missions were coming quite fast now and on Friday 31 December crews were given a dubious New Year's Eve treat with 'milk-runs' to airfields in France.

Robert 'Peck' Wilcox, the bombardier on *Iron Ass* in the 510th Squadron, 351st Group, at Polebrook, sat bolt upright in his bunk. The sergeant with his GI flashlight was awakening crews. He said, 'Lieutenant Wilcox, Lieutenant Freeman, breakfast is being served. Briefing at 0230 hours.' Wilcox shook his head, trying to clear the cobwebs and get awake. 'My gosh! I hadn't been in the sack very long,' he recalls.

> I had got back from Peterborough about midnight and had been on a mission over Germany the day before. I hadn't hardly figured on another mission today but oh well! Get these missions over with and back to the States. I had qualified for the Air Medal the previous day so I only had twenty to go.
>
> We met Captain Marvin H. Grupp, our pilot, and co-pilot at the mess hall and had our bacon and eggs with plenty of coffee and not much talk. About everyone figured we would 'sir down' on this, the last day of the year and almost everyone was planning a New Year's Eve party. I know Andy our engineer, Harold Long the assistant engineer and I were looking forward to going back to Peterborough for a gala New Year's Eve. In the briefing room was another surprise. A lot of high brass were there in their flying clothes and the briefing officer told us, "We're going on a milk-run to bomb the docks at Bordeaux. We'll be flying over water most of the way at 12,000 feet. You won't have to wear oxygen masks all the time and you won't have to wear the heavy flying suits until we get ready to go in over the target area. If clouds should sock in the target, we'll come back and hit the secondary target, the airport at Cognac. Major Blaylock will lead the mission. Colonel Hatcher [the CO] will be in the lead plane."

Larry Goldstein recalls:

> The 388th was assigned an airfield on the outskirts of Paris. When we were briefed, Colonel William B. David made a point that none of us was to spend New Year's Eve in Paris: "It's an order!" A little humour to ease the tension. However, we were told to expect heavy fighter opposition and as heavy flak, as the actual target was an aircraft engine plant and would be heavily defended. The flak was not as bad as we had been led to believe. We really hit the plant with everything. From the reports we heard later our bombing was excellent. Pictures showed all bombs on the target and none in the city. The French would be madder than hell if we did. The support was excellent and we returned with no battle damage.

For 'Peck' Wilcox, the trip to Bordeaux went well.

> It was good to do without flak so heavy you could get out and walk on it. We made our turn and went in over France and sure enough, the Bordeaux area was

covered with a thick cloud cover so we headed for Cognac. It wouldn't take too long to get there because Cognac is only about 75 to 80 miles from Bordeaux. The formation was in good shape and was pulled in close. There were some scattered clouds but no flak and no fighters. Up ahead I saw our target. Already the lead bombardier was sighting in on it and on we flew. I wondered why we weren't taking any evasive action. We were closing fast when, all of a sudden, all hell broke loose. The lead plane was the victim of a direct hit. Our plane was hit; the air was turbulent. A big hole had been blasted in the nose. I dropped our bombs but no one had a chance to look down. Planes seemed to be going down all over. The formation was shot to pieces, I would say. We had an engine on fire. We made a circle all by ourselves and we were all alone. I mean all alone. What was left of the formation had headed for England. Then it was Bender over the intercom. He said, "We will be unable to make it back to England. We are too far from Switzerland and the plane may explode at any time." So he gave the order to bail out. No one questioned it. I went out through the bomb bay after Freeman and Andy. I was a long way from home and I wasn't going to be in Peterborough for any New Year's Eve party.

Two of the twenty-five bombers that were lost were from the 614th Squadron in the 401st. *Hey Lou*, flown by 2nd Lieutenant Donald B. Lawry, was hit by flak and fighters on the mission to Bordeaux and went down just beyond St Catherine's Point in the English Channel. All that was found was wreckage and the body of 2nd Lieutenant James S. Dockendorf, the co-pilot. The names of the crew were posted at the Cambridge Military Cemetery at Madingley. *Flak Rat* was piloted by 2nd Lieutenant Homer E. McDanal, who, along with Major I. W. Eveland, flying as co-pilot, and two other members of his crew, evaded capture and returned to Deenethorpe weeks later. Eveland related the story of *Flak Rat*'s demise, which was pieced together by intelligence officers on the base.

Soon after we made landfall near Arcachon we experienced light flak and further damage in one engine. (The supercharger had already gone out on one engine). By this time we were under attack by German fighters. Since we were a cripple and could not hold tight formation, we were singled out for special attention and we were 'worked over' thoroughly from front to rear. Our 50 calibres made quite a chatter as they responded to each attack. We could also feel the 20mm's as they hit us – and something went through the cockpit above the din. Our gunners were busy – but not for long. Suddenly the steering column leaped back in our laps and the aircraft's nose went up. McDanal and I together managed to get enough downward pressure to bring her nose down, but there was no doubt about it – something was wrong. Our flight controls did not function. There was only one thing to do – so I gave the 'Bail out' order on the intercom. McDanal also hit the 'Bail out' switch on the panel in front of him. We received acknowledgement from the nose but not from the gunners in the rear. Then I realised that the intercom was out and the aircraft was alternatively heading nose down and nose up in spite of all we could do. Also the fighters continued to attack. I had a hard time getting McDanal to bail out. He seemed to delay too long (in his efforts to assist me with the controls) and I was mad! With no intercom he could not, or would not, understand. Finally, he disengaged his seat belt, oxygen, etc., and headed to the compartment below, where he would go out the bottom hatch. I had great difficulty getting disengaged because every time I tried to take a hand off the wheel the plane would head for the blue sky up position – or try to spin leftwards. After what seemed a lifetime (and what almost was), I also made it to the bottom hatch. The plane was almost inverted and it required all the strength I had to pull myself through the hatch and free of the aircraft.

The 448th's target was La Rochelle airfield, a Luftwaffe training base, in south-west France. Sixteen B-24s loaded with ten 500lb GP (General Purpose) bombs and 2,700 gallons of gas took off from Seething at around 0730 on this, the last mission of the year. Bill McCullah in Paul Helander's crew recalled that:

It was touted by briefing officers as a 'milk run' – a minimum effort. The Group would do it alone. We were always glad when we drew targets other than German but the mission deep into southern France would be an exceptionally long 1,200-mile trip. Again Crew 11 would fly No. 2 Group lead, first section. I attended bombardiers' briefing with Snyder. I would be the togglier-gunner in the nose turret. Again I had a seat up front. We flew the mission over water, deep into the Bay of Biscay to a point south of Cognac. There we turned east into France. Our run on the airfield would be from south to north. Because La Rochelle was an advanced fighter base, we expected them to come up. Many flying minutes ahead, we could clearly see the airfield. We banked into a slow left turn, beginning a long bomb run. It looked easy. It was a beautifully clear, sunshiny day, not a cloud in the sky. The surrounding scene was peaceful and serene.

Wallace Patterson adds:

The point at which we were to turn into our bombing run was of all places, Royan where I spent a summer over ten years before. We got near our first flak over the Brest Peninsula on the way down but it was too far away to harm us. We were all the way over dense cloud cover except for one large clear patch. As luck would have it the target was in the dead centre of that patch. The target was smoked up with bombs from previous groups when we started our run. P-38s were buzzing around, the flak was accurate as hell and very thick and we were right in the middle of it. Halfway down the run I saw at least fifty bomb bursts smack in the middle of the field and on some of the buildings and I watched the ack-ack guns flash around the edge of the field. I could not see where our bombs hit but as they left the ship I heard something hit the ship. We got found flak holes in the aileron, left rudder and right bomb bay door.

Bill McCullah continues:

Breaking my search area into quadrants, I systematically scanned the sky for fighters. All was clear. Returning my eyes to the front, the sky had changed. Five miles ahead of us, a slimy, greasy black blob hung over the airfield. It was a cloud, actually a wall, big and black, a solid mass and a textbook example of concentrated fire! In the clear sky around us it was out of context, out of place. It happened suddenly.

"Goddam it's flak!"

The realisation hit me. I jerked my body straight up on my seat, staring at it. We bored ahead, closing the distance. I donned my flak vest when we crossed the French coast. I had only to drop my left shoulder and the jacket would slide to the floor. I went through all of my flak procedures, door half-open, hunkering between my gun receivers, turning my turret to the right, lacing it. I knew it would be a bastard! I was as ready as possible.

Already fighters were attacking the rear of our formation. I could hear their positions called over intercom. There was an out of range Me 109 flying 2,000 yards to our left, parallel and dead level. He must have been calling our altitude to the ack-ack gunners below. Then we were into it! All that was missing was a brass band and a military drum-roll! I was breathing it; smelling it. We flew into heavy smoke. I could see fireballs from the centres of new explosions. Red and yellow centres framed against a dirty, black backdrop. Breaking out of smoke, we found ourselves at the leading edge of new explosions. There was no let-up. Ground gunners tracked us to perfection. 'To kill a snake, cut off its head and the body will die.' In a bomber formation, the lead element is the primary target. We were the No. 2 in the lead element. So far everything was OK. I again scanned the sky for fighters. Returning my gaze to the front, our No. 1 lead plane was gone. He was no longer there! "Where the hell was he?" I frantically thought. Shaken, I half-stood in my turret, peering downward. There he was 100 feet beneath us, burning, going down. The long Davis wing was disintegrating, breaking apart in slow-motion collapse. Everything but the nose turret and pilot's compartment was enveloped in flames. Fire was consuming the plane and crew! "Number one going down," I said; a redundant statement because Helander had seen it. "He's breaking-up and burning."

"Roger," said Helander.

The plane had taken a direct hit. There could be no survivors. At that moment, we became No. 1 lead. Snyder would drop the bombs. He was glued to his sight, tracking the target. A moment later, the plane flying our right wing took a direct hit. The slow-motion honour show began anew. It was a replay of the first. "Number 2 going down," I announced. The second plane was a real close-up. Flaming 100 yards, I watched the huge wing crumple from the tremendous heat and saw the thick aluminium alloy plate at the centre wing section melt and run like water! God it was awful!

"Bucket man going down.[8] He took a direct hit," Ray Giwojna, tail gunner, announced.

He was trailing us below, just off our right rear. It was all so close. Impossibly done on a bright, sunshiny day over Southern France. This was my first close-up of the true honour of war. It was terrible as I watched 448th airmen die in their planes.[9]

Having dropped our bombs, out of the target area, fighters attacked us in earnest. A Messerschmitt 109, out of range, angled toward us from the 2 o'clock position, acting as if he would attack. Seeing him early, I slewed my turret to pick him up but he veered, changing his course. My turret, hard against stops, would go no further. All I could do was watch. Snyder, seeing the fighter, hammered on my turret, shouting, pointing.

"Fighter, goddam it! Fighter!" he screamed.

I could hear him above our engine noise. I nodded. "I see him!"

Wallace Patterson wrote:

Going back, Bill Trunnell[10] adjusted the mixture a little too lean and the two starboard engines cut out and the ship fell into a steep dive to the right. Al

Northrup pulled it out all right but announced shortly after that we were nearly out of gas. We sweated hard over that as we were still over enemy territory. We struggled all the way back to over England, waiting for our fighters or theirs, neither of which showed up. Al had us buckle our chutes on and prepare to bail out but finally our distress signals connected with a fighter base and two P-51s came up and led us down through the overcast. We saw one field that was not ready for a landing, being under construction but we saw another farther off. Al made a beautiful landing on an uphill grass field much too short for a B-24. It was Worthy Down, a Royal Navy Fleet Air Arm training field. As it was late, they told us to spend the night.

Bill McCullah adds: 'Other than for landing at Seething almost out of fuel there were no other incidents. The mission had exceeded 11 hours and 20 minutes, the longest mission that we ever flew. Only two planes made it back to Seething – us and one other. As group lead, Helander thought it essential that we get back to debrief the mission.'

At Seething, two damaged B-24s were beyond repair and five others were repairable. *Bomb Boogie*, which was badly damaged when *Cold Turkey* exploded and riddled with 150 flak holes, crash-landed at Predannack. Both the pilots had carried their Class 'A' uniforms with them on the mission and they caught a train to London to welcome in the New Year. *Baby Shoes* was landed at RAF Brize Norton while *Crazy Mary*, damaged by flak, limped home and was put down at Yeovilton naval air station and written off. Short of fuel, *Lady From Bristol* only got as far as an airfield near Oxford, where Lieutenant Elmer Hammer's crew, who were on their first mission, spent a week as guests of RAF Mount Farm. Too badly damaged to fly back to Seething, the battered B-24 remained behind until after repairs were carried out. At ground school two days later, crews were told that they had not bombed La Rochelle at all but the alternate target, Cognac airport. And there were pictures to prove it. They also managed to bomb some French villages. Bill McCullah wrote:

Now whenever I saw the name 'Cognac' on a bottle, it transported me back to that day every time. The mission was a wake-up call. For the first time I got the picture. What we were doing was 'for real'. Why, I could get my Missouri ass shot off. What was different about Cognac? Why was that mission so bad? I had seen more people killed on our way to Osnabrück when the planes were crewed with strangers. But Cognac happened in our backyard. They killed our friends; people we knew. Cognac happened close; so close it could have been us! It could have been me! The briefers learned one thing for a certainty; "Cognac was no milk-run." We could continue to say, "Run for the roundhouse, Nelly! He can't corner you there." We had been in the roundhouse where locomotive engines were turned around. By the Grace of God, there sure enough had been no corner.

In his diary, Bo Bottoms wrote that 'at one minute into the New Year some of the men in our hut opened up their .45 pistols for seven shots each and it sounded like we were at war. Ha.'

Fog and rain prevented any further missions until Tuesday 4 January. Russell F. Beach in the 'Hells Angels' at Molesworth reported for the mission. However, Flight Operations showed that the engineer/waist gunner was still on grounded status after suffering badly frozen feet, hands and face on his thirteenth mission and they would not let him go. Beach had flown some tough missions, including the one to Schweinfurt on 14 October with Fred C. Humphreys' crew, all of whom were 'wonderful guys and no mistake'. Humphreys, who was from Paris, Texas, and the rest of the crew of *Sweet Ana* went to briefing, where they discovered that the target for over 500 bombers was the very important U-boat port and ship building facility at Kiel. Tech Sergeant Fred J. Janisch would take Beach's place as engineer on the crew.

At Knettishall the 388th briefing was earlier than ever before, with crews being awakened at 2 a.m. 'Goldie' Goldstein wrote: 'Most believed it was Berlin and started sweating it out.' However, the 388th was part of a diversionary force attacking Münster while the 1st Division hit Kiel and unescorted groups in the 3rd Division pounded targets in France. By now the crew had nicknamed their faithful 42-30241 *The Worry Wart* but no-one ever got around to painting it on the nose of their B-17. Goldstein continues: 'The 388th were in the air by 7 a.m. Flak over the target came very close and Kent Keith, our bombardier, had a rather close call. While Keith was watching for 'bombs away' a piece of flak hit the nose of the ship. As the Plexiglas shattered, a small piece hit him just over the left eye. He was extremely lucky.'

Eight of the crew of *Carolyne*, the 401st lead ship flown by Major William C. Garland, had a lucky escape when their B-17 was ditched after an engine failure. Major Garland was flying on this mission with Major M. K. Martin as the Air Commander. Over the North Sea the aircraft developed engine trouble and they were forced to ditch. Garland landed near two British trawlers, but it was mid-winter and it was an hour before the rescue could be completed. It was said to have been the coldest, roughest day of that winter at sea and it seemed a minor miracle that only two of the crew of ten lost their lives. 2nd Lieutenant F. G. Howe, the bombardier, was dead when he was taken from the water and S/Sgt R. D. Newton's body was never found.

This was the first raid for Lieutenant Harry L. Cornell's crew in the 305th at Chelveston. His waist gunner, John D. Kettman, would never forget it. Everything seemed to go wrong. Fog and rain had grounded the bombers, including those at Chelveston, whose Forts took off on the 4th at around 0800 hours. Cornell's bombardier passed out over target; Sergeant Darius A. Logan, the waist gunner, found that his mask had frozen in the -40° temperature at 25,000 feet and he almost passed out. The ball turret jammed over target and Pete Wolak had to be lifted out of the cramped turret. The flak was really close and Kettman saw four Junkers Ju 88s over the target and one B-17 go down. Cornell's bombs would not release so Wolak toggled them out over the North Sea. Some of the crew thought that he had fallen through the bomb bay while toggling the bombs and it was a relief to see him coming through the radio room. Logan and Kettman had frostbitten faces and necks and when they got back they had their faces bandaged. George A. Mayer, bombardier, also had frostbite and Leo Hartman, navigator, was taken to hospital with a frozen toe. After being shot at, Kettman now knew what a clay-pigeon felt like. 'Up there, there's so much going on that there isn't time to get very scared. When the wheels hit the ground I felt like a little kid. There is nothing like the good earth. I said to myself, "John, you have only to go through twenty-four more of these." Yes it's a funny thing this war.'

The crew were given the usual twenty-four-hour pass after flying a first mission and their next would have to wait for another few days. As it was, the next day bad weather interfered with the mission and only 216 bombers of the 1st Bomb Division returned to Kiel. The 91st lifted off from Bassingbourn to become the first Group to complete 100 missions, although it had paid dearly for the privilege, losing more aircraft and crews on mission than any other group. Four B-17s in the 94th did not make it home. Neither did Fred Humphreys' crew. *Sweet Anna* was shot down over the North Sea and nothing was heard from them again. At Molesworth, Russell F. Beach was then permanently grounded.

When, on 5 January, the 91st lifted off from Bassingbourn they became the first group in the 8th to complete 100 missions, although it had paid dearly for the privilege, losing more aircraft and crews on mission than any other group.

Sergeant John D. Kettman in the 305th Bomb Group, which went to Brunswick, wrote:

> Brunswick is the place where they lost fifty-nine planes the last time they went. It's about 120 miles from Berlin. This was one rough son of a bitch. On the way over there was a little light flak but on the bomb run all hell broke loose! And it was accurate too. They briefed us for twenty-nine flak guns; there must have been 329! A burst broke just below us and we thought sure as hell we'd had it.

Fortresses in the 3rd Division, meanwhile, flew to airfields in France. The 94th was assigned Bordeaux airfield and the route as briefed was to fly straight in as if they were going to Germany and then turn due south and fly the whole length and breadth of France and out to sea, hitting the target as they went. Ralph K. Patton, the co-pilot in Glenn B. Johnson's crew, whose usual ship, the *Horrible Hanks*, was out of commission with a cracked air intake and their replacement ship, '212, had been badly shot up and had only just managed to make it back to England on a previous mission, wrote:

> We had been briefed that we could expect heavy flak and it wasn't very reassuring. There was also an operational training group of young fighter pilots about sixty miles south of Bordeaux and they had at least sixty fighters. Our fighter escort wouldn't be able to stay with us over the target because of fuel limitations. We could expect the 'schoolboys' to be there in force. The 94th came under constant enemy attack from the time we hit France until we headed out to sea. Just after we had dumped our bomb load a shock hit the 'plane. Johnson and I struggled to right it. Black anti-aircraft puffs were all around us. As we moved out of range the call came in over the intercom – "Bandits, 12 o'clock high!" Then they came in at 3 o'clock. Suddenly, five Fw 190s in single file came in from 1 o'clock level. On the second pass we knocked one of them down. On the third pass they fired four cannon shots in the tail before turning and heading back. Suddenly the tail assembly began shuddering and we had to reduce our speed to 150 mph. The formation slowly pulled ahead of us. When we reached the Breton coast the rest of the formation was almost eight to ten miles ahead of us. Suddenly, as anti-aircraft fire began to burst close to us and as we swerved to elude it, our gunners spotted two Fw 190s hiding in the glare of the sun. Our tail gunner called out: "Here he comes!" As he released his microphone switch I could hear his guns open fire. Those were the last words I heard him speak.

The Fortress was raked by 20 mm cannon fire and the tail gunner and Jim Stewart, the ball-turret gunner, were killed. Johnson felt the control pressure go limp as the nose shot up violently and gave the order to bail out.[11]

Still under attack, the remaining B-17s in the 94th headed for the temporary safety of the sea until the time came to re-cross the Normandy Peninsula.

The 448th flew its fifth and sixth missions on 4 and 5 January, when the Eighth bombed the port area, the U-boat yards and the industrial area of Kiel. Münster was also attacked and on the second day targets in France were also bombed. About twenty-five bombers were lost over the two days. On 4 January Colonel James Thompson, the CO, led the Group on the first Kiel raid in Alvin Skaggs' B-24, which carried a bomb load of magnesium incendiary bombs. The target, however, was overcast so it was necessary to bomb on PFF. Just as the bombs cleared the bomb bay doors, the housings separated from the magnesium sticks, allowing them to scatter all over the sky. The flak was fairly heavy over the target but not accurate. Colonel Thompson suffered frostbite injuries and one B-24 received minor flak damage but the Group suffered no losses. Wednesday was a different story. Fourteen crews suffered the usual Army game of hurry-up-and-wait as they awaited take off. Finally, the Liberators lifted off and climbed through the blinding overcast for thousands of feet before they broke through the clouds and reached the dazzling sunshine to join the huge fleet of bombers assembling for the raid. The pilot of *Sequoia Gal* returned to base early to replace a faulty oxygen mask for the bombardier and was written off in a crash landing. Three more B-24s in the Group also aborted. Two hundred and thirty-five aircraft were to attack Kiel: 131 B-17s from the 1st Bomb Division and 114 from the Second. The First had been designated to lead the raid, but somehow a group of B-24s had got into the forward position instead of the B 17 group. They departed the English coast over Cromer and headed out over the North Sea. The clearing weather revealed whitecaps on the sea below. It looked cold and ominous. The long flight eastward over water kept them out of German territory as long as possible. An in-flight 360° turn by the 448th failed to correct the group alignment and the B-24s would be the first to go in over the target. The entire formation turned 90° to the south and the first bursts of flak were seen as they approached the islands off the northern coast of Germany and the Jutland Peninsula. The Group was under attack for thirty-six minutes and in that time *Maid of Tin* and three others were shot down by flak and fighters. One of the victims exploded in mid-air after being hit by flak. There were no survivors from two of the other B-24s and only two men escaped from a third Liberator that went down. William Ferguson, the pilot of *Maid of Tin*, Major Kenneth Squyres, the 715th Squadron CO, and all the crew were killed. Only six Liberators returned to Seething, where the shock was total.

Crew losses were bad enough but when they came in multiples of three from the same hut it had a disquieting effect on men like Staff Sergeant 'Bo' Bottoms in Barracks 4. On 30 December he had watched Crew 61 go down and Lieutenant Abraham Kittredge's Crew 54 went missing after their B-24 fell out of formation after having two engines shot out. Bottoms took leave in London from 5 to 7 January and he returned to find that Lieutenant Walter Yuengert and Crew 53 had been lost over Kiel on the Wednesday. Bottoms wrote that they were 'a very good bunch of boys'.[12] It meant that Crew 55 were now the only original crew left in Barracks 4. Bottoms added, 'I ask God to go with us on our missions and protect us from all harm. I ask him to go with us while we are in the ETO. My utmost prayer is, "May He see us to our respective homes to loved ones."'

Bill McCullah, irritated by lead-crew flying limitations, saw mission numbers mount slowly.

Flying every fourth mission was limiting, it slowed us down and I especially did not like it. Always in a hurry, I wanted to be home with momma. I liked England but I wanted the war finished and the sooner the better. I do not recall the date or the target of our fourth mission, nor do I remember the second or third missions. Unless something made a truly unique impression, the sameness of missions causes them to run-together. (There were no easy missions.) My distinct recollections are those where 'God checked our hole cards!' How could I forget this one? We were in take-off position at the end of the long runway. Our pilots had completed the pre-flight drill. I was sitting on the flight deck as we began our take-off roll. I could see both pilots' heads below the compartment divider.

Carroll stood in the doorway behind and between the two pilots, his normal take-off position. Carroll's was the third set of eyes scanning the multiple clusters of instruments on the front instrument panel. A second panel of dials, cranks and wheels was mounted on the ceiling above the pilots' heads. There were four throttles and numerous controls on a pedestal separating the two pilots' seats. In front of each pilot was a wheel, mounted to a movable yoke, dual controls for manoeuvring the plane in flight. Beneath their feet were rudder pedals and toe, brake actuators. If one were untrained in such things, the picture presented an intimidating, intricate, confusing array. Dials and needles took the pulse of Boomerang, indicating her speed, direction, rate-of-climb, altitude and her attitude in relation to the ground. Importantly, they measured the beat and well being of her engines. The cockpit was a busy place. Helander lifted *Boomerang* off the runway. Everything routine, the landing gear was coming up and we were flying. I settled onto the padded bench in a mode of comparative relaxation. I do not know what tipped me but I knew that something was dreadfully wrong! I stood up, apprehensively looking into the cockpit to see Helander and Schneider standing on the rudder pedals and backs arched and straining, as they pulled on the two yokes (wheels)! They were trying to horse *Boomerang* to a higher altitude. We were 50 feet off the deck and about to go into the ground! The pilots were struggling, pulling with all of their strength, fighting for our lives! They did it quietly, unobtrusively, no fuss, no muss, no panic. Even with all of their pulling, *Boomerang* would not budge. Thank God there were no hills or tall trees in our path. We were trapped in an aerodynamic lock that prevented us from climbing. Boomerang was trying to kill us!

"Jerry, give us a hand," Helander quietly said to Carroll.

Carroll calmly grasped both control wheels, pulling rearward. The three of them pulled with all of their strength but Boomerang would not budge! God how I wanted to help but there was no room! Richmond, our radioman stood beside me. He was white. I may have been, too. We flew thusly for three to five minutes (an eternity), when Helander, seemingly resigned, said to Carroll, "Jerry, stand-by to cut the master shut-off valve!" Helander considered the probability that we would clobber and we could have. Carroll stopped pulling and calmly placed his right hand on the red knurled knob above the cockpit entry door. He displayed no change of expression; he was calm as a rock. Placidly he watched and waited. He awaited the command spin the knob to the 'off' position that would cut fuel to all four engines! If Carroll closed the master shut-off valve, we were dead! If our plane went-in first, we were dead! If we went-in at all, our ass was grass and Boomerang was the lawnmower! Our speed and load were against us. There would be no survivors! I remained standing, watching. The lock that held Boomerang let go and we climbed hard! The 'G' force of the climb slammed me to my knees, holding me to the floor of the plane. Thank you, Jesus!

Only then did I hear the source of trouble. Our No. 2 engine, revved to its limits, was running away. It was uncontrollable. The engine could not be shut down. It emitted a high and pulsating whine, as the engine ran out of sync with the other engines. The danger then was that the prop would shear its shaft, flinging the propeller through the side of the plane. Runaway engines were common to the B-24. That and a tendency to blow-up were a bad combination.

A runaway engine on take-off, fully loaded with fuel and bombs, was a bad scene. A runaway engine that cannot be shutdown creates drag, far worse than an engine with a feathered propeller (an engine deliberately shut-down, with prop edge facing into the wind). Helander banked Boomerang into its two good engines, saying to Richmond, "Call the tower and clear the active runway for a downwind landing. Have the crash-wagons ready."

On downwind landings, you must 'fly' (not stall) the plane onto the runway. This required a high-speed approach. Richmond, face still white with fear, froze! He could not move! Helander himself called the tower. He brought *Boomerang* onto the active runway, downwind, fast and smooth. Crew 11 of course was not credited for our aborted fourth mission attempt. To be credited we had to draw fire over enemy territory. We had to do the 'fourth' mission again. It would be 'our second-time-around,' a down-and-dirty encore!

Safely on the ground, Richmond called Helander aside, telling him that he was through! He could not and would not continue to fly. The big brass busted him from Technical Sergeant (five stripes) to private (a slick sleeve) and assigned him to ground radio maintenance. From that moment forward the spirit went out of Richmond. He was a defeated person who continually sought Crew 11's reassurance. He was ostracised, cut-off and ignored by most flying personnel. I did not condemn Richmond because he showed certain kind-of-guts for having the nerve to quit. At one time or other following a particularly bad mission, with the exception of Helander and Means, everyone on Crew 11 had said, "I will not fly again! I'm through!" That statement was often accompanied by violent cursing and wild gesticulation. We were blowing-smoke, running our mouths, letting-off steam, venting. With several days' break behind us come the next mission, we would find ourselves climbing aboard again, wondering why in hell we were doing it. We must have been retarded!

Richmond's replacement was Staff Sergeant Kenneth L. Dyer from Indiana. Having a lot of traits in common, Kenneth and I quickly became fast friends and buddied together. Kenneth was the only person on the crew with whom I ever had real rapport, though Benny Means and Mike Duginske were decent, likable people. Kenneth and I made several trips to Norwich with a trip to London thrown in. Kenneth's mother in Indiana would call my mother in Missouri, trading crew information. They developed a close telephone relationship. On our trip to London, Kenneth and I stood under the metal roof of the Norwich boarding station, waiting for our train. While waiting, German bombers passed overhead on their way to some inland target. Searchlights framed the planes above us, as nearby anti-aircraft batteries opened up. Not wanting to miss our train, we remained where we were, the metal roof coming alive from falling shell fragments. It was dumb not to seek shelter because the rail-yard could have been the target. Kenneth flew several missions with us. We were standing down and were not scheduled to fly again for several days.

The first mission under the auspices of the USSAFE[13] was flown on Friday 7 January, when 420 B-17s and B-24s caused considerable damage to chemical and substitute war material plants at Ludwigshafen and the engineering and transport industries in the twin city of Mannheim. Major James M. Stewart, a Princeton honours graduate and famous Hollywood actor, who in 1940 had won an Academy Award for his role in *The Philadelphia Story*, now CO of the 703rd Squadron, led forty-eight B-24s to the IG Farbenindustrie plant at Ludwigshafen. As the bombs doors opened a shell burst directly under his wing but Stewart managed to regain control and complete the bomb run. Beyond the target he joined the wayward 389th, which had strayed off course. Although the 'Sky Scorpions' lost eight aircraft, his action probably prevented total annihilation. *Trouble* in the 'Sky Scorpions', flown by Captain David L. Wilhite with Major Kenneth Caldwell in the co-pilot's seat, was lost when it was attacked by a rocket-firing Fw 190 near Paris. A rocket exploded in the cockpit and other hits signalled the end of the bomber. Staff Sergeant Robert H. Sweatt was the only survivor.[14] Altogether, the 8th lost seven Liberators, five Forts and seven fighters on the 7 January raids. Four of the B-24s – *Blunder Buss*, *Los Angeles City Limits* and *Heavy Date*, in addition to *Trouble* – were from the 'Sky Scorpions'. In the 'Travelling Circus', *On The Ball* and *Ole King Cole*, which Lieutenant David M. Richardson landed at Dübendorf in Switzerland, and a third Liberator were lost. All were from the 328th Squadron.

John Butler, who was flying his fifteenth mission, was tail gunner in *Tennessee Rambler*, piloted by Lieutenant Lange. In the bomb bay were twelve 500lb M-47 incendiaries. Butler wrote:

Took off at 8.40 to bomb the chemical works. It is like the Du Pont in the United States. The temperature was minus 37. We ran into flak quite a number of times around the target area. It was really hot. We had P-47s for escorts and they sure look good. The clouds were very thick and you couldn't see the ground. When we were about 200 miles in from the French coast the cloud cover was gone could see the ground very clearly. We passed over quite a few big cities. You could see the trains on the ground barges on the canals. Once in a while some German flak gunners would send up a few bursts to let us know that they still had ammunition. We were now without fighter cover. As we passed over two German airdromes you could see the German fighters taking off in pairs from the fields. We were in for a very hot welcome. These fighters were very good, as they were called the Abbeville kids. Two of the three B-24s from our group that they shot down were flying on our wing. They really were very hot pilots and they didn't scare very easy. I noticed four Me 109s at about 1,200 yards at 7 o'clock. I had my guns set on them to see what they would do. They were just milling around. Then one peeled off and came into attack I held my fire until he was about five hundred yards. Then I open up. I fired about 70 rounds. He was then in to about 200 yards. He started to burn and he peeled off toward 8 o'clock. He then threw his belly up. I then let loose about thirty rounds. He bailed out and the plane started down and then exploded. My right waist gunner shot down a Fw 190 and the pilot bailed out as the plane exploded. I received my second oak leaf cluster to the Air Medal also I was credited with one plane destroyed, so I also received another oak leaf cluster.

On Saturday 8 January Wallace Patterson and others in Al Northrup's crew caught the 2.10 train bound for London, his first visit there in nearly eight years.

After a wild cab ride from the Liverpool Street Station, we put up at the Red Crown in Clifford Street. Immediately we washed, had supper and went to the Regent Palace for a drink and to watch the Piccadilly Commandos at work. There were more of them inside the hotel and on the streets. They'll back the boys up in an alley for £2; take them home for from £3 to £20. They're a pretty sorry lot, most of them, but a few people said some of them had to do what they do or starve, while others are financing future businesses. We went to a few clubs. I got a horse steak with onions and a bottle of scotch and just made it home. Rising late Sunday, we went sightseeing – Piccadilly, the government houses, Buckingham Palace, Whitehall, Trafalgar Square, Cleopatra's Needle, the Tower, London Bridge, the Cheshire Cheese, Westminster Abbey, St. Paul's. We took a cab and saw everything from the outside because all except the churches were closed. In the evening we clubbed again, had a Chinese dinner and were pretty disappointed because we couldn't get theatre tickets. Monday morning I tried Hobson's (no insignia), Dunhill's (no pipes) and Liberty's where I got Bobbie two of their famous print scarves. At another store I got me some handkerchiefs and a strictly non-military red plaid woollen muffler. We had lunch at Simpsons – roast turkey and sausage, beautifully done. Then we visited the Services Museum and the waxworks of Mme. Tussaud. Our train left at 4 p.m. and we stood for two hours before we could find us a seat for the last hour. Norwich was very dead. We saw a movie with Lawrence Olivier and as it let out quite early, took a taxi back to the mud hole. We are alerted for what promises to be a pretty tough job tomorrow; so I'd better try to get some sleep. I'm using the last of my sherry for a sleeping potion.

The rumours were true. Tuesday 11 January was a maximum effort involving more than 570 B-17s and B-24s that attempted to destroy aircraft factories at Waggum, Halberstadt and Oschersleben in the Brunswick area, a city notorious for its flak and fighter defences. Morning came early. At Kimbolton Bob Singer, a B-17 radio operator in the 379th, was awakened at 0400 to fly his fourth mission. 'At 0430 we went to the mess hall for breakfast of eggs and ham. At 0530 we were briefed and told that our mission was to bomb the aircraft factories in Oschersleben. Our plane was loaded with eighteen 50lb incendiaries. Take off was at 0630 with twenty-five other B-17s. We would meet ninety-six other planes to make a formation of 120.'

At Rattlesden crews were awakened at 0300 hours with briefing at 0430. It was dark, cold and damp as usual as thirty-six crews walked to the mess halls and made their way to the briefing room. This was the largest contingent to prepare for a mission in the 447th's short experience. The Forts were loaded with 61 tons of GP and incendiary bombs. Take off began at 0710 hours. Eighteen to twenty minutes were required to get the force into the air. Lieutenant John H. Cole, flying with Lieutenant Herschell A. Jarrell's lead crew as navigator, recalled:

> Shortly after take off we developed trouble in the No. 3 engine. Lieutenant Colonel Charles H. Bowman, Deputy Group Commander, instructed the deputy lead to continue forming the Group. When we returned to the field, the Group had not completed its takeoff. It was still pitch dark and we circled the base until the last plane was off the ground. We were rushed to another ship, a silver job. I remember remarking that when the Jerries saw the silver ship they would say, "I want one of those." I was kidding and didn't realise the truth of my statement.

Jarrell eventually caught up with the rest of the Group and followed in their proper spot. It was completely under cast as they flew over the North Sea in the bright sunshine at the planned altitude of 21,000 feet.[15]

The American fighter escort soon become lost in the cloud layers over England and many were forced to abort the mission. Two hours into the mission the 2nd and 3rd Divisions were ordered to abandon the operation but the 1st Division, which was about 100 miles from Brunswick, was allowed to continue with disastrous results, as Bob Singer recalls.

We flew at 21,500 where the temperature was -35 degrees. The weather was bad and the mission was aborted from headquarters but none of our planes ever received this order. As soon as we passed the English Channel we were over France and were attacked by 109s or Focke Wulf 190s and Ju 88s all the way to the target. Many of our planes on our right and left were shot down. We would sometimes see parachutes and sometimes not. By the time we got to target and dropped our bombs, flak had hit our plane and knocked out our oxygen lines which caused the waist gunner and tail gunner to go on portable oxygen. Going home things got worse; more B-17s were hit. Flak hit the left waist gunner's flak suit and he passed out. I dragged him out and revived him with portable oxygen. Our top turret gunner was given credit for two 109s shot down and so was the tail gunner credited with two 109s. Only sixty bombers returned, which were shot up very badly. For this mission we were awarded the President's Citation and when I finished my twenty-ninth mission I was awarded the Distinguished Flying Cross.

Joe Wroblewski, pilot, 351st, recalled:

Any bomber that fell out of formation was a dead duck. I watched a B-17 off to our right by itself. A Me 110 got on its tail and really poured tracers into the bomber. It caught fire and as the flames licked around the tail I could see the tail-gunner still firing back at the Jerry. Finally, the bomber climbed straight up and fell off into a spin, burning and breaking up. One yellow nosed Me 109 came in between us and our wingman with his guns blazing. He must have put a few holes in our tail, but no one was hurt. Our waist gunner fell back away from his gun for a second when he saw this plane so close and when he did start shooting again he shot through our tail and through the B-17 flying next to us. The enemy fighters kept falling and exploding all around us, but still they kept coming in without giving us a breathing spell. They tried real hard to break up our formation but we hung together for dear life. All I could hear over the intercom was, "Fighter coming in at five o'clock, one at seven o'clock, another at nine o'clock low. Fighter coming in at 10 o'clock level!" It was almost useless to call them out. There were so many coming in from every direction.

At about this time many thoughts began to go through my mind. My parachute was just behind my seat and the temptation to snap it on and get the hell out of it was very strong. But then I thought about the other crewmembers. I don't doubt that they were just as scared as I was, but at least they could shoot back. I thought about my training that led to our present situation and about looking forward to being in combat. But that was before all this. Right then I would have settled for being just a potato peeler, mess cook or whatever, washing kettles for the duration.

Somehow, one of our P-51s got separated from his group and he tagged along with us. We were very grateful because he fought as long as his fuel permitted; chasing the enemy until his ammunition was gone. Then he just dived after the fighters to divert them from the B-17s. Watching this one fighter escort bolstered our confidence for survival and we all admired his guts to hang in there with us. Later we learned his name was Major Howard.[16] He got back to base safely.

Four B-17s in the 401st did not return to Deenethorpe from the mission to Oschersleben. At 1129 hours, about thirty minutes before the target, *Pee-Tey-Kuh*, flown by 2nd Lieutenant Steven G. Nason, suffered a fire in the No. 3 engine. The bomb bay doors were opened and the bomb loads was jettisoned. Nason and seven of his crew bailed out before the Fortress blew up. The radio operator and the ball turret gunner never made it. A minute later the B-17 flown by Captain James B. Foster went down to enemy fighters. A concentrated burst of fire hit the right wing behind the No. 4 engine and gasoline poured out. Both wings caught fire. Foster, who was from Spokane, Washington, pulled out of formation and the bomber was then attacked by three Ju 88s. All the crew bailed out successfully and they were taken into captivity. Ten minutes later, after the target, 10 miles south of Oschersleben, the B-17 piloted by 2nd Lieutenant Donald C. Sprecher was attacked by fighters, who killed two of the crew. A fire started in the No. 4 engine and the aircraft flew on for about five minutes before the bomb bay doors were opened. Fire came out of the bomb bay and increased as the B-17 carried on. Two men got out from up front and their parachutes opened immediately. The flaming Fortress then left the formation and turned to starboard, staying with the Wing formation for about three minutes before the aircraft started to come apart. Six more men got out before the aircraft exploded. Last to go was *Carolina Queen*, piloted by 1st Lieutenant Harold J. Chapman, of Pontiac, MI, which at twelve noon was shot down over the target shortly after 'bombs away' in a head-on attack by two Bf 109s. Sergeant D. D. Johnson, the right waist gunner, recalled that 'Lieutenant D. G. Wallis the bombardier, of Richmond Hills, New York, was hit by 20 mm shells and killed. The controls were shot away and we were ordered to bail out. The ship lost a wing near the ground but landed almost intact.' Three gunners and the radio operator also were killed.

Andy J. Coroles, bombardier in Crew 19 in the 331st Squadron in the 94th, who was flying his eleventh mission, wrote:

Brunswick was the deepest penetration the group had made into Germany unescorted since Schweinfurt. The weather over England was very bad when we took off and assembled. The mission was recalled about the time we left the English coast, but Colonel Thorup did not receive the message. As a result, our Wing and two others that did not receive the message apparently went on into the target, not knowing the mission had been scrubbed and the fighter escorts recalled. It was a costly mix-up and cost us several good crews. The weather began clearing up as soon as we reached Germany and was perfectly clear in the area of the target. We made a 'dry run' and had to do a 360 degree turn and come in again. As we started our second bomb run the Me 110s began attacking us. The other two groups in our Wing had dropped their bombs on the first run and headed for home, leaving our group alone. We had a running battle for about an hour – the Me 110s attacking from 3 o'clock around to 9 o'clock with rockets and 20 mms. One by one the ships around us would be knocked out of formation. The enemy fighters would then 'gang up' on these cripples and finish them off. Our group was heavily hit by Me 110s and Fw 190s and lost eight ships and crews. Our squadron lost three crews – Butler, Rubin and Service. Bloyd and Cox were doing violent evasive action all through these attacks and again and again I saw clouds of 20 mm shells explode where we had been only a second before. It looked as if our group was going to be picked off one at a time. I was expecting our turn to come at any moment.

About 90 miles from the coast, six P-47s suddenly appeared and scared away the Jerries. Our formation was a sad sight – only ten planes were left out of the original twenty-one. Besides the eight ships from our group that went down, our formation lost two from the 447th which had tacked on to us. I saw one of the 447th ships go down. It was an all silver B-17. The entire tail of this ship from the waist back was blazing fiercely and one Me 110 was sitting on his tail not more than 200 yards out, slugging it out with the tail gunner. The tail gunner finally hit the Me 110 and it peeled off and started down smoking heavily. I watched the flames eat their way forward on the ship as it flew on in formation for one or two minutes. Then, it suddenly nosed up, fell off on its back and went straight down. I saw no chutes come out of it. It was a fascinating sight and one I'd never forget. Our ship came through the entire battle with one small flak hole. The Lord must have been watching over us and I'm thankful to be back front that raid in one piece.

One of the B-17s that the 447th lost was piloted by 2nd Lieutenant Claude L. Hickey[17] and the silver ship Coroles saw go down[18] was flown by 1st Lieutenant Herschell A. Jarrell. Jack Cole, the lead navigator, who had unknowingly predicted that the enemy fighters would take a liking to their sleek silver job, recalled:

We were easy prey for rocket-firing fighters. Violent evasive action left us by ourselves most of the time, weaving back and forth and up and down. All attacks were from the tail; the interphone was busy with chatter from the rear of the ship – "Fighters coming in at 5 o'clock high" or "There goes another 17" or "Another fighter going down". They came in by twos and threes, staying out of our range to fire their salvos of rockets and then boring in close with their 20 mm guns blazing in the wings. Flak and rockets were bursting all around and since there were no nose attacks, I had to just sit and navigate and listen to the rattle of 20 mm and rocket bursts as they hit the ship. I caught an occasional glimpse of fighters coming in at 4 o'clock. The first time I knew we were really in a tough spot was when there was an explosion to the right of the nose and I felt as though my leg had been plugged, but was not serious. The nose to my right slightly resembled a sieve; the hydraulic line had been hit and fluid was spurting all over my legs. A burst at the same time hit part of the oxygen system and soon we had a call from Jarrel saying that Colonel Bowman's oxygen system was getting very low. I heard Jarrel ask how he was doing and he replied slowly, "I still know what's going on." Since I was busy keeping track of our position, about this time a fire must have broken out in the bomb bay. Thomas Tate, the bombardier, came scurrying back to the nose and, on order from the pilot, told us to get set to bail out. The nose was filled with smoke and the smell of cordite. As we buckled on our chest pack chutes, the ship seemed to go out of control and started a steep turn to the left. Tate and I worked together, opening the escape hatch. We had to jerk the release three times before it slipped. While kicking out the hatch I noticed Tate behind me and Jarrell's legs getting out of the cockpit. I wasted no time, going out head first with the ripcord handle in my left hand and floated on my back for about ten seconds before pulling the cord, releasing the chute allowing it to blossom out overhead. It was amazingly quiet and peaceful. I had bailed out at about 22,000 feet and breathed hard for a long time. I observed no other chutes or the plane but saw a few fragments falling. It must have taken me 20 minutes to drift down.[19]

Wallace Patterson wrote.

We assembled our usual ragged formation over Splasher 5 and proceeded over a Channel we couldn't see. Over Holland they tracked us with some black flak but it was too low and between groups so no one got hurt. Then about a half-hour from the target, with all sorts of P-47s covering us, the Pathfinder ship dumped its bombs and flares, a few other ships salvoed their loads and the whole division turned off course and ran like mad for home. For some reason Skaggs continued on course. We had to follow and a few moments later we all dumped our bombs in a swamp and turned for home. Then we ran into trouble. We were quite a way in German property when a bunch of Me 109s came up, looked us over and jumped us. I never saw a single one attack as all the fun was going on behind me. I never got in a shot but I was very busy trying to keep my armoured glass between the stuff and me. No. 3 engine was smoking badly most of the way but we did not have to feather it. The hydraulic landing gear system was shot out and we had to let the wheels down manually. The bomb bay was flooded with hydraulic fluid. Al made a beautiful landing and we sweated out the mud at the end of the runway. We thought we'd have no brakes but we did. After we parked we got out to survey the damage. A whole group of B-17s landed shortly after we did; out of gas, I guess. It would have been a 900-mile trip and there were 6,000 lbs of TNT aboard.[20]

Next day the real yarn came out. The Division was called home because of weather over the proposed target. But Captain Jack Edwards, [Operations Officer] flying with Skaggs, thought he saw a target of opportunity and called the bombardier to bomb it. We all dropped our bombs together. Photos showed we bombed a sugar beet refinery near Meppen and other bombs previously salvoed landed in a couple of villages, probably Dutch.[21] The raid cost the group two more crews, not to mention the six sieves we came back in, which would be out of action for some time.

As far as I am concerned they can call this war off any time now, give me my pay and send me home.

Vast banks of stratocumulus clouds covering most of Germany prevented the visual bombing of targets, so throughout the remainder of January attacks on targets in France became the order of the day. On the 14th almost 530 heavies bombed twenty V-1 weapon sites in the Pas de Calais. 'BJ' Keirsted's crew reached double figures with a mission to the Pas de Calais. The crew had been alerted for a ferrying mission in the morning but a briefing at 11.30 changed this to a 1.30 afternoon take-off to France to bomb Noball targets. Bombing was completed from 12,000 feet. With no enemy fighters or flak, 'Goldie' Goldstein wrote that it was 'the prefect milk-run'. All of the crew added clusters to their Air Medals.

Of the twenty-nine missions flown during January and February 1944, thirteen were to V-1 rocket sites. Soon these strikes would no longer be regarded as 'milk runs' because the Germans, having realised their vulnerability to air attack, had moved in additional flak batteries and the bombing altitude was raised to 15,000 feet and higher. But Harry Cornell's crew at Chelveston and Claude Campbell in the 303rd all thought that the 14 January mission would be a 'milk run'. Campbell, who had completed his tour, volunteered for the mission to the V-1 site at Meillard.

I got tired sitting around and decided to take another trip with the boys. I led the 359th Squadron, which flew low. We bombed by squadrons from an altitude of 12,000 feet. Naturally the flak was very heavy and accurate. We hit a barrage just inside France and Captain Merle Hungerford's ship [*Wallaroo*] was hit by a burst that disintegrated the tail surface and must have killed the tail gunner. He was right in front of me. His ship went into a steep vertical climb, stalled out at the top, dropped off on one wing and went into a dive which developed into a flat spin. 'Chutes came out and it is presumed that most of the crew got out.[22]

John Kettman, on Harry Cornell's crew, reported that the mission, close to Lille, was a 'milk run'.

We were last to take off, as a plane in front of us ran off the runway and blocked our way. We caught up with the 92nd and bombed with them. There was no flak near to us but some of the other groups ran into a lot of it. We didn't see any enemy fighters but we did see our own P-47s and P-38s. It was a nice short mission, the kind we like. Everything went very smoothly. We were only on oxygen one hour. On 21 January our third mission was the same, except that it was a little longer. Mayer, our bombardier, flew with another crew. Robert Sage, radio operator, didn't fly as he was grounded. We were supposed to go over the coast and hit the rocket installations. When we got there, there was a lot of cloud and we had to make three runs over the target. Each time we went over we caught flak, the last time was worst. We really heard it and it bounced the ship around quite a lot. A piece came in and missed Darwin Gidel, the engineer, by a fraction of an inch. He felt it brush by his pant leg. We did not see any enemy fighters as we had good P-47 support. After the second run everyone got disgusted and started to sing Pistol Packin' Momma on the interphone, Vogel, the bombardier, started it. All of our squadron got back. We had to circle the field a long time as a couple of planes blocked the runway due to blowouts on landing.

The 388th returned to the Pas de Calais for another strike at Noball targets. This was Keirsted's crew's eleventh mission and it tested their luck as Larry Goldstein recalled:

This mission was scrubbed two consecutive times and the briefing was the same as for the past few days. It was a rather important day for the crew. Firstly, our ship *241* was taken away from us. Secondly, we took off with the heaviest bomb load that a B-17 had ever carried. These were twelve 500-pounders inside and two 1,000-pounders externally. This was 8,000 lbs of bombs. To add to this, we had a Lieutenant-Colonel from the Signal Corps riding with us as an observer. It was a heavy load but 'BJ' handled the ship okay. Unexpected cloud cover crept in and we were forced to make three bomb runs before hearing 'bombs away' at 12,000 feet. No enemy fighters or flak so this was another 'milk run'. At this point eleven missions completed and fourteen to go. Never once did we discuss our chances for survival. You could say we lived from day to day, never expecting the worst.

On our twelfth mission on Monday 24 January we had an exceptionally early briefing at 4 a.m. Our target was Frankfurt, a very long flight. Our pilots prided themselves for good formation flying but soon after flying into a cloud bank there were B-17s all over the sky. 'BJ' decided to abort as there was no formation to join. We were over enemy territory and just the danger of mid-air collision was enough to make that decision. Kent Keith wanted to unload the bombs on an airfield located between two small towns but without a bombsight he did not want to chance hitting the towns. To add a little extra excitement we had a new crewmember flying in the ball turret on his first mission. He became airsick and Jack Kings and I managed to get him out of the turret and into the radio room.

This was not easy at 20,000 feet. We all returned to Knettishall safely with a full bomb load. The mission was scrubbed but next day we received credit for a mission.

Meg Cole was twenty years old when she received news of her husband Woody's death, which occurred on Friday 21 January after a bombing raid on Escalles-Sur-Buchy in France. He was flying as bombardier on the crew of *Liberty Belle* in the 67th Squadron in the 'Flying Eightballs', which was piloted by 1st Lieutenant Keith Cookus from Eugene, Oregon. Meg had met Woodrow 'Woody' Cole when she lived in Hollywood, California, working at RKO Studios, first as an actress and later as a publicist. He was an air cadet in the flying school at Roswell, New Mexico, and received his bombardier wings in March 1943, shortly after they were engaged. Woody and Meg were married in Kingman, Arizona, on Easter Sunday of 1943 and they spent their three-day honeymoon in a dusty little motel. Then he was off to one of the many bases where he would be stationed preparatory to going overseas. Meg spent the next three months following him throughout the western part of the US. She was not unlike thousands of other young war brides, riding on trains and buses, sitting and sleeping on her luggage in the aisles, scrambling for food and drink at little out-of-the-way stations all over the western part of the country. Upon reaching one base, Meg would be told that Woody's group had just been transferred, so it was back on board after waiting in long lines for tickets. Once on the train they could be side-tracked while waiting for a troop train to pass. Many times Meg was taken off the train, having been 'bumped' for a serviceman who was en route to his designated place of embarkation.

Meg finally caught up to 'Woody' in Casper, Wyoming and they had only three weeks together before he left for overseas. From then on, their marriage consisted of a few phone calls and heavily censored mail as Meg tried to fill in those deleted passages that would give her an idea of where he might be. She listened to the music of Glenn Miller ('At Last' was their song); hostessed at the Hollywood Canteen; performed in USO shows at military bases up and down the West Coast; and went on bond-selling tours with other Hollywood actors. Since there were no nylons, she painted her legs with makeup and drew seams up the backs with eyebrow pencils; and wore shoes with soles made of rope and other compositions. She walked to work, because gasoline was rationed; stayed slim because there was no butter, sugar or meat; and lived the civilian side of a war that would, hopefully, mean that her future children would never have to fight in another. How very naive!

Meg, along with thousands of other women, took this new way of life in her stride, refusing to tell their husbands, fathers, brothers and sons how tough it was because their plight would sound ridiculous to those who were 'over there.' Their troubles were miniscule by comparison, so most tried to make light of it in their letters. Those poignant letters were sometimes difficult to compose, as they tried to let their men know how they felt, yearning to profess their love and longings without making them so homesick that they might be endangered in some way. 'Who was the general who said, "War is hell!" Sherman?'[23]

1st Lieutenant 'Woody' Woodrow was more familiarly known on the crew of *Liberty Belle* as 'Junior'. His pilot, Keith Cookus, who was better known as 'Buck', wrote:

We were out over the Pas de Calais. I was leading a section of our B-24s and I had aboard the command pilot, an experienced guy who picks secondary targets for the section and keeps the formation together. The command pilot was Major William N. Anderson from Taylorville, Illinois who stood between the second pilot and me. I also had Captain Robert L. Agar the group bombardier and 1st Lieutenant Henry A. Weiser along for the ride to see how we worked. We met little opposition. We had cloud cover, anyway. We were trying to bomb through cloud and made five runs but we could not make sure, so we turned back with our bombs.

As we were crossing the French coast we found the Jerries had moved in a bunch of mobile ack-ack. They must have been tracking us quite a time. The first burst was so close I heard it and I started evasive action. There were twelve of us in the formation but 30 seconds after that first burst we got it at 11,000 feet. It happened so fast that we were thrown around completely out of control by the smack of the explosions. Jerry soon got us with seven hits in a bunch. I put the plane into a dive as soon as I got some sort of control and went down as fast as I could 3,000 feet to 8,000 feet to get out of the area as quickly as possible and we were not hit again. But I realised at once that there wasn't much of my plane left – that burst had practically blown us to pieces. One of the shells had burst right inside the bomb bay, ripping out the catwalk, which holds the bottom of the fuselage together. It also blew Staff Sergeant Richard Trechel the radioman, out of the machine; we never saw him again. It wounded the navigator, Franklin

'Chubby' Campbell and the tail turret gunner, Hermann 'Moe' Becker. There was a hole in the middle of the plane just as if a shark had taken a bite out of it.

Neither Howard 'Tiny' Holladay, my co-pilot, or me were touched. Major Anderson had slumped to the floor of the cockpit and was lying in a heap. "Take care of the major," I said to Tiny. I couldn't get any news from the rest of the plane because nothing was working. No. 1 engine had been shot to pieces; that was the second direct hit. It was hanging in shreds but I managed to feather the airscrew before I lost all of the pressure there. The third direct hit had blown out half of my No. 2 engine. There was nothing left to feather there. I then saw that No. 3 engine was on fire. Andrew Kowalski the engineer saw the hit on this engine. The flash of the explosion had set it on fire and it was blazing furiously, leaving a long lick of black smoke trailing back, streaked with red. I had to leave it to burn because I couldn't get back to the English coast without letting the motor run as long as it would. I just left it and looked the other way. But I couldn't forget it because it began to fill the plane with gas and oil smoke.

"The major's in a bad way, Buck," Tiny yelled. "He's been hit in the legs and through the back. He's asking for morphia." We gave the major two shots on the way back to the English coast but it was clear that he was in bad shape. There had been a direct hit in the base of the nose turret. Splinters sailed up all round Staff Sergeant Eugene Seifried but by a miracle he wasn't hit, although it blew the top right off his turret. He managed to extricate himself from the wreckage and reach the cockpit. He pointed out that we had a direct hit, which had gone clean through the right wing. The shell – the seventh they pumped into us – took the right main landing gear with it and part of it is metal as thick round as your thigh. Tiny shouted at me, "No use trying to get it down Buck. We ain't got it with us now." All the hydraulics were out anyway. I had to keep that blazing motor going to get us home. I couldn't ditch because we had wounded aboard. I still thought the major would live. So we strung along, going very gingerly. We weren't being attacked anyway. I couldn't give anyone orders about haling out, because the electrical system was shot away. The group bombardier and the group gunnery officer took a jump when they saw half the middle of the ship, go west. We were over the coast and the wind should have taken them to land in France.[24]

Just about this time, when we were settling down to the job of getting home safe, 'Junior' Cole crawled up on the flight deck. 'Junior', a big guy, was covered with blood. His face looked awful and he didn't look like 'Junior' at all. The blast had tossed him around but we found out that he had crawled into the bomb-bay, holding on with his hands and toes to the pieces of twisted metal and wires; anything he could find that was still rooted firmly to the rest of the plane. He had been tossing out what he could of the mass of shattered bombs in there. The emergency release mechanism was gone. He'd cut his hands to ribbons. He'd come to say there was some he couldn't shift. Then he flopped down. He couldn't see; he couldn't talk and we couldn't get him to move. He just lay there, staring at nothing. While all this had been going on, the ball turret gunner, Staff Sergeant Thomas Fong, had managed to get himself out of the ball turret. How he did it, I don't know! His turret was a jangle of twisted stuff like a train wreck and he thought it was time to move when it began filling with blazing oil from the hydraulics. Fong joined Walter E. 'Watbe' Boyd the left waist gunner and the tail gunner.

We were going along all right, heading straight for home and not losing too much height. Then Tiny shouted in my ear: "Coast!" And I looked and there it was! At that moment there was a whoosh and a smack that made the plane shake like jelly; what kept her together I couldn't say. I saw that I had no power from No. 3: the engine had blown up. It was white hot but it had got us home. A petrol pipe exploded and the fire began to look really nasty. It was still burning round the remains of the engine.

I said to Tiny: "How's Anderson?"

He said: "The landing won't hurt him. He's dead."

I had brought a plane in on one engine before but this time the machine was more like a sieve and practically nothing was working; so what with losing height too fast for me to care much about it, I had to pick a landing spot pretty quickly. We came down in a field [at Brambling Down, Wingham in Kent] – not too bad – but that field went up and down and up and down again like a switchback. My stalling speed was 140 on account of all the damage she had taken. We shot across that field and its ups and downs like a piece of soap on a bathroom floor but we were absolutely okay and slowing up in fine shape when I saw a wire fence ahead. We took it and it shook us up. We crashed through it and when Tiny and I looked up from where we had ducked our heads, we saw a ditch and a hedge ahead. And it was in this ditch that we finished up.

The men in the rear of the Liberator – Fong, Watbe and Kowalski – were sent off to hospital. Cookus, who clambered out of a side window, and Tiny Holladay were uninjured but 'Junior' Cole died from suffocation in the crash. The rest of the men on the flight deck were trapped as the wrecked Liberator burned. Campbell and Becker were crushed up between the floor and the top, with the sides caved in too. Campbell's wounded legs were held in a vice between the crushed-in roof and the floor, with Anderson's body on one side and Cole's on the other; he was bent double with his head forced down on his knees and he stayed this way for three hours. British workers – there were about sixty of them at one time – worked like beavers but they could not put the fire out. When RAF lorries with cranes arrived, they were released and taken to hospital. Tiny, Seifried and Cookus sat in the field, exhausted. Somehow, against all the odds, *Liberty Belle* had made it back. Cookus was awarded the DFC.

'Woody' was laid to rest in Cambridge Military Cemetery at Madingley.

CHAPTER 2

All The Fine Young Men

We were on oxygen four and half-hours. We used pathfinders this trip, as there was thick cloud coverage. The flak was way off, which was a big relief to us. After the bomb run enemy fighters followed us for about an hour. Eight 109s jumped *Shady Lady* and they headed for the clouds. When we got back *Shady Lady* was simply riddled. On landing their No. 2 prop fell off and all their tyres were flat. They claimed seven fighters and had over 200 holes in the ship. They flew clear across Germany at 2,100 feet. They even did a little strafing. Right after 'bombs away' I saw a P-38 shoot hell out of a 109; it was a pretty sight. Our bomb bay doors stuck and Darwin Gidel had a hell of a time cranking them up. We were over enemy territory hours and that ain't hay. It was just a little easier than we thought it would be. Later, news broadcasts said that we lost 39 B-17s, so some guys caught hell. The tail gunner and ball turret got in a few, I didn't.

Sergeant John D. Kettman, waist gunner, Frankfurt, Saturday 29 January 1944
– his fourth mission.

Smoke drifted upward from beneath Warren Bruce's bunk and spread out like fluffy clouds in a summer breeze. The clouds of smoke brought a sense of peace into an apprehensive night that stretched into early morning. Sleep was impossible and the best the young Liberator pilot could do was to keep the tension in tow. He heard the familiar sound of fleece-lined boots shuffling between their barracks in the Bungay Buckaroos' 704th Squadron area. The duty officer was coming to summon them. The agony of the long night's wait was over. It was 'get dressed, get breakfast and get going'. Second Lieutenant Ernest Warren Bruce rolled out of his upper bunk and admonished 2nd Lieutenant Thomas J. Pretty, the bombardier-nose gunner, from Memphis, Tennessee, to quit smoking. 'Those things will kill you before Jerry does'. Quiet, likable, an only child – Pretty just wanted to get back to the telephone company and have six kids. Bruce, who was from San Bernardino, California, gave 2nd Lieutenant David H. 'Grish' Grisham, the handsome, temperamental co-pilot, a hard shake and his morning greeting: 'You will never get transferred to fighters if you don't learn how to get out of bed.' Grisham was deeply hurt at having been assigned as co-pilot, having graduated from fighter school. The first time Bruce took him up on an orientation flight he looked at him and shouted, 'Well, this is like sitting on your front porch and flying your house.'

Second Lieutenant John P. Wheelis Jr, short, cocky, everyone's friend, a good navigator, of Jackson, Mississippi, rolled out of bed with a faraway look: 'I am not going to get home today.' Warren Bruce looked him in the eye and asked: 'Who are you going to fly with?' He smiled.

As they walked to the briefing room, Bruce noted that 'the charcoal sky was pierced with specks of silver'. Every bomber base was carefully blended into the countryside, with the barracks dispersed in wooded areas to minimise damage and loss of life in the event of enemy attack. The several housing sites were separated by distances ranging up to a half-mile or more. It was estimated for a man working on the flight line to get from the place where he worked, ate and slept, he would travel an average of 7 miles per day. They travelled on trucks, bicycles and shanks' mare.[1]

It was eight days since the crew's first mission – their battle christening. They entered the 446th Bomb Group briefing room. A hush fell over the crews as the intelligence officer raised the screen covering the Royal Air Force map. The red ribbon reached deep into Germany … Frankfurt-on-Main. It was to be a long and tough one; another maximum effort. When formation positions were assigned, Warren Bruce drew the tail-end Charlie slot. The colonel suggested he 'hold it up in there'. The Group was at the end of the striking force and Bruce and his crew were at the end of their Group. They would be the last crew to cross the target. 'Don't worry' he thought to himself, 'the flight leader's tail gunner and my bombardier will be able to play tick-tack-toe with each other on their turret windows.'

'The Continent will be covered with clouds to an altitude of 5,000 feet. Bombing will be done by radar,' they were told. At Hardwick it was the same story. Clarence 'Bill' Neumann, in Lieutenant Roy Dahl's crew in the 'Travelling Circus', was disgruntled and the young bombardier was not alone. The orderly had woken them at 0415, telling them to 'to rise and shine'. 'What a comedian he was', Neumann retorted. The Ploesti veteran's crew dressed, ate breakfast and then to briefing at 0530. Over 760 B-24s and B-17s led by Pathfinders were to hit the IG Farben and Vereinigte Deutsche Metallwerke war industries in Frankfurt, which had escaped five days earlier when unpredicted multi-layer clouds and haze impeded assemblies and only half the large force were dispatched. Neumann shuddered to think how many times they had prepared for Frankfurt only to have the mission scrubbed. Cloud formations and dense contrails over the English Channel had made holding formation impossible and the force had been recalled. This time the 'Circus' would be leading the 20th Combat Wing. They completed their pre-flight and climbed aboard the aircraft, hoping that this mission would not be scrubbed. Dahl taxied out to the runway and was airborne at 0830.

At Flixton, the briefing over, Warren Bruce's crew and Sergeant Edward W. Schuller, a combat photographer, gathered their gear and boarded a truck that took them to the dispersal where *Hula Wahina*, their B-24 Liberator, was waiting. Pre-flight inspection was made. They boarded the B-24 and waited for the go-signal. Engines were started one by one. They responded and Bruce taxied to the take-off position. The next to last ship rolled down the runway. Bruce released the brakes and the plane began inching forward. Thirty seconds went by on the clock. With a roar, they rolled into their take-off. The slow agony of earthbound lethargy was transformed into the grace of flight.[2]

Not everyone made it. William McGinley, the tail gunner on the crew of Lieutenant John Stukus, flying *Sally Ann* in the 578th Squadron at Wendling, recalls:

> The misfortune began during assembly over East Anglia when one of our ships from the 577th Squadron had a terrible mid air collision in cloud with one of the 482nd Pathfinder B-24s with one of our original 392nd crews on board. From the two ships, a total of only three men managed to escape from the tumbling wreckage of the Pathfinder and survive. Due to those same clouds which extended all along our route, with a few breaks, we lost contact with our group formation en route to Frankfurt. We decided to turn back when we failed to locate any other B-24s with which we could have joined up and so complete the mission as briefed.

Warren Bruce, meanwhile, had crossed the North Sea and *Hula Wahina* headed into Germany.

I alerted the crew that we were over enemy territory. The lonesomeness of flying tail-end Charlie set in. I asked Sergeant John H. Pfaffenberger, the tail gunner, how it felt to be at the end of the line. "Very alone," he answered. He had nothing to look at but the emptiness of where we had been, no matter what we did. He was always the last to do it, but he was first rate. Didn't play poker. Loaned his money to Sergeant Jesse P. Fleming, radio operator, tall, blond, good-natured, addicted to poker, was always broke.

The silence was broken, with a chilling thought. We were not alone and we were not safe. I wondered how many radar scanners were plotting our course and reporting our position to flak batteries and Luftwaffe fighters along the way. Surely the Luftwaffe was not going to allow this to go unopposed. They still had the capability of hitting hard, and there was no lack of determination on their part. We knew they could inflict severe damage at points of their choosing. Some of our crews would suffer all the hell that is war; others would have nothing but the dirty brown flak with which to contend.

Our fighter cover was up front protecting those under attack. If we were to see them at all, it would be on their run for home to refuel. They would return to escort us to the coast. Our peaceful entry into enemy territory seemed unreal. Our first mission had been relatively calm, though we had been bracketed with well-placed anti-aircraft.

"Navigator to pilot."

"Yes."

"The IP is dead ahead."

It was the initial point. We ceased all evasive action and flew straight and level to the time of 'bombs away!' From there to the target the lead ships went on autopilot and the bombardiers flew the ships with their bomb sights. It was an uncanny device that determined exactly when the payload was to be released.

Except for the take-off, landing and the bomb run, the co-pilot and I flew in half-hour shifts. When I had the controls he assumed the role of fire-control officer.

The Group was increasing air speed and it became very difficult for us to 'hold it up in there.' I had no intention of becoming a straggler. We increased our power considerably above cruising as we moved toward the target.

Over the target, huge black belching clouds were broiling up through the white cloud cover. The blue sky was full of flak. The morning's tranquillity had ended.

"Open bomb bay doors." The bombardier called. The co-pilot opened the doors and exposed our belly to the German gunners. I continued to inch up my power and it seemed as though the Group was determined to run away from us. Number two cylinder head pressure needle swept to the left. Supercharger out! At our altitude, it equated to engine power nil. Twelve hundred horses gone from the team. I advanced the pressure on the remaining three. The co-pilot advanced engine rpm. We began to trail and lose power. There was no need to feather the prop. There was just enough manifold pressure to equalise the propeller drag. I alerted the crew of our problem. We were becoming more alone every second. The number three needle swept left and we had one-half the power we needed to maintain altitude. At least we were well-balanced. Two and three were inboard. It could have been worse – both losses could have been on the same side. The co-pilot and I advanced to full-rated power. The engines worked valiantly as though they could sense the desperateness of our situation. It looked as though we were going to make a lone assault on the target.

"Bombs away," the bombardier called. "Close bomb bay doors."

"Bomb bay doors closed."

In rapid succession, one and four turbos gave out. Four manifold pressure needles all in a row, on the wrong side of the dials.

"Pilot to crew – stand by for a fast, steep dive. We're headed for the clouds. We've lost all four superchargers and I have to get these horses down where they can breathe again. Watch for bandits and hang on tight. Keep yawning to equalise pressure on your eardrums." Ten men and 25 tons of airplane hurtled toward earth at 300 miles an hour.

I scanned the sky for bandits and spotted two. "Pilot to crew. Bandits at two o'clock high – bearing down fast – ready for action!" There was another 10,000 feet to go before we could nestle into the gentle protective folds of the clouds. The bandits closed in fast. Our co-pilot called 'Little Friends' for help. I risked three hundred twenty-five and asked him for the air speed.

Two silver Me-210s in tight formation dropped down to within a hundred feet of our tail, swinging in at 3 o'clock and pointing their gun-loaded noses at us. Two of our gun positions could have been brought to bear, but nothing happened. The right waist gunner opened up. His bullets tore up the right engine, across the wing and into the cockpit of the plane. It rolled over and spun in on fire. The other Me disappeared with a P-38 on its tail. At our air speed and flight altitude they could have finished us.

I wanted to enter the cloud bank almost straight and level. Europe is fairly flat country, but 5,000 feet wasn't the greatest altitude for instrument flying.

"Pilot to navigator, I need a heading to the nearest English coast."

"Have it in a second."

"Pilot to crew – check in."

From nose to tail, all was well.

"Navigator to pilot, hold two nine zero."

"Roger – two nine zero."

Then there was silence. Ten men in ten separate worlds with ten different reactions to an unreal situation.

"Pilot to crew, weather is gone; we're going to make the rest of the trip on the deck. Hold tight again, I'm going down as fast as I can."

At 1,000 feet I began to break our descent, inched the throttles forward, levelled off at tree top, set the throttles for cruising and trimmed the ship.

"Pilot to crew, check in."

Everyone was okay.

"Pilot to belly – Renfro, get out of your turret, you're too close to the ground for comfort." Hardy B. Renfro was the youngest member of the crew. When things were quiet, he was always asking for permission to shoot at something on the ground. I'd answer: "Fine, if you can figure the ballistics for 20,000 feet and 100 mph." That always stopped him.

We shot across Germany and for a short while it was very peaceful.

Grisham yelled: "Hey, there's a little old man in a donkey cart."

"Bandits at 8 o'clock," shouted Sergeant Leslie M. Jones, left waist gunner, the tallest man on the crew and the oldest. The eternal good-natured griper, he thoroughly detested the army and the war. There was a fierce battle going on back there. It was a strange feeling not being able to see your attackers and having someone else doing the fighting. All I could do was fly a little lower and avoid the trees and rooftops.

Directly behind me there was a dull explosion and a sickening thud. Sergeant Eugene D. McGuire, engineer and top gunner from Minneapolis, Minnesota, quiet, withdrawn, efficient, a comfort to have along, slumped on the flight deck, was writhing in pain. His arm and neck were badly torn. Fleming jumped to his aid. I ordered him to the turret.

"Pilot to navigator, need you on the flight deck – engineer wounded."

"Belly to pilot, Jones badly wounded and his gun knocked out."

Wheelis swung on to the flight deck to care for McGuire. Fleming dropped out of the top turret. "Turret is blown up and won't function."

I turned McGuire back over to Fleming and sent Wheelis to the waist to verify its condition.

Jerry was still with us! Sergeant Forrest R. McLaughlin, right waist gunner, shortest man on the crew, full of fun, always smiling, addicted to poker, was hit and his gun silenced.

"Navigator to pilot. Waist gunners are in bad shape, but alive. We've given them morphine and bandaged their wounds. It must have been a 20 mm cannon shell that hit us. I can see daylight everywhere I look back here. Be gentle with this tub!"

"Pilot to radio. Call for help! We could use an escort to shepherd us home."

After a brief silence, "Radio to pilot, my transmitter is knocked out sir, try command radio."

I called and called and called, but no answer. All of our transmitters had been shot out.

"Pilot to crew, all radios are out, there won't be anyone coming to help us. It's up to us to make it alone." Dead ahead laid a huge city that seemed to fill the entire horizon. I knew it was bound to be full of anti-aircraft guns.

"Pilot to navigator, we're approaching a large city at 12 o'clock. I'm going to swing to the left and try to sneak by. Do you know where we are? We've been indicating 200."

"Navigator to pilot. It's Liège."

Our luck held out and we flew by uneventfully. I had flown every inch of the way since I took over at the IP. I asked Grisham: "You want to take it awhile?" He stretched his arms, and reached for the control column. It slipped all the way out of the instrument panel and into his lap. His cables had been shot out! I immediately tried a few gentle manoeuvres with mine. They were firm and working.

With the shock still registered on his face, Grish looked at me and pleaded: "Let's get this thing down somewhere and get out of it."

"Not as long as all four engines are turning." He must have forgotten about the wounded.

I received a very calm call from the tail: "Bandit pulling up at 6 o'clock level. My hydraulic system is out and one gun won't function. When I fire, the other gun sweeps out of control. What shall I do?"

"Crank it over manually, make a sweep, crank it over manually, and make a sweep. Keep him occupied."

Before I could decide which way to turn to throw off our attacker, we were flying in an inferno. All around us, cherry red balls of fire, as big as oranges, were flashing by in an endless stream. It seemed to go on forever. I thought we were going to explode.

I was snapped back to reality with a jolt. Directly ahead of us sat a thatched roof, half-timber farm house. Beyond was a yard filled with chickens. Hundreds of white chickens. The cherry red balls crawled across the thatched roof and into the yard. Chickens and feathers filled the air. I did a steep bank within inches of the house and churned up a mess of feathers and frantic chickens.

The Luftwaffe pilot did not get us. I could have laughed had it not been so sad. There had to be people in the house. The farmer just stood spellbound at the far side of the fence. If our prop wash didn't kill them, his chickens must have laid curdled eggs.

"Pilot to crew, check in." No more casualties.

"Belly gunner to pilot. He left us with a hole behind number three engine big enough to drive a jeep into."

Three men wounded; a gaping hole in our wing, the waist was severed, and radios were inoperative. We were left with a nose turret, one erratic tail gun and a co-pilot without controls. All four engines were still performing and that was a good feeling.

As I scanned the horizon, I spotted a plane at 9 o'clock level. One lone Fw 190. He was checking our speed, flying abreast of what seemed forever.

"Pilot to bombardier. I think you're going to get a chance at an FW 190. As soon as he rolls into his attack, I'm going to go after him. The rest is up to you."

"Roger, I'm ready," he answered.

The German pilot made his decision and rolled into his attack. When he reached 45 degrees and was in full top silhouette, I rolled in to attack. He didn't expect it. He winged over and flew away parallel again. I rolled back to our previous two nine zero heading.

He tried again. I turned steeply into another attack. He rolled out and we flew parallel once more. Now I attacked first. He pulled away forward and began a wide, slow sweep to the right, through 11 o'clock, through 12 o'clock, 1 o'clock, and 2 o'clock.

"Pilot to bombardier. It looks as though he's going to try our other side. This time I'm going to wait until he rolls out level and is totally committed to his attack, and then we'll go after him."

"Roger, I read you."

At 3 o'clock he made his decision, rolled into his attack, rolled out level and bore in.

I wanted him to think we were going to sit and take it bomber fashion. Then I banked over steep and rolled out fast. It all became very personal. He was after me and I was after him. At tree tops, bomber and fighter, crashing headlong toward one another. Four engines against one. Two guns against six. Somebody had to go. One of us was about to die. Space diminished. No one budged. We were both welded to our course by purpose and determination. His radial nacelle got larger and larger.

"He's close enough to tear us to bits."

"He's not shooting."

"Good God. He's going to ram us!"

"Now Pretty," I shouted and once again his half-inch slugs tore up an engine nacelle, crawled across the fuselage and entered the cockpit. His reflexes pulled him up over our right wing. He flipped over and rolled in.

"Tail to pilot. He's done for, scattered all over the countryside. Scratch one Fw."

I swung back to our escape heading, peered into the distance and saw the coast. A beautiful blanket of low clouds moved in from the Channel at about 1,000 feet. I went home in it. The climb became an agonising struggle. With no superchargers it was a tough fight to reach that beautiful fluff. We made it.

"Wheelis, ETA England?"

"14.45."

Fifteen minutes to go. I squeezed the control wheel with deep affection.

"Six Spitfires on collision course at 10 o'clock," Pretty called. I dove, they climbed. Two lucky decisions. Grish and I waved to their leader as they crossed over us and we were on instruments again.

"Navigator to pilot. We should have crossed the English coast."

"Pilot to crew. We are going to let down. I want to get the wounded to the nearest hospital. It's a long way to base and the weather might be worse up there."

We broke out with a 50 foot ceiling, visibility one-quarter mile. We had to land somewhere fast.

I called on intercom: "Somebody find an airfield!"

"Bombardier to pilot. Fighter at 10 o'clock, going away with his gear down. Follow him." I turned gently to the left and the pilot took us down to the centre of an RAF fighter strip at Detling. I made one pass to have a look. I swung around and made one more pass to get the feel of the runway. We fired red flares asking for an ambulance.

McGuire squeezed my shoulder.

"Gas is very low. Let's not go around again."

I called for landing check list. All went well until we reached 'gear down.' Gear would not come down. Emergency procedures would not work. I rocked the ship in a desperate attempt to shake those rubber donuts loose. They refused to leave their wells.

"Pilot to crew. Prepare for belly landing, gear won't come down. We are low on gas and have to go in." I rolled out on the final approach.

"Pilot to crew. Everybody set?"

The waist answered, "Everybody set."

I called for full flaps and reduced air speed. "Co-pilot, call air speed."

"One thirty – one twenty…"

The tower fired red flares telling us "your gear is up, don't land". We fired red flares asking for an ambulance. The sky was full of red flares. "Sorry, we can't talk to you, but we're coming in."

"One ten. One hundred. Ninety." We touched down gently.

"Switches off!"

The props stopped. The plane stopped sliding. Six hours and fifty minutes after take-off, tail-end Charlie was back on the ground. It was *Hula Wahine*'s thirteenth mission. She would never fly again.[3]

In East Anglia bomber after bomber touched down, rubber and runway meeting with a squeal and a puff of smoke. Chalk up another mission. And then the long roll down the runway and taxi to the hardstand. Back on the line, engineering officers with the crew chiefs would be assessing the damage to the aircraft and determining how many planes would be available for the next mission. The photo lab would be printing the strike photos to be rushed to Group Operations for assessment. Trucks met the exhausted crews and took them to Interrogation. Before talking to the debriefing officers they would have a cup of coffee or maybe down a Scotch to calm their nerves and possibly some Paraguayan corned beef on a biscuit, compliments of the Red Cross girls, if they were lucky. Men were soon pouring out their stories to the S-2s. Did you encounter flak and enemy fighters? Did you get any enemy planes? Where did the friendly escort pick you up? Did you see any planes go down? Did you count the number of chutes leaving the plane? And the important question: 'Did you hit the target?' There was always the same answer about the flak: 'The flak was so thick you could walk on it!' Slowly and methodically, the overall picture of the raid, the first in which more than 700 aircraft attacked targets, was pieced together. Forty-six of the bombers had bombed the target of opportunity at Ludwigshafen after deviating from the planned bomb route. In one thing crews were unanimous; fighter opposition had been fierce. Twenty-four B-17s and five B-24s were missing.

The 401st at Deenethorpe had lost four Fortresses. *Little Boots* flown by Captain William R. Beers, another B-17 flown by 2nd Lieutenant Leon G. Van Syckle and 2nd Lieutenant Donald T. Nicklawsky's Fortress, comprising an element of the low box, were all shot down at the same time, which was witnessed by S/Sgt W. E. Merritt, who told his interrogation officer:

These aircraft were attacked by seven or eight twin-engined enemy aircraft at about 1130 hours and just past the target. One was observed to blow up at once and the other two were damaged and went down simultaneously, one being observed to explode before reaching the undercast, the tops of which were approximately 19,000 feet, the other being reported as exploding and also as disappearing into the clouds. No chutes were seen from any of these aircraft.[4]

Captain Beers related:

The situation after take-off and crossing into enemy territory was normal prior to crossing the French-German border. At this time No. 3 engine failed due to mechanical difficulties. Upon arrival over the IP and the subsequent 360° turn, No. 2 engine failed because of flak damage. Our aircraft, with a flight of two, straggled after leaving the target. Friendly fighters left the vicinity shortly after this and our three aircraft came under an enemy fighter attack by twelve Me 110s and Me 210s. The enemy fighters made two attacks in which our aircraft was set on fire in the right wing, cockpit and bomb-bay, where two incendiary clusters had failed to release. The top turret gunner, T/Sgt C. E. Young, me, the tail gunner, S/Sgt J. E. Turvey and the navigator, 1st Lieutenant E. Gershon were wounded. All communication throughout the aircraft was destroyed during the attack. The 'Bail out' signal was given by means of the emergency system. The forward part of the ship was evacuated with the exception of myself and I attempted to leave the ship by the bomb bay after assuring myself that all crew members alive in the rear part of the ship had jumped. However, I was unable to make my way to, or go through the bomb bay because of the intense heat, fire and exploding ammunition. I then returned to the navigator's hatch and bailed out. Almost immediately after this the aircraft exploded.[5]

2nd Lieutenant John Tannahill Jr's B-17 was shot down by fighters near Bonn and only 2nd Lieutenant W. C. Frye, the bombardier, and Sergeant T. E. Brennan, the right waist gunner, survived. Frye related:

> Over the target we had two engines out (one was on fire). We were under heavy fighter attack previous to the explosion. I believe that the pilots may have been hit for I heard shells exploding in the cockpit. The ship went into a steep dive. I started for the cockpit to try to lend assistance. The plane started to spin. I pulled the emergency escape hatch and was blown out by the plane exploding. As I attempted to get to the cockpit I could see the top turret gunner – or at least the lower half of him. As far as I could tell he was uninjured at the time of the explosion.

'Bill' Neumann, whose pilot after leading the 93rd to their base, touched down at Alconbury at 1405, exactly five hours twenty minutes since taking off, said:

> Our P-38 fighter cover was a sight to behold. No problems passing over Holland but as we entered German air space everything changed. About twenty German fighters jumped us but our P-38s drove them off. As we approached our Initial Point the flak became intense. Sergeant Schrock from his position in the tail reported several B-24s were hit and going down. Cloud cover over the target was completely overcast so I bombed the target using radar. As soon as the bomb bay doors were closed we made a wide turn and headed for home. No major problems on the way out as the P-38s were joined by P-47s and furnished us super cover. God bless those guys. I understood we lost five aircraft. One of these was a Pathfinder from our outfit. A mid-air collision was the cause. Had a shot to calm the nerves and then headed to the chow hall. You guessed it; our next stop was the sack for much needed rest.[6]

Staff Sergeant John W. Butler, who flew his eighteenth mission as left waist gunner in *Naughty Nan*, flown by J. J. Collins of Lancaster, Pennsylvania, said:

> We hit flak two or three times on the way to the target. Over the target the flak was really heavy. We bombed with PFF through $^{10}/_{10}$ clouds. We had P-38s, P-47s and Spitfires for escorts. Saw a P-38 shoot down a FW 190. The FW 190 started a dive and the P-38 right on his tail. Flames started out his plane as he exploded. I also saw a P-38 shot down. Also saw a German fighter pilot floating down in his parachute.

At Wendling there was no word from Lieutenant John Stukus and the crew of *Sally Ann*. William McGinley, the tail gunner, who was on his ninth mission, recalled:

> Shortly after turning back, we came under attack by a swarm of German fighters and a running battle ensued for the next 20 minutes or so, in and out of the clouds at high altitude, but as our ship sustained and absorbed more damage we were forced down to 2,000 feet, losing altitude and on fire.
>
> Our navigator and bombardier had been killed during the battle, our gunners were completely out of ammunition and three German fighters were coming in fast and lining us up in their gun sights, so we survivors had no alternative but to bail out. I scrambled from the tail gun turret, went forward and hauled the ball gunner up from his Plexiglas turret. After standing at the open waist exit door for a moment, absolutely terrified, as I looked down at the open countryside slowly passing below, I jumped into space. I would never forget getting out of that burning bomber. I had no idea where I was as I floated down and landed clumsily in an open, freshly ploughed field. Quickly unbuckling my chute harness, I started running across the field, looking for a hiding place. As I was stumbling my way over the ploughed furrows, I saw someone waving frantically at me from the edge of the field to get down and stay down. Little did I know that this was my first contact with the Belgian Resistance movement. Immediately I flopped forward, face down on the soft soil and checked my wristwatch. It was 1100 hours. I stayed as still as possible, face down and hugging the cold, damp ground while hearing the distant shouting and yelling from German patrols as they travelled along the surrounding country roads, tracks and through woodland searching for me and the other survivors from our crashed plane. We'd been told back at Wendling that if we could manage to get through the first 12 hours in enemy-occupied territory without getting caught, there was a reasonable chance that the underground movement would make contact.[7]

It had been Mission Thirteen for the crew of *The Worry Wart*. Safely back at Knettishall, Larry Goldstein wrote:

> We went all the way this time. Not much flak and no enemy fighters. P-38s and 47s galore. The sky over Europe belongs to the 8th Air Force. I was given the job of throwing chaff out of the radio chute. Our ball gunner got sicker than hell again and Jack, 'BJ' and I had quite a time with him. Can't go on like this. A fellow gets quite exhausted at 20,000 feet pulling another fellow around.

Mission completed, he concluded, 'Over the hump and on the way home.'

When on Sunday 30 January a record 778 heavies were dispatched to the aircraft factories at Brunswick, Larry Goldstein recalled:

When the crews heard this at the briefing we remembered the heavy losses the 8th Air Force suffered on their last visit. We all tightened up and our stomachs began to churn. The breakfast did not go down and doubts set in. Surprise, little flak and few fighters but bombing by our group and all the sweat and strain was for nought. We were supposed to bomb from 20,000 feet but we were forced to go to 29,000 feet to get out of cloud cover. Our bomb pattern seemed poor so I expected another visit to this place.

About 700 aircraft bombed using PFF techniques, while fifty-one dropped their bombs on targets of opportunity. Twenty aircraft were lost on the mission. John Kettman in Harry Cornell's crew recalls:

Brunswick was the place where we lost fifty-nine planes the last time. This was one rough son of a bitch. On the way over there was a little light flak but on the bomb run all hell broke loose! And it was accurate too. They briefed us for twenty-nine flak guns; there must have been 329! A burst broke just below us and we thought sure as hell we'd had it. The bombs were just released and the concussion blew the radio room open and knocked Robert Sage, radio operator, on the head. Just before the bomb run a few 190s came in. Pete Wolak, Gidel and I got a few shots at them. They shot rockets from the ground. Clelland Martinson, tail gunner, saw a B-17 go down in back of us. P-38s picked us up after the bomb run. After the flak area we didn't see Hayward's B-17. Later we heard he landed at another field pretty well shot up. They had a rough time. They went into a tailspin and pulled out at 8,000 feet. We had a hole in each wing, one in the stabiliser, one on my side of the waist a yard away from me, another two feet from Logan and Martinson had a large one just at the back of his fanny, which brushed his leg. All our squadron came back. One of the 365th ships was missing. This was a rough place and I was glad to be back. We bombed by pathfinder so we never saw the ground. I hope to hell we hit the plane factory down there, we travelled almost 1,000 miles.

John Butler, who flew his nineteenth mission on 30 January as left waist gunner in *Naughty Nan*, flown by J. J. Collins, recalled:

We took off at 09.15 to bomb some factories at Brunswick that were making parts for planes. We ran into flak quite a lot on the way to the target. Over the target the flak wasn't too bad. We had to bomb by PFF through $^{10}/_{10}$ cloud cover. We had P-38s, P-51s, P-47s and Spitfires. Only saw one enemy fighter. He made one pass at a B-17 but some P-47s showed up. The German ran for home. The last time we hit this target we lost 58 planes. Next day we took off at 11.55 to bomb V-weapon construction works at Siracourt in France with twelve 500 pounders. It was a very nice day and we could see our target real good, as visibility was perfect. There was no flak or fighters. We also had good fighter protection. So it was a milk run as a whole. One plane was lost through mechanical failure.[8]

From an aesthetic point of view the big Liberator wasn't pretty. She had a turned-up nose. Her curves weren't graceful. She wasn't sleek. She had been patched up and coiffured many times. But *Heavenly Daze* – how she got that name no one can explain – had done a commendable job of bombing and slugging on twenty-four missions over Hitler's fortress. She had roared proudly over Vegesack, Danzig, Oslo, Bremen, Kiel, Brunswick, etc. and had acquired a personality as well as a reputation. 'She's a wonderful ship,' her pilot, 1st Lieutenant Walter McCartie, of Oskaloosa, Iowa, often boasted. 'She always comes through – because she's got a lot of heart in her.' But *Heavenly Daze*'s last flight, on a crisp February morning, was destined to be a strange odyssey. The big Liberator headed out over England on her twenty-fifth operational mission, piloted for the first time by 1st Lieutenant Richard J. Pettit, of Los Angeles, California; she developed a conglomeration of mechanical troubles ranging from runaway propellers to a 'conked-out' electrical system. The plane lurched forward and began climbing with the speed of a thunderbolt. 'We had one engine runaway shortly after we got off the ground, so I started to circle back for a landing,' explained Pettit, 'but at 4,000 feet, with two more runaways, it looked like the vibration would tear the ship apart. We were climbing at 200 miles an hour at about 1,500 feet per minute with a full bomb load.'

Pettit and his co-pilot, 2nd Lieutenant Humphrey J. Elliot of Richmond, Virginia, wrestled desperately with the controls. They were above the overcast and had no idea where they were – except near the North Sea coast. They didn't dare risk jettisoning the bombs because of the possibility of English towns down below. They couldn't crash-land because visibility was less than 2,000 feet and the ceiling 800 feet. Time for split-second thinking. Figuring the best way to save his crew was to have them jump, Pettit steadied *Heavenly Daze* as best he could and then gave the bail out order. Parachutes blossomed under the ship, as the crew dropped away from her. 'I 'trimmed' her and headed her out to sea before going over the side,' the pilot said later, 'and as I floated into the overcast, I saw the ship wheel into a gentle bank.'

The crescendo of the whining radials reverberated in the ears of the 'chutists as they descended through the cloud blanket on to the East Anglian countryside. And then, as if deciding she'd been temperamental long-enough, *Heavenly Daze* levelled off at medium altitude and wandered aimlessly over East Anglia and the North Sea coast. Townspeople who were disturbed when they heard her distressing drone now heard her normal purr. So they resumed their workaday tasks. Just another airplane. The Royal Observer Corps heard her too but couldn't spot her. She was still above the overcast. Because her electrical system was out, she couldn't have identified herself as 'friendly', even if her crewmen had been aboard.

Several Spitfires of the RAF were sent up when the 'intruder' failed to answer radio calls. British ack-ack gunners were alerted. The RAF pilots radioed back the startling report that there apparently was nobody in the plane. Still the bomb-laden B-24 droned on over the coastal sector. The Spit pilots were in a dilemma, because there was no way to tell for sure that there was no one in the big ship. One by one, the crew members who had bailed out landed and telephoned base. The bombardier, 2nd Lieutenant Robert F. Leesley of Chicago, Illinois, landed in a WAAF camp where girls eyed his silk with wistful lust. Co-pilot Elliot landed in a tree and the navigator, 2nd Lieutenant Leslie A. Jacobson, landed in a field, started down the road, was picked up and subsequently wound up in the hospital, where he became conscious the next morning. He had remembered nothing after he'd pulled the rip cord. The waist gunners, sergeants John P. Kogut of Clayville, New York, and Erharot D. Lange of Marinette, Wisconsin, landed near a haystack and Staff Sergeant James R. Stanley, of Midland, Texas, the engineer-gunner, was challenged by a youngster who 'took some convincing that I was a Yank – not a Jerry'.

Staff Sergeant Peter Bortua, of Palmerton, Pa., the radio operator, and Sergeant Joseph A. D'Atri, of Brooklyn, New York, dropped into farmyards. Pettit landed in a drainage ditch, a bare 100 yards from the sea. When he checked into base via telephone, he told the officers that he was the last man out of the ship.

Crewless, *Heavenly Daze* continued to soar above the clouds. All the while she was under the watchful eyes of the Spits. A lively exchange of views commenced over the radio telephone between the Spitfire pilots, their ground station and the

Liberator base. Finally, everyone decided that the abandoned B-24 with her 6,000-lb cargo of high explosives should be disposed of.

A sergeant-gunner carried the news to McCartie, 'non-operational' that day and 'sweatin' 'em out.' He ground his cigarette stub into the muddy turf and sped for the control tower.

The Spits circled the lumbering Liberator until she headed out to sea again. She had been flying alone for over an hour and a half now. The RAF pilots debated over the radio who was to go in first, for they didn't like the idea of bombs exploding in their faces. Finally, they went to work. They learned quickly that Libs aren't an easy aircraft to shoot down. They made pass after pass on the helpless bomber. No evasive action for *Heavenly Daze* now. No hair-breadth exploits for her gunners. One fighter even ran out of 20 mm ammunition as the point-blank cannon fire ripped into the wings.

The big Lib finally plummeted into the icy sea – her wings clipped, chewed off. That night the communiqué might have read, 'One of our bombers is missing – due to "friendly" action.' The commanding officer was trying to figure out how to enter the weird flight on the books. Out 'on the line', in a lonely Nissen engineering hut, *Heavenly Daze*'s crew chief, Master Sergeant Raymond L. Bader, of Columbus, Ohio, sat idly whittling shavings into a coal bucket. He went to the window and looked out across the windswept airdrome. The dispersal site was empty where *Heavenly Daze* once proudly squatted day and night when she wasn't delivering calling cards.

Bader fumbled the blackout curtain. The darkness bore down. 'She was a great ship,' he shrugged. 'I don't blame those guys. I'd probably have gotten out sooner myself. But she'd never let anybody down, though. You just hadda know her...'[9]

By now 'BJ' Keirsted's crew in the 388th were veterans and their fifteenth mission was on Thursday 3 February, when the 8th was assigned Wilhelmshaven. Larry Goldstein recalled:

The briefing again was early and getting out of a warm bed at 4.45 a.m. and stepping into an English February morning can leave you chilled for the whole day. For some reason this was an easy mission. Picked up a flak hole in the right wing but there was no other damage. The worst part was the extreme cold, which was about 47 below zero. We were supposed to bomb from 27,500 feet but bad weather forced us to bomb from 22,000 feet. Because of a shortage of gunners we had to fly with a nine-man crew, without ball and waist gunners.

Operations wanted to cancel us but 'BJ' was eager to get the mission in. When we went into the combat area we released the turret from a locked position and Jack Kings gave the turret a shove every once in a while to make it appear occupied. Fortunately, the enemy fighters did not take on the 388th today.

John Kettman, in Harry Cornell's crew, recalled:

We dropped the cookies at 29,000 feet, which was the highest we'd been so far. We had beautiful fighter support to the target; P-38s and P-47s and P-51s. We didn't see a single enemy fighter the whole trip. The flak was light around the target. We were throwing out chaff to goof up their radar. I really heaved it out too. Coming out of Germany we were supposed to go out over the North Sea. Well, the lead navigator goofed up and we went over Holland. We caught flak and were really surprised as we thought we were nearly home. Eddy Donald, our co-pilot, was back in the waist foolin' about with Darius Logan and when he saw the flak he came through the plane like a bat out of hell. We flew low over the Channel and had to sweat out the gas. We made it with a few pints to spare. It wasn't a bad raid and I hoped we get more like it.

Keirsted's crew sewed on their second cluster and prepared for the sixteenth mission. It came the following day, when 433 bombers in fifteen combat wings of B-17s and B-24s were dispatched to Frankfurt on the Main River, escorted by fifteen fighter groups. Frankfurt was almost within P-47 range, although target support could only be carried out by the few long-range P-38 Lightning and Mustang groups while eight Spitfire squadrons covered the final stages of the return flight. The Main River presented a clear return on the H_2S radar carried by PFF aircraft and it was enough to allow the bombers to drop their loads through overcast with a fair degree of accuracy. However, H_2S failures and high crosswinds prevented accurate bombing while several combat wings came under intense AA fire over the Ruhr. It was Keirsted's crew's seventh raid in eight days. The lead navigator could not locate the target and the 388th bombed the secondary. Goldstein noted:

We went through the southern part of the Ruhr Valley and it was an awful experience. The 'Happy Valley Boys' can really throw up a heavy barrage of flak. It was very heavy today and Jack Kings had a close call. Flak entered just below his gun position but armour plate deflected it. After 'bombs away' the pilots used evasive action and really threw the plane around the sky. It was the heaviest flak

I have yet to see. Thank God there was no fighter opposition. We sweated this one out. Many planes went down and we settled for quite a few flak holes, one of which necessitated a wingtip change.

1st Lieutenant Thomas Keene's crew in the 448th were flying their fourth mission, in *No Name Jive*. It was one Crew 55 would not forget as 'Bo' Bottoms explains.

We started out and got to the enemy coast about 1130 and encountered light flak there and thereabout for 30 minutes after that. We got the heck knocked out of us. I had never seen such flak, it knocked out our No. 3 engine and we had to feather. It also put a couple of holes in our wing and one in the fuselage beside the left waist window. But with one engine gone we stayed with the formation until we arrived at the target. When we tried to open the bomb bay doors, one of them did not open and one side of the bombs – twenty-six of them, and incendiaries at that – fell into the bomb bay. Edwin Moran hung onto the bomb rack with one hand and dropped thirteen of them out the side that was open with the other. It took three of us to throw the rest out the escape hatch in the rear. It was 47 degrees below zero and 'Pappy' Blanton and I got frostbite on our faces. We came all the way back on three engines and made the landing fine and dandy.

Fortunately the Luftwaffe was limited in its operations by the weather, though JG 26 claimed seven of the total of ten bombers shot down by the German fighters.[10]

The crew of *The Worry Wart* only had nine more missions to go. One of the barrack room jokes was 'sixteen missions and no rest home yet'. Crews that had battle fatigue were sent to a rest home for a week or ten days and then came back to combat flying. 'Goldie' Goldstein recalls:

We reached seventeen without anybody suggesting a rest home to us. We went on a two-day pass to London and we arrived in town late in the evening. When we woke up in the morning we read in the papers that American air forces had heavy losses on the raid the day before. It made us relieved that we were safe in London while our friends may have gone down or were PoWs.

On Saturday 5 February 450 B-17s and B-24s attacked airfields at Châteauroux, Avord, Tours, Châteaudun, Orleans and Villacoublay. 2nd Lieutenant E. A. Christensen's B-17 in the 401st was attacked by fighters on the mission to

Châteauroux but the pilot managed to bring his badly damaged bomber back and he landed at RAF Abingdon near Oxford, as he recalled:

A Me109 attacked from the one o' clock position and hit us with a burst of cannon fire. Shortly after this a Fw 190 came at us vertically, raked us with 20 mm cannon fire from a range of about 20 yards then stalled away. One shell struck the ball turret and a fragment went through the forehead of S/Sgt Jack Nonemaker. Other fragments wounded him in the back of the neck and right hand and yet another tore a finger from his left hand. Despite being shot through the head, he managed to get out of the ball turret and get to the radio room for help. The radio operator himself had been hit in the right leg by a 20 mm shell, shattering his leg badly. At the same time S/Sgt B. J. Fatica, the right waist gunner, was hit below the hip by another 20 mm shell, which exploded and blew his leg off. The bombardier, 2nd Lieutenant Reynolds, and the left waist gunner, Sergeant Batson, gave first aid to the three injured men but Fatica died of his injuries about 45 minutes after being hit.[11]

The bomber formations included for the first time B-17s and B-24s of the 452nd and 453rd Bomb Groups, based near Norwich, at Deopham Green and Old Buckenham respectively.[12] In January the arrival of the 452nd had brought cheer to twelve-year-old Jim Matsell and his pals who lived near the base.

There was a faint drumming in the air, a far-off buzzing and we knew they were coming. When the Yanks arrived, us youngsters stood open-mouthed as these huge aircraft filled the skies overhead. The noise was tremendous; it was very daunting and quite an awesome sight. We hopped on our bikes and rode off following them to the airfield, to their dispersal point. The end of the aircraft opened as it landed and these crewmen threw out chewing gum and candies for us. They had heard these terrible stories that the English were starving and on rations; we didn't mind playing on it a little bit. Then they threw out a bundle of 10-shilling notes and there was a right free for all.

Tom Brittan had just turned twelve and was living in Carleton Rode, a Norfolk village sandwiched between Tibenham and Old Buckenham, when the 453rd arrived. His house in Norwich had been damaged in a German air raid.

The news that the Yanks in huge four-engined bombers had arrived at Old Buckenham spread like wild fire through the village. Our toy rifles and homemade uniforms, with which we played soldiers, were quickly discarded. We jumped onto our bicycles and peddled furiously up to the airfield. THERE THEY WERE! Some already parked at their dispersal points, and others circling the base for landing. We watched in wonder as one came to a halt only a few feet from the hedge by the roadside. The roar ceased as the engines were switched off and the crew emerged, carrying boxes. They threw oranges over the hedge for us to catch. We had almost forgotten that the fruit existed. I shall never forget my mother's expression of surprise on seeing my orange and being told that an American had given it to me. In the ensuing months, Old Buckenham airbase was the centre of attraction. Many hours were spent watching the Liberators return from their missions and waiting for a hand wave from the crew as they parked their aircraft. We each had favourite Liberators. Mine were *El Flako* and *Ohio Silver*. When *El Flako* failed to return in November 1944, I was terribly sad as I cycled home. The aircrews and groundcrews who serviced the aircraft became our friends and it was thrilling to be allowed to go inside a Liberator.

On Sunday 6 February 206 bombers bombed airfields and No Ball sites in France. Bad weather prevented more than 400 other heavies from completing their missions. 'BJ' Keirsted's crew flew their seventeenth mission when the 388th went to Romilly-sur-Seine, However, the Group failed to find the target in the cloudy conditions prevailing and crews brought their bombs back. Despite the failure the mission counted and the crew now had only eight missions to go. Six bombers failed to return.[13] On the 7th the Bomb Groups were stood down. On the Tuesday 237 bombers attacked Frankfurt-on-Main using blind bombing techniques and 127 bombers attacked V-1 sites at Watten and Siracourt. Another seventy-eight heavies bombed targets of opportunity. 'BJ' Keirsted's crew flew the mission in *Screamin' Red Ass.* 'Goldie' Goldstein recalls:

It was almost a routine combat mission except for the fighter and the extremely heavy flak. The cold was tremendous and my heated gloves and shoes went on the blink. The gloves were plugged in at the wrists and the boots plugged in at the ankles. If one of these shorted out the other three extremities shorted out. This day my left boot shorted out. However, some genius had had the foresight to supply a plug which we carried and when used it closed the circuit for the other three limbs. It took me some time to realise that it was the left boot; the heavy clothes and manning the radio and a gun made this somewhat difficult to accomplish. I did, however, find the right limb and when the plug was inserted I closed the circuit. It was 47 below and I really had to do quite a bit of stomping and clapping all the way to the target and all the way back to keep my limbs warm. I like to think that I walked from France to Frankfurt and back to England.

Apart from the cold the young American from Brooklyn was also scared at the sight of one of the engines smoking on the way to the target, but the aircraft returned safely to Knettishall. Goldstein noted that he was 'rather tired of visiting Frankfurt' and hoped that 'perhaps it has been finished off by now'.

It was another long haul for Harry Cornell's crew, which went to Frankfurt, as John Kettman recalled.

There weren't as many of us as usual and we were to have excellent fighter support. Everything went smoothly until we hit the target and then all hell broke loose. The sky was black with flak. We waded through it then started home with P-47 and P-51 support. We got to Amiens, France and caught more flak. After that our escort left and enemy fighters started on us, they made a nose attack right through the formation. One came through and wasn't ten feet from us. He blasted the nose off our right wing man. We were leading the second element. Then they picked on another group and knocked down a B-17. I saw two chutes come out before the B-17 burst into flames and went into a spin. The fighters started to cue into us again when our P-47s showed up. The navigator and bombardier both got shots at them. They were really after us. There must have been about fifty of them Me 109s around. We only had two holes in the ship in spite of all that. Damn lucky! Donald Eddy got excited and all he could yell was 'hit the son of a bitch' over and over again. The bombardier was injured on the plane that had its nose shot off. It was a rough one; I was glad when it was all over.[14]

Another city which was very unpopular with fliers was Brunswick. A mission to the city was scrubbed on 9 February but 'BJ' Keirsted's crew were one of twenty-two 388th crews assigned the target on Thursday the 10th. It was their nineteenth mission and a significant one for Larry Goldstein, whose twenty-second birthday it was.

Today was the roughest mission of all my eighteen missions. We hit the French coast and picked up enemy opposition and they continued to attack all the way to the target and back again to the coast. I saw more fighters today than ever before. There were 109s, 190s, 110s and Ju 88s. We had good fighter support of 38s, 48s and 51s but I'm afraid that we need more of them. They did a swell job of protecting us but the German fighter pilots were determined to knock down as many Forts as possible. Quite a few planes did go down and even saw our own fighters taking it on the chin. 'The target was hit very hard and I believe that it was a shack job. I really sweated today. The flak at the target was not too heavy, but plenty accurate. It was about 54 below and that's plenty cold. Returned safely with very minor damage. Believe me, I am not ashamed to say that I was scared today and never prayed harder to come through. Nineteen missions completed.

Three crews in the 388th failed to return.

One of the replacement crews who arrived at Snetterton Heath to join the 'Falcons' during the month was captained by 2nd Lieutenant Sherman Gillespie. S/Sgt Ernest J. Richardson, the radio operator, recalls:

It had taken a little time getting lined up with my crew because we were all doing our own thing, but eventually our crew started to come together. My pilot was Sherman Gillespie; co-pilot Robert Ketcham, bombardier Glenn Fister. I don't remember the original navigator's name but I do remember him as quite a character. His favourite line was: "Ah don't wanta be the best navigator in the world – Ah just wanta be the ol'est." He got us lost one night right over Spokane so shortly after that Gillespie requested another one whose name was Chester Schultz. Top-turret was Steve Condur, waist gun-gunners were Robert Christiansen and Willard Berg, James Schroeder was the ball-turret, Jack Fletcher tail-gunner. That was the crew until we got to England and Schroeder left our crew and went with the ground personnel; from then on we had a new ball-turret man for almost every raid. We wondered how we would make out? Would we be as lucky as the crew we were sharing the hut with? Wonder if they're chicken here? With all that running through my mind it was quite a while before I fell asleep.

The non-coms in Gillespie's crew shared a hut with 2nd Lieutenant Robert H. Dickert's enlisted crewmembers. Dickert's crew had been assigned to the Group in October 1943 and by early February had only three missions to go to complete their tour of twenty-five missions. When he woke up the next morning Ernie Richardson saw that Dickert's crew was gone.

I began to wonder if I'd ever get to know when there might be a raid. Everything was new to me. Going to chow that morning I saw one of the most beautiful sights of my life. Groups were forming overhead and every so often the lead plane and the planes following in the same group would shoot certain coloured flares that against a very blue sky, with more planes than I had ever seen before, was a fantastic sight. I couldn't believe the power I was witnessing. Our first day we were introduced to our CO. We liked him right from the start. When he spoke of a crew that didn't make it back from a raid he made it sound like it was the crew's own fault, as we didn't know any better we thought he might be telling the truth, hell what did we know. He did seem to take a personal interest in all that were there. We were shown where each of us was supposed to go if scheduled for school and the different areas around the base that we should know about. It was also mentioned what time the group would be back in case we wanted to watch them come in. The raid happened to be an easy one and everyone got back safe.

Well, this was great; maybe combat wouldn't be so rough after all, remembering the beautiful sight I had seen that morning. Dickert's crew was ecstatic that night in the hut. Only two more raids to go and back to the States for them. We shared their happiness. A fella called 'Rosie' that worked in ordnance hung around our hut a lot, mentioned to Dickert's crew he would supply them with parachute flares that they could shoot off when they came back from their last mission. It was all planned; all they had to do was get back. Charlie Gafford the tail gunner had written a letter to his wife that was to be sent in case he shouldn't come back. I remember him waving it around and saying, "Two more raids and I can rip this to hell." Yep, everyone was in fine spirits. Could you blame them?

There was no raid the next day because of the weather. Although the weather was nasty, Condur and I went down to the line to look at the planes. "Boy, just think these ships have been over Germany and have probably been shot at." It was really exciting just looking at them. Frightening too.

The next raid was somewhere in France. The 96th got hit by a few fighters but no one was hurt. Dickert's crew was telling us about it that night, seemed Jerry had something new. It was a fighter that was real fast and looked just like a Fw 190 except that it had a longer nose. But in that no one was hurt, why worry?

"One more raid and we're through, they can't get us now."

Everyone was sweating out their last one.

The constellation of Orion was low in the western sky as crews in the 447th walked in the dark to the mess hall at Rattlesden on 10 February, in preparation

for a 0430 hours briefing. The low rumble of voices was silenced as Colonel
Hunter Harris came into the room and everyone was called to attention. After
preliminaries, the intelligence officer removed the cover from the mission map.
The black ribbon left the English coast at Great Yarmouth and continued across
the North Sea and the Zuider Zee to Brunswick.

At Seething 1st Lieutenant Helander and Crew 11 were stood down but the
CQ awakened Lieutenant Robert Ayrest's crew to fly the mission to Rijen airfield
in Holland in *Boomerang*. No one, least of all Bill McCullah, envied them. Rain,
sleet and snow discouraged everyone from going outside but after several hours
of high winds and driving snow, crews received orders to take off. Snow flurries
delayed take-offs but eventually all the B-24s departed and climbed toward
the assembly area. Two aircraft returned to Seething early due to mechanical
problems but the remainder of the 448th struggled to assemble, as did the other
Groups. Continuing in these conditions for an hour, Ayrest and the crew of
Boomerang finally spotted the Group at 2 o'clock high. Ayrest initiated a turn
to join the Group when a flash of another B-24 forced him to violently push
forward on the controls to avoid a collision. Pulling the aircraft back to level
flight after the abrupt manoeuvre exceeded the structural limits of the Liberator
and *Boomerang*'s tail broke off between the waist and the tail. It pitched up into
a stall and then the wingtips folded. *Boomerang* was doomed. It entered a spin
and the centrifugal forces pinned Sergeant Edward Schroeder, one of the waist
gunners, to the floor with Sergeant Leonard Snell, the other waist gunner, pinned
on top of him. As suddenly as it started, the powerful forces subsided. The waist
section of the airplane disintegrated, freeing Schroeder from its death-like grip.
Slipping backwards, he fell out of the aircraft where the tail section and the tail
gunner used to be. Falling free of the aircraft, he groped for his chest pack. Finding
the ripcord between his legs (he had connected only one buckle of his chest pack),
he pulled it. Following the opening shock, he looked above his head to see the
parachute. Schroeder landed and was dragged over an embankment and across a
field by the wind before the chute became entangled in a hedgerow.

An eighteen-year-old English girl witnessed his landing; to Schroeder she was
an angel. The girl helped him to a gate where Mrs Chinnery, her mother, was
waiting with a car and she began driving toward the smoking wreckage of the
Liberator, which had crashed at Oaken Hill Farm, Badingham. Schroeder said he
did not want to go to the crash site so the woman drove him to her farmhouse
nearby, where they had watched two chutes coming down and wreckage falling.
Later, an ambulance carrying Leonard Snell picked up Schroeder and carried them

to Seething. Lieutenant Ronald McAllister had also survived with just a broken ankle. The ball turret gunner had broken free of the B-24 but his parachute was damaged and only partly opened. He and the six other crewmembers lost their lives.[15] Bill McCullah was angry at the loss of *Boomerang*.

That stricken crew were deader than a hammer! Deader than Tom Mix's horse, Tony! It could have been us! It should have been us! *Boomerang* was our plane. We pre-flighted her. It was a goddam rotten shame! It cost a crew and our airplane!

Boomerang came back all right; in little pieces!

At Snetterton Heath 'Red', a ball-turret man from another crew, came into Ernie Richardson's hut at about ten o'clock and said his B-17 had to abort because of an engine problem.

"Where were you going today?"

"Don't know," he said, "the other planes aren't back yet," indicating to us that we wouldn't find out, at least not from him.

Ernie Richardson wondered if he thought they were spies.

After lunch Condur and I were supposed to fly. We were still being checked out in certain areas. Down at the line our pilots were just about ready but we just weren't supposed to fly that day. First the engines wouldn't start and then when we did make it to the runway the other planes started coming back from the raid so the tower told us our flight was called off. Steve and I went to get our parachutes when we noticed Jim White on Dickert's crew from our hut unloading a bunch of A-3 bags and flying equipment from a truck. We thought it must have been a short raid.

"What say White?"

"Hi," he answered. He seemed to have a strange look on his face, also he seemed rather distant toward us but we didn't pay too much attention to it. We went inside to get our chutes and saw Dickert's bombardier taking off his heated suit. We heard someone ask him where our fighters were. "Yeah we had fighter cover, but they were fighting Germans way above us."

What the hell was going on here? We still didn't know what had happened. We started back out to our plane when we saw a big crowd gathered around one of the other ships. We asked someone what was going on at that plane and he told us that it had just come back and was all shot up and that the radio operator had been killed. Oh no, not Charlie Rayburn. It hit me what he was saying. "What happened to the rest of the crew?"

"They bailed out over France or Belgium."

Wow! So that's why White was acting the way he did. I had that awful feeling inside of me. Well, combat wasn't so wonderful after all. This was terrible. After seeing this Condur and I didn't feel much like flying; also we were anxious to see how badly the plane had been hit. Condur and I jumped out of the plane and took off for Dickert's ship, to just look at it you would swear it could never fly. Dickert did a great job getting it back. Charlie dead, the radio compartment was full of holes; a 20 mm had gone through the waist and exploded just as it entered the radio room. I was all choked up inside. "Did the ball-turret man get out OK?" I asked someone near the plane.

"I think so," was the answer. "Guess they all did."[16]

That didn't make me feel any better. Maybe they were dead too. Boy, what chance had we got? All kinds of things were running through my head. So this is aerial warfare. Condur and I started back to our hut. On the way we passed White and his four officers heading for the Officer's Club. No one said anything. If I was them I think I would want a drink too. If we had known what was in store for us back at the hut I don't think we would have gone there. 'Red' was sitting on a bed crying, I hadn't seen a man cry in a long time. 'Rosie' was there with a blank look on his face. The rest of our crew was standing around. No one was saying anything. Supply was picking up the personal belongings of the crew members that had bailed out. Later, with everyone feeling lousy, White came in. He looked at us – his eyes were red and he reeled a little. We sort of expected him to say something. There was still a lot of mystery as to why the rest of the crew had bailed out. How many fighters had hit them? Where was the raid? 'Red' answered most of the questions for us. White hit the sack. The raid was about a hundred miles west of Berlin; a place called Brunswick. They had been hit bad and Dickert let the wheels down thinking they would all have to bail out. When Willie, Herman and Gafford saw that, they just went. The last thing they heard Herman say was "Charlie's down!" They had been hit by Goering's 'yellow noses', which were his pet fighters at that time stationed in France. We started thinking of our own skins. What the hell chance had we got? We hadn't even flown our first raid yet. Now we were more aware of what we would be up against. We wished we would get our first raid in so we could see what it was like for ourselves.

It was on Friday 11 February that the first P-51 Mustangs joined VIII Fighter Command. At Frankfurt-Main 180 B-17s of the 1st Division attacked industrial targets. A V-weapon site at St-Pol-Siracourt was also bombed and 130 heavies bombed Ludwigshafen and other targets of opportunity after the blind bombing equipment failed. The 3rd Division was rested and the 2nd Division bombed targets in the Pas de Calais. John Kettman wrote:

My third trip to Frankfurt. It was a smooth trip. We had beautiful escort all the way, P-51s and P-47s. At the IP we picked up fighters but they didn't come in. It was quiet until we were over the city and then the sky just got black with flak. They shot a few rockets up from the ground. It was really thick. We picked up 47s after the target and they took us all the way home. I saw a 47 shoot down an enemy fighter. A 110 came in close just before the target but didn't bother us. We caught a little more flak at Amiens. We had a big hole in the wing, just at the back of No. 4 nacelle. There was one in the nose but it was from an empty cartridge. Our plane would be out for a week or more, as it hit the main spar and Tokyo tank valve.

Next day we were surprised to hear that we weren't bombing Frankfurt. We hit Ludwigshafen instead, which was some distance away. The lead navigator got mixed up so there we were. We saw the bomb pictures and we made a good job of it! They sure had as much flak as Frankfurt!

Eighty-five B-24s returned to the St-Pol-Siracourt area and bombed the V-1 sites again. John Butler, who was flying his twenty-fifth and final mission of his tour, was right waist gunner in *Reddy Teddy*, piloted by Lieutenant Glenn E. Tedford in the 'Travelling Circus'. He wrote:

We took off at 0730 to bomb Siracourt from 18,000 feet. Flak was pretty good but none was close to us. It was minus 22. When I left the French coast behind, I was very happy. I never wanted to see the French coast again except on a postcard or on a newsreel. It was a good mission to finish up on. I was a pretty happy guy when I landed.

Major General Jimmy Doolittle, who had recently replaced Ira Eaker as chief of the 8th Air Force, had been biding his time, waiting for a period of relatively fine weather in which to mount a series of raids on the German aircraft industry. Myron Keilman recalls:

The weather had been so bad that the 392nd had flown only sixteen missions since 1 January. But by 20 February we had been both alerted and briefed and had taxied for take-off nearly every morning since General Doolittle had taken command. We waited for hours in the dense fog before the red flare fired from the control tower signalled 'mission cancelled'. Then back to airplanes' dispersal pads; back to the dank Nissen huts and back to the damp, ice-cold cots for needed sleep and tomorrow's alert. Damn the foggy weather, damn the war and damn General Doolittle too.

After his Tokyo Raid on 18 April 1942, for which he was awarded the Medal of Honor, Doolittle had commanded the 4th Bomb Wing from June to August 1942 before being given command of the 12th Air Force. The forty-seven-year-old, 5 foot 4 inch, famed air racer was given command of the 8th Air Force on 6 January. On 13 February the Chiefs of Staff accepted a revision of the CBO Plan when targets were reduced to a number that could be decisively attacked and target lists were revised to keep up with the effort of the enemy to relocate vital industrial plant. Disruption of lines of communication and a reduction of the Luftwaffe fighter strength were now given high priority. General Carl 'Tooey' Spaatz and his subordinate commanders, Jimmy Doolittle (8th Air Force) and Major General Nathan F. Twining (15th Air Force), planned a series of coordinated raids known as Operation Argument on the German aircraft industry, supported by RAF night bombing, at the earliest possible date. But only good weather would permit the first battle involving the mass use of bomb groups of the Strategic Air Forces (USSTAF). The meteorologists informed their commanders that the week of 20–25 February, which was to go down in history as 'Big Week', would be ideal for such an offensive.

Like so many mornings in England, the sky in the early hours of Sunday 20 February was clear but a few stray clouds drifting in from the North Sea gave warning of an instrument assembly above $^{10}/_{10}$ cloud by take-off time. At Snetterton Heath S/Sgt Ernie Richardson on Sherman Gillespie's crew, who had yet to fly a mission, recalls that they were awakened around 02.30, went to breakfast and then down to the line for briefing. Richardson continues:

In the briefing room a large curtain covered a map, that is it was supposed to, but this morning it covered just half of it. A ribbon ran from England up the North Sea and disappeared behind the curtain. Everyone wondered where we could be going. Seemed like the more experienced crews weren't used to seeing the ribbon take off in such an odd direction from England before. It scared the hell out of us. All the crews had worried looks on their faces, I heard one of them say, "Never saw anything like this before, looks like a long one." We were there groaning about what might be in store for us when an S-2 officer walked in and pulled the rest of the curtain back. Wow! "Today gentlemen, you're going to a place called Tutow; you will cross Denmark here," indicating with his pointer where the ribbon crossed. "Flak, if you stay on course shouldn't be too bad. You will probably be hit by fighters, but we don't think you will see too many of them, you're to destroy an airfield here," indicating again with his pointer, "the 2nd Division is going after an aircraft factory located here," pointing to a place just below where we were scheduled to go. "You'll have flak over the target, we're not sure how much, but as Colonel Limely says you can tell about that when you get back." We were supposed to laugh.

Tutow was located about 150 miles north-east of Berlin. A combat experienced pilot named Schneider would be flying with us on our first raid and Gillespie would fly co-pilot. I thought Schneider was a very brave man to take a new crew on their very first raid. Being a radio operator, I had to go to another briefing where I received a flimsy, which gave me my radio call signs, frequencies for the day and a lot of other data for that particular raid. By the time I got to the plane the rest of the crew were putting in their guns and making sure everything was in working order around their positions. White was there mentioning things he thought would be helpful, I really liked him for it.

A force of over 1,000 heavies was assembled as the anticipated cloud scudded across eastern England, bringing snow squalls, which threatened to disrupt the mission. The 1st and 2nd Bomb Divisions were briefed to hit the Bf 109 plants at Leipzig, which had been bombed only a few hours earlier by RAF Bomber Command. The 3rd Division, meanwhile, would fly an equally long and arduous route, to Poznan in Poland. At Knettishall Lieutenant Lowell Watts, pilot of *Blitzin' Betsy*, was flying his nineteenth mission that day. He viewed the map in the briefing room with a sense of foreboding.

The map was covered as always, but there was an extension on the right hand side of it. Our regular map, which reached from England to east of Berlin, was too small for this raid! The cover was pulled away and there it was! The red tape ran out from England over the North Sea to Denmark, across it, out over the Baltic Sea, then back in over eastern Germany and into Poland. Poznan was our target. It lay almost 1,000 miles away.

"Men," Colonel William B. David was saying, "Your bomb load is 5,000 lbs, gas load, naturally maximum. Don't start your engines before you have to. You'll need all the gas you have. Altitude is 11,000 feet. Over the Baltic you'll climb to 17,000, which is your bombing altitude. If you lose an engine over or near to the target, check your gas and if you don't think you can make it, head for Sweden. Our wing is bombing Poznan. The 13th Wing will go part of the way but are bombing about where you will hit the German coast, so you'll be alone all the way back. The rest of the 8th will be bombing targets all over central and southern Germany. You'll have no fighter escort so shoot at anything you see in the way of a fighter. Keep on the ball and good luck to all of you."

Lowell Watts recalls:

Just before taxi time we started the engines. There was no point using any gas we could save. We took off, climbed through the clouds and assembled. The rendezvous time was cut in half and we started out over the North Sea, tightening up the formation more as we went along and climbing to 11,000 feet before levelling off. We used the lowest possible power setting and the lowest rpm possible and flew as smoothly as we could in an effort to make our gas last. Near Denmark the clouds began breaking up and by the time we crossed the Danish coast it was as clear as a bell beneath us. Something else met us besides good weather: Jerry fighters. Off on our left a group was under heavy fighter attack. Two bombers went down. Later, we saw ten 'chutes drop from another crippled 'plane but, pilotless as it was, this ship, slowly losing altitude, continued on eastwards and not until we were across the Danish peninsula did we lose sight of it.

The Fw 190s attacking us kept sweeping in until we were well out over the Baltic and the quaint red-roofed villages of Denmark had blended into the horizon beneath us. We changed course to the south-east and climbed to 17,000 feet. Clouds were piling up beneath us again and the German coast was covered by them. On and on we flew. We were almost to Poland now and Ju 88s, Me 110s and Me 210s had replaced the Focke-Wulfs, making steady, unrelenting diving attacks on our formation. Nowhere could we see a break in the undercast. There was a ruling that no target in occupied country would be bombed except by contact bombing. Targets in Poland came under this category, so after flying those hundreds of miles, many of them under fighter attack, we had to turn back, still carrying our bombs, tired, hungry, with the fighters still on us and a feeling of frustration in the knowledge that Poznan's factories would still be turning out Focke-Wulfs on the morrow.

The formation was still at 17,000 feet and using a lot more fuel than it would had the Forts dropped their bombs and gone back down to 11,000. Sixteen of the Group's twenty-one B-17s were still in formation. One of them was 'BJ' Keirsted's flying *Cock of the Walk*. 'There were quite a few enemy fighters,' recalled Larry Goldstein, 'but somehow they were not too eager and did not pester us.'

Lowell Watts continues:

We checked our gas tanks. They were less than half full and we were still lugging our bombs. The loss of only one engine would be enough to make us run out of gas. As it was, it would be nip and tuck. We should just make it, but maybe we wouldn't. We were still at 17,000 feet, using a lot more gas than we would had we dropped our bombs and gone back down to 11,000. Sixteen of our twenty-one 'planes were still in formation. Our other two groups were a little better off. We had lost the left wing and the 'diamond' ships in our element, the second element of the low squadron. The VHF crackled to life. "Wolfgang Yellow, Wolfgang Yellow, this is Wolfgang White calling. Open bomb bay doors. We're approaching our target."

Now over Germany, we were going to bomb a secondary target by PFF through clouds.

Our bomb doors swung open as we fell in behind the 96th, which had the PFF ship. Suddenly, flak appeared: big, ugly, mushrooming billows of black, blossoming out around the angry red flash of the shell's explosions. The flak became thicker and more accurate as we neared the point of bomb release. Our ship bounced as the sound of ripping metal brought a lump to our throats. A big jagged hole had made its appearance between our number one and two engines. The number two gas gauge still showed no indication of a leak. There were two rips in the number two cowling, but the oil pressure was up and the engine was running smoothly. Up ahead two long streams of white arched down beneath the lead ship in the 96th formation. Those were the marker bombs of the PFF ship. In a few seconds we were nearing those markers. As we passed them we dumped our bombs, happy to feel the 'plane leap upwards, free of its load. The flak pounded us for about a minute longer and then it began to disappear. At last we were heading home, free of our bombs and able to cut down on our power settings. Only a few Ju 88s were around. Now and then they would lob a rocket at us, careful to stay out of range of our .50s. One formation of 88s lined up behind us and started pumping rockets at us. The projectiles sailed into the high squadron, bursting like flak. Fire broke out on the right wing of [Lieutenant Richard F. Reed's] B-17 after it was hit by a 20 mm shell. It flew for a minute longer and then rolled up on one wing and started down. [Reed and his co-pilot W. E. Osness got the bomber under control and opened the bomb doors for bail out]. Suddenly, there was flash, a huge billowy puff of smoke and jagged pieces of broken, twisted metal fluttered aimlessly earthwards.[17]

Ernest Richardson, in the 96th formation, continues:

The ride across the North Sea to Denmark took us about three hours. I think I started looking for Germans as soon as we left the ground in England, I think the other guys were too. There was a cloud cover below us so I couldn't see when we crossed into enemy territory.

"Flak eight o'clock; our level."

It made me jump. I wanted to see what it actually looked like. I'd never seen it before except in the movies.

Yep, there it was, six or seven black burst off to our left but it was quite a distance away. Just think, Germans are shooting that stuff at us. It was hard for me to believe that someone was trying to kill me. I'm not sure I was trained to kill. Being in the air force things were more impersonal; we were killing machines and bombing the factories that made them.

"Four contrails passing over us keep your eyes peeled, they're enemy."

The German fighters were Me 110s. They seemed reluctant about coming in very close, but they did shoot at us. I really didn't blame them when I saw all the fire power we could throw at them.

My first mission was good experience, we saw both fighters and flak, two of the things we were expected to see on our future raids.

Lowell Watts continues:

The hours dragged on. We'd been up almost eight hours now and we were crossing Denmark with the North Sea still separating us from England. Leaving the coast, we let down to 10,000 feet and loosened the formation as the fighters fell away. A glance at the gas gauge was anything but heartening. It would be a close one getting back today. We checked everything we might need if we should have to ditch.

The sun was riding low in the west as we neared England. Every few minutes one of our 'planes would drop out of formation to save gas. A few we heard calling pitifully to Air Sea Rescue and soon below us one of the lone 'planes would glide with a splash into the sea, its gas exhausted. Emmett J. Murphy said on intercom:

"Pilot from navigator, we're over England. You can see a spot of coastline off to our right through that little hole in the clouds."

"Good deal. Guess we'll make it if this let down doesn't take too long."

We watched the radio compass swing around, telling us we were passing over our field. Our squadron leader zoomed gently up and down. His left wing ship peeled off and was followed by the squadron lead ship, his right wing ship and then our 'plane. The ships were letting down on a heading of 90° disappearing one by one into the fluffy folds of white below us. Soon we were skimming the clouds and then we were in the soup, dark, lonely and uninviting. I was watching only the instruments now, heading 90°, flaps one third down, wheels down, airspeed 150, vertical speed 500 feet per minute. Down, down, down we went, the gloom darkening each second. At 1,000 feet we were still on instruments. We were all dead tired, but during the let-down we forgot it for the moment while eager eyes tried to pierce the murk for signs of the ground or other 'planes which might hit us. At 750 feet we broke out. It was raining but visibility was fair. We turned almost 180° until the radio compass read '0' and we flew until landmarks became familiar. Finally, we saw flares up ahead and soon the runway became visible. A 'plane was on his approach. Another, too close to him, pulled up and went around again. We started our approach and let down with the fuel warning lights on and the gas gauges reading almost empty. We couldn't stay up much longer. Kennedy, the co-pilot, turned the turbos full on in case we should need the power if we had to go around again. Old *Blitzin' Betsy* settled down, floated a second and touched the runway. We rolled to the end of the runway, another mission completed. Then we realised how tired we were.

'BJ' Keirsted also had to nurse his bomber back with rapidly diminishing fuel reserves. Larry Goldstein recalls:

We landed at dear old Knettishall in a heavy late afternoon haze and in almost total darkness. I believe we stretched the B-17 to its maximum and as always it brought us home in one piece. The mission count at this point was twenty. We started thinking about it but did not say it out loud: "Can we as a crew make it through twenty-five?" No-one talked about it, but I'm sure we all thought about it.

As the 1st Division formation crossed into Germany, it encountered single- and twin-engined fighters of almost every type. The German pilots adopted American single-engined fighter tactics in an effort to gain favourable attacking positions. In a last attempt to deter the 1st Division, the Germans employed cable-bombing methods. It did not work. The leading 401st Bomb Group, led by Colonel Harold W. Bowman, the CO, leading the 94th Wing, flew on to the briefed point west of Brunswick and diverged to bomb the target. Despite a heavy flak barrage during the bomb run, which heavily damaged Colonel Bowman's aircraft, the formation bombed with excellent results. Direct hits were achieved on the principal assembly shop at the Erla Maschinenwerk Messerschmitt production factory at Heiterblick, and its other large assembly building at Mockau was observed to be on fire as the bombers left the target area. Forty-two Bf 109s, just completed and sitting on an airfield nearby, were destroyed by American bombs and 450 workers in slit trenches and poorly constructed air-raid shelters were killed. *Doolittle's Doughboys* in the 615th Squadron, flown by 2nd Lieutenant Edward T. Gardner, who was killed, failed to return to Deenethorpe. 2nd Lieutenant C. A. Couger, the navigator, recalls what happened:

A strong formation of enemy fighters attacked us from a 12 o'clock position near Magdeburg. The ship was hit by 20 mm shells directly behind the navigator's compartment and the electrical generators were knocked out. The engines lost power and we dropped back out of formation. I crawled up to the cockpit to advise the pilot of the damage because the intercom had also been knocked out. He decided to 'hit the deck' and try to make it to Sweden, but at that moment the fighters, seeing we had left formation, made a concentrated attack on us. We were hit throughout by 20 mm cannon fire and the No. 3 engine burst into flames. At that time Gardner gave the order to abandon ship. I shook hands with Gardner in a farewell gesture and then went forward to inform the bombardier to bail out. Gardner sent the engineer, S/Sgt Minard, back to the rear of the ship to inform the rest of the crew to bail out. He found Sergeant Fred Monnes, the radio operator, mortally wounded in the radio room and Sergeant Trupia, one of the waist gunners, dead from a direct hit from a 20 mm shell. The three others had already bailed out. Sergeants Durben and Piazza had taken the badly wounded tail gunner, Sergeant Bosovski, out of his turret to find his right leg almost blown off. They had bailed him out near Magdeburg, where he was found and rushed to hospital and had his leg amputated. The Germans found the body of Lieutenant Gardner three weeks later near Pilm, Germany. His chute had failed to operate or he had left it too late to bail out.

In all, twenty-one bombers failed to return and others crash-landed in England. Brigadier-General Robert Williams, in his critique of the Leipzig mission, described it as the most successful mission carried out so far by the 8th Air Force. Three medals of Honor were awarded to 1st Division airmen this day. Despite being badly hit in the face, twenty-three-year-old Lieutenant William R. Lawley of Leeds, Alabama, a pilot in the 305th, brought his badly disabled B-17 back with a dead co-pilot and eight wounded crew. In the 351st the ball-turret gunner, Staff Sergeant Archie Mathies, a Pennsylvania coal miner's son, born in Stonehouse, Scotland, who had a few hours' flying experience, and the navigator, 2nd Lieutenant Walter E. Truemper, a former accounting clerk from Aurora, Illinois, were posthumously awarded the Medal of Honor for gallantly flying *Ten Horsepower*[18], their severely damaged bomber, back to England after Ronald E. Bartley, the co-pilot, had been decapitated and 2nd Lieutenant Clarence R. Nelson, the pilot, rendered unconscious. Mathies had once patted the side of the Fortress and said that, 'Someday this big girl will get me a medal.' Despite a valiant attempt to land the aircraft, both men were killed on their third attempt to crash-land the crippled bomber at Polebrook. Nelson, the right-hand side of whose face had been sheared off, survived for only another hour or so. After the war the Pittsburgh Coal Company renamed one of its mines for Archie Mathies, who had worked beside his father in a bituminous seam in Liberty, Pennsylvania, after graduating from Monongahela High School.

At 2100 hours on the night of 20 February a brief teletype message was sent to all 8th Air Force bases: 'Favourable weather forecast for tomorrow. We will fly another maximum effort mission.' The principal targets were the MIAG aircraft factories at Brunswick, which produced component parts for the Bf 110, and the fighter park at Diepholz, railway yards at Lingen and Luftwaffe airfields at Hanover, Achmer and Hopten. Once again the 15th Air Force was grounded because of bad weather over the Foggia area that prevented the bombers from taking off. In England, the bomber stream would be swelled by thirty-six B-17s of the 457th Bomb Group, otherwise known as the 'Fireball Outfit', commanded by Colonel James R. Luper and based at Glatton, Huntingdonshire, which was making its debut.

At Snetterton Heath, Sherman Gillespie's crew prepared for their second mission. When Ernest Richardson, the radio operator, had seen saw the route they had planned for his crew's first mission, he did not think they wanted him to go on very many raids.

When I went to the briefing for our second raid, I was sure of it.

"This morning gentlemen, you are going to Brunswick." I think my eyes must have popped out of my head, but I was worried more about the lump in my throat and the weakening in my knees; it was like getting a death sentence thrown at you. Brunswick, Charlie's death, Dickert's plane all shot up, part of the crew bailing out; all the ships that didn't make it back. I was really frightened.

"You should have fighter escort most of the way. There won't be much flak if you stay on the briefed course, except at the target."

Walking to the ship that morning, I was wondering if I would be walking over the same ground that night. I remember looking up at the sky and praying a little.

Gillespie's B-17 had just crossed the Channel and was making its way into Europe when, looking up through his hatch, Ernie Richardson saw the sky in back and above filled with single-engine contrails and they were coming toward him.

I quickly turned to interphone on my jack-box. (As radio operator I was supposed to listen to my liaison receiver which was our communication with our base in England. It was real exciting when the guys would test fire their guns without letting me know ahead of time, every time it happened I thought we were being attacked.)

"Fighters – lots of them – six o'clock high, keep your eyes on them."

The fighters were passing over the group in back of us. I wondered why they didn't attack them. Then I figured they would probably come up to hit our group first then circle back and hit the group behind us. Our formation started tightening up; all the turrets were swinging to six o'clock. They will sure mix in a fight when they do hit us. All this was running through my mind when just before they reached our group they started zigzagging back and forth, four abreast. They were P-47s. I was so excited about going on this particular raid that I had completely forgotten the briefing where they mentioned we would have fighter escort. The relief that went through me was tremendous; I just sat down and looked at them. It was a beautiful sight.

"Sure is a bunch of them, aren't they beautiful."

"Yeah and they're all ours."

The combined effort of fighters and bombers looked like a tough combination to tangle with, the Germans must have thought so too because we didn't see one fighter.

"Boy, look at that flak up ahead." The sky was almost black.

"Yeah, they sure have enough of it."

The worst thing about flak was there wasn't anything you could do about it except throw out chaff. Fighters you could shoot back at; it gave you something to do. But flak was always there at every target pounding away at you and there was very little evasion action you could take against it when you are lined up on the target. They threw a lot at us that day and when you looked out at it you wondered how a plane could possibly get through it. It always managed to scare you. When it was close you could hear the muffled burst and almost always hear it hitting the ship, it sounded like hail hitting against a window.

Outside of seeing a lot of flak and our fighters, number two was just about like the first one. We were glad to get back – maybe it won't be so bad after all.

The same sentiments were shared by 'BJ' Keirsted and the *Worry Wart* crew, who flew their twenty-first mission, in *Pegasus II*, to Brunswick, but the omens had not been good. 'Goldie' Goldstein recalled: 'I'm sure that all my fellow crewmembers felt the same as I did: "Will we survive this one, will we come home to our own beds?" It seemed from past experiences that every time the 8th went to Brunswick it was a bloodbath. Our last mission to this city was a nightmare.' But he need not have worried. 'Our fighter support was plentiful and did a magnificent job protecting us. The rest of the mission wasn't too bad and I recorded this as an 'easy' mission. We were very tired flyers. We had been flying many missions, mostly long flights to heavily defended targets and all major aircraft component plants.'

Some 924 bombers and 679 fighters fought their way through dense contrails and biting cold to get there but thick cloud obscured the objectives and 764 bombers bombed using PFF. Many groups attacked targets of opportunity and airfields and aircraft depots were heavily bombed. Sixty German fighters were claimed shot down. Nineteen bombers and five fighters failed to return. Two of the B-17s that were lost were from the 'Fireball Outfit', which split into two formations to attack Lippstadt and Gütersloh.[19]

That evening Doolittle and his staff evaluated the day's missions. The large air park at Diepholz was seriously damaged but at Brunswick most of the bombs had fallen on the city and not the aircraft factories. Weather reports for 22 February continued to indicate excellent prospects for visual bombing at Regensburg and Schweinfurt and the Erkner ball-bearing plant near Berlin. Major General Frederick L. Anderson suggested to Doolittle that all three targets should be bombed simultaneously; Doolittle disagreed, saying that it would spread the bombers too thin and that it would also split the fighter escort. Finally, it was decided not to bomb Erkner and that the main attacks would be concentrated on Schweinfurt and Regensburg, but late that same evening news reached High Wycombe that the 15th Air Force could participate in the next day's raids so 183 of General Twining's bombers were detailed to attack the Messerschmitt factory at Obertraubling near Regensburg and the 8th, Schweinfurt, Gotha, Bernburg, Oschesleben, Ashersleben and Halberstadt. A small diversionary force would bomb Aalborg airfield in Denmark.

Almost 800 bombers set out from East Anglia but low-hanging clouds caused collisions during assembly and chaos ensued. From his HQ, General Curtis E. LeMay soon ordered the 3rd Division to abandon the raid on Schweinfurt. The 2nd Division bomber stream became so strung out that it also received a recall while flying a scattered formation over the Low Countries. Some groups dropped their bombs on targets of opportunity, while two B-24s in the 445th, which did not receive the recall, bombed the assigned target at Gotha. A Liberator group bombed Nijmegen in Holland in error and caused 200 Dutch civilian casualties. The 1st Division, led by Colonel 'Mo' Preston, CO of the 379th, continued to the Junkers works at Aschersleben and Bernberg. Only ninety-nine B-17s of the 289 Fortresses got their bombs away at their primary targets because of dense cloud but the Junkers 88 works at Aschersleben was so badly damaged that production was cut by half for two months. Nine B-17s in the 306th, heading for Bernburg, had aborted and on the bomb run seven were shot down and each of the remaining twenty-three aircraft were damaged, some seriously, but Ju 88 production was temporarily reduced by 70 to 80 per cent.

Harry Cornell's crew had a long mission when the Wing pulled the diversion to Aalborg, as John Kettman recalled.

We didn't have any fighter escort on this mission at all and it was around a 1,000-mile trip. We were over the North Sea most of the time. When we got to Denmark it was quite covered with clouds. They hunted for some time for the target but didn't find it. On our way back the fighters started in on a few stragglers. They were 109s and 210s. One B-17 went down in flames. I saw six chutes come out and someone else saw nine. That was a horrible sight seeing them go down in flames. Even though they did bail out, they landed in the North Sea about 40 miles from land.[20] One of the other straggling Forts knocked down a 109. A 210 was knocked down right in front of us. I got a burst in on a 109. So did Pete and Logan. We dropped our bombs into the sea when the fighters attacked.

In the 401st formation on the mission to Oschersleben, two B-17s were shot down by a combination of flak and fighters. 2nd Lieutenant Alfred P. Mayne, the co-pilot of the B-17 flown by 2nd Lieutenant Roy M. Shanks, recalls:

We were attacked by fighters early on in the mission and then severely damaged by flak at about 1200 to 1230 hours. Two engines were lost and we began to fall back out of formation. Our ball turret gunner, Sergeant Hardney A. Gibson, took a bad wound to the right ankle and it was in such a state that we gave him a shot of morphine, dressed the wound and bailed him out. Later we found that he was picked up by the Germans and taken to a small hospital, where a German lady doctor saved his leg by an operation instead of amputating it. The attack by fighters still went on and when a fire started in the wing the order was given to bail out. All the crew except Tech Sergeant William R. Jarret, the engineer-top turret gunner, made a safe landing. Shanks accidently pulled his ripcord inside the aircraft so Jarrett gave him his and went back to the waist and put on a spare chute. For some reason the chute never opened and he was killed. We were picked up by the Germans and spent the rest of the war as PoWs.

The second B-17 in the 401st that was lost was piloted by 2nd Lieutenant Vernon A. Arneson of Benicia, California. The aircraft left the formation just before the target and then returned to the fold, joining the rear of the Low Squadron at a lower level, Arneson taking the No. 1 position after three fighters had worked him over. Some P-51s then came in to help him. He was last seen heading for home with one prop feathered and two enemy fighters attacking him. When S/Sgt Richard C. Schmidt of Oak Lawn, Illinois, went to put his chute on he found that it had been riddled with machine-gun fire. Unable to jump, he made his way to the cockpit to find all other crew members had bailed out. Although the controls were shot away, the Fortress landed itself and Schmidt survived the crash-landing without any injuries.[21]

This day proved the worst of 'Big Week', the 1st Division losing thirty-eight Forts and the 2nd Division three B-24s. The 15th Air Force lost fourteen bombers.

On Wednesday 23 February 8th Air Force crews received a much-needed respite when weather conditions were the prime reason for keeping the heavies on the ground. In Italy, Twining managed to dispatch 102 bombers on a mission to Austria to attack the Steyr Walzlagerwerke ball-bearing plant. Reconnaissance photos indicated that 20 per cent of the factory was destroyed. In East Anglia maintenance crews worked around the clock, attempting to get every bomber possible ready for combat. They were needed the next day, 24 February, when Doolittle dispatched 867 bombers to targets throughout the Reich. Hearts sank at 1st Division bases when the briefing curtains were pulled back to reveal that the target was the ball bearing plant at Schweinfurt. The name of this city was well known to crews in the 305th at Chelveston, even to crews who had not been there yet, as John Kettman recalls.

> Our group hit this target in October with fifteen ships and only two got back. We expected this to be the roughest so far. We were briefed for 1,100 enemy fighters. Only our division was going down there; the rest were hitting other targets near Berlin. It turned out we had wonderful fighter support, all the way to and from the target. We didn't see one enemy fighter! Over the target there was plenty of flak and a couple of rockets but I'd seen worse over Frankfurt. We blew the ball bearing plant to ribbons. Just past the target we saw six chutes come out of a '17; he was hit by flak. We believe they all got out as the plane was still under control. We saw pictures of the target and we blew it to hell. It was clear all the way. It was a 'good' mission.[22]

At Gotha, 420 miles due east of the White Cliffs of Dover, 238 B-24s attacked the aircraft factories. Eight groups crossed the target and a ninth, the 458th at Horsham St Faith near Norwich, flew a diversionary sweep over the North Sea. Some twenty-eight B-24s in the 445th joined with the 'Sky Scorpions' and the 453rd to form the leading 2nd Wing. The 14th Wing's 44th and 392nd Bomb Groups flew behind them, while the 20th Wing brought up the rear. Flak was heavy over Lingen, Holland, and the Liberators encountered persistent attacks by the Luftwaffe. Even the arrival of three P-47 Thunderbolt groups just after 1200 was unable to prevent five 445th Liberators being shot down in the space of six minutes. Over 150 enemy fighters ferociously attacked the formation all the way to the target, despite close attention from escorting fighters. The Division beat off incessant attacks as it flew on over the Dummer Lake, where it veered south-eastwards to Osnabrück and the bombed-out airfields near Hanover. Three more B-24s in the 445th were shot down before the formation turned south near Gottingen at 1235. Nine minutes later, the Group's ninth Liberator loss occurred.

Lockheed P-38 Lightnings and P-51 Mustangs took over from the hard-pressed P-47s near Hannover and orbited the formation as it proceeded to Gotha. Undaunted, German fighters attacked and raked the B-24s with cannon and rocket fire. Using the Liberators' dense vapour trails to excellent advantage, they often struck at any lagging bomber from below and behind. The Luftwaffe even attempted to disrupt the large and unwieldy combat wings. At 1309 the Division changed course to the south-east, with a feint towards Meinegen. Some confusion arose at the IP when the navigator in the 'Sky Scorpions" lead ship suffered oxygen failure and the aircraft veered off course. The bombardier slumped over his bombsight and accidentally tripped the bombs. Altogether, twenty-five Liberators bombed the secondary target at Eisenach. Before the small 445th formation reached the target, its tenth and eleventh victims fell to the German guns. By now the 445th consisted of only fourteen Liberators, three having aborted before entering Germany. Another 445th B-24 was shot down just after leaving Eisenach. The thirteen remaining B-24 crews realised that they had veered off course and they continued alone and arrived over the target at 1325. During an eight-minute bomb run they dropped 180 500-pounders from 12,000 feet, which inflicted considerable damage on the Gotha plant. Another 171 B-24s dropped 468 tons of assorted bombs from varying altitudes and directions. A thirteenth B-24 in the 445th fell victim to the German defences minutes after 'bombs away'.

Myron Keilman, who was flying deputy lead to Lieutenant Colonel Lorin J. Johnson, recalls:

The weather was very clear as we turned to the target. Red flares from the lead ship signalled 'bomb bay doors open'. The bombardier removed the heated covers from the bombsight. (They had heated blankets before we did!) He checked his gyroscope's stabilisation and all bombing switches 'on'. Our high and low squadron fell in trail and all seemed great. Then pilotage navigator Kenny in the nose turret observed the lead wing formations veering away from the target heading. A fast and anxious cross-check with lead crew navigator Swangren and a recheck of compass heading and reference points assured command pilot Lorin Johnson that the target was dead ahead. Within minutes, Good, the lead bombardier, called over the intercom: "I've got the target!"

Lead pilot Jim McGregor checked his flight instruments for precise 18,000 feet altitude and carefully levelled the aircraft on autopilot. He then called back: "On airspeed, on altitude. You've got the aircraft." Making a final level of his bombsight, Good took over control of steering the aircraft with the bombsight.

At 18,000 feet it was 40° below zero but the bombardier never felt the cold as his fingers delicately operated the azimuth and range controls. He cross-checked all the bomb and camera switches to the 'on' position, especially the radio bomb-release signal switch that simultaneously releases all the bombs of the other aircraft in the formation. Maintaining perfect formation, the 392nd fought its way through the German flak defences and bombed the Gotha works with pinpoint accuracy. After Good had dropped the bomb load the camera recorded the impact of the bombs. Jim McGregor took over and swung the formation to the outbound heading and the rallying point. Despite the now accurate flak, the second and third squadron bombardiers, Ziccarrilli and Jackson, steered their squadrons to the precise bomb delivery points too. Of the thirty-two B-24s which took off that morning, twenty-nine of them delivered their twelve 500-pounders precisely on target as briefed.

The 392nd was extremely accurate, dropping 98 per cent of its bombs within 2,000 feet of the aiming point.[23] The 'Eightballs' had also achieved a highly accurate bomb run. Intelligence described Gotha as 'the most valuable single target in the enemy twin-engine fighter complex' and later estimated that six to seven weeks' production of Me 110s was lost. However, the 392nd paid dearly for its accuracy. Strung out in trail and with some B-24s slowed down by flak damage, the three squadrons became vulnerable to vicious fighter attacks. For an hour after bombing, the 392nd was subjected to head-on passes and tail attacks from singles and gaggles of Luftwaffe fighters. When the group returned to Wendling at 1530, seven hours after take-off, seven B-24s were missing and another thirteen returned badly damaged. Sixteen enemy fighters were confirmed destroyed by 392nd gunners. Six 'Sky Scorpions' were also shot down in quick succession during the raid, while the survivors received further punishment on the homeward journey. The thirteen surviving 445th Liberators, nine of them battle damaged, limped into Tibenham at about 1545. Altogether, they had lost 122 men on the bloody mission.[24]

The 3rd Division was assigned Rostock but heavy cloud over the target forced the Fortresses to head for their secondary target at Poznan, missed four days before. Ernest Richardson in the 96th recalled:

It was our longest raid and one of the longest ever pulled by the 8th Air Force, twelve hours and fifteen minutes. We were on oxygen six hours. The route was plotted about the same as the first and it went about the same. We saw a few fighters and flak and of course, plenty of other things to scare you. I don't think there is anyone who went on a bombing raid that wasn't scared. I mean really scared. I don't think the 8th Air Force has many atheists.

Larry Goldstein wrote:

We ran into some flak along the route and one particular barrage hit us in the right wing. Luckily, it was not in an engine. We were hit by fighters and as we had no support all the way we had a battle on our hands. I did quite a bit of shooting today. A few fighters kept pecking away at us and there were a few 17s that went down. Bombs were dropped in a scattered manner. I do not think we did a good job at all. The mission was long and tiresome. We had a heading set for Sweden in case we could not make it back to England. We were airborne for over eleven hours and the fact that we landed at Knettishall in almost total darkness was in itself a miracle. Our pilots were really great people. They knew how to fly and they knew how to get us home. We were exhausted and could hardly get to the mess hall for the evening meal. At this point we as a crew figured that the next three missions to bring us to the magic number of twenty-five, would, by the law of averages be simple, light missions. How wrong we were.

Lieutenant Gillespie's crew went on pass after the Poznan raid as Ernest Richardson recalls.

We were glad to get away for a while. I went to Norwich, about 19 miles from our base. I had a feeling of pride when I was sitting in the Red Cross Club looking around at the other GIs there. I wondered how many of them were part of a combat crew, if they were, how many might have been on the Brunswick raid two days before. To me that was just about the worst raid anyone could go on remembering what happened to Dickert's crew. That night I just wandered around the town. It was blacked out of course. Later I went to a dance and tried to have a good time. There were some pretty girls there.

Friday 25 February marked the culmination of 'Big Week', when the USSTAF readied 1,154 bombers and 1,000 fighters for the deepest raid into Germany thus far. The 1st Bomb Division was assigned the Messerschmitt experimental and assembly plants at Augsburg and the VFK ball-bearing plant at Stuttgart, while the 2nd Bomb Division attacked Furth, near Nürnburg. Despite the long and dangerous mission to Poznan, tired and weary crews at all 3rd Bomb Division bases were tumbled out of their warm cots at 0300 hours the following morning, Friday 25 February, for an equally arduous mission. Crews were mortified to learn that their target was the Bf 109 plant at Regensburg-Prüfening. This was the first time the B-17 crews had the need to return to the city since the fateful raid on 17 August 1943, when they had suffered devastating losses. The Germans had given top priority to the reconstruction of the Regensburg plant and within six months had restored production to something like its previous output. Although most of the old buildings had been destroyed, several main buildings had been rebuilt, including a long assembly shop on a site where three had once stood. This time the Italy-based 15th Air Force would bomb the target before the England-based force arrived over the city.

Beautiful weather greeted crews as they assembled over England and headed for the Continent at 21,000 feet. John Kettman who flew in Harry Cornell's crew, recalls.

This was our deepest penetration over Germany so far. We were six hours and thirteen minutes over enemy territory. This was the roughest raid I ever hoped to be on. As soon as we hit France the fighters started to work on us. Right off the start I saw three B-17s get knocked down; one of them blew up in mid-air. We fought on our own all the way in; our escort really goofed up royally. We were firing all the time. P-38s finally caught up with us over the target. The flak was intense but not too accurate. We hit the target without a doubt. Just before the target the lead ship fell out and headed for Switzerland with engine trouble. The deputy leader took over and took us right over the heart of Stuttgart! Boy what flak they had there; we didn't think we'd get out but we did! After that, the fighters started on in again. We fought them for another half an hour. Then went right over Saarbrücken! More flak! We ploughed through that and finally picked up some escort P-47s. Six hours plus of sweating over Germany and France. We lost two ships – Safranek's and Czarnecki's[25] – from our squadron, four from the group. We are really getting the long rides of late.

In the 3rd Division formation, flak had bracketed the 388th as they crossed the French coast near Le Havre and some ships sustained hits. Soon the B-17s flew out of range and crews peered into the distance in search of their fighter escorts, but they failed to show. For another 30 minutes the 388th flew on eastwards but still it found itself alone. Suddenly, fighters appeared, but they were Focke-Wulf 190s, Ju 88s and Bf 109s. They circled in ever increasing numbers and then they pulled up ahead of the B-17s and started their attacks. It was almost 1200 hours when the 388th sighted a column of smoke rising almost to their altitude from fires at Regensburg left by the 15th Air Force. The Alps could be seen quite clearly to the south. The 388th added its bombs to the conflagration and headed for home through thick flak and heavy fighter attacks. A new tiredness seeped through crews' bodies as the strain of flying several long combat missions during the week began to tell. Larry Goldstein recalls:

The flak had been mostly scattered and ineffective but at one point over the target it was intensive and very accurate. Some aircraft were hit. Luckily not ours. A few enemy fighters pecked away but fortunately we were not the group to be hit. Our fighter support was supposed to be there but they only showed up when it was too late. This was one of those fouled-up missions. The only thing right was our bombing. The raid was a great morale booster at a time when it was needed. As it turned out this raid was also important for the invasion which was to come later. My brother was in the US Army tank forces and he later told me that when his unit entered Regensburg the plant was in a shambles.

Very considerable damage was caused to the Bf 109 plants, first by 149 B-17s and B-24s of the 15th Air Force and then by the 3rd Bomb Division. They arrived over Regensburg an hour after the 15th Air Force bombers, to see smoke pouring upward and rising to about 20,000 feet. Unlike their Italy-based colleagues, the 3rd Bomb Division met only token fighter opposition. The joint bombing was highly effective and output was severely reduced for four months following the raids. Also, the 1st Bomb Division heavily damaged the Messerschmitt plants at Augsburg and the ball-bearing plants at Stuttgart. The raids cost the 8th Air Force thirty-one bombers. Thereafter, cloudbanks over the Continent brought a premature end to 'Big Week'.

On leap year day, Tuesday 29 February, the target for 215 B-17s was aircraft production plants at Brunswick and thirty-eight B-24s bombed a V-weapon site at Lottinghen. At Deopham Green, *Panda-monium* in the 730th Squadron in the 452nd and 2nd Lieutenant Jake S. Colvin's crew had flown six missions but the vicissitudes of war dictated that the crew leave their beloved B-17 at Deopham Green while they were trucked on down to the 388th to man *Cock o' The Walk*, one of the Knettishall group's old war-wearies, in place of a crew which was on stand-down. Allan E. Johnson, the navigator, recalled:

Our crew was one of the original, charter-member crews of the 452nd, having been a part of the group since its formation at Pendleton, Oregon, from personnel supplied by the replacement depot at Moses Lake, Washington. In the early

training days in the Pacific North-west our B-17, a beautiful G model with a chin
turret, didn't have a name, but our crew was acquiring an identity, nonetheless.
Jake Colvin was not the most highly co-ordinated individual in the world and this
fact became evident during formation flight practice, especially when we were in
the tail-end Charlie slot. We'd begin to fall further and further back until Jake
would realise that he had to do something and he'd ram the bottles ahead, we'd
come steaming back into the formation, much too fast, and suddenly Jake would
drop the wheels to slow down. But then he'd hold the wheels down position
too long and we'd begin to fall behind once again, so he'd raise the wheels and
the whole process would begin all over again. Sometimes, in the course of this
see-sawing, we'd get into the configuration where our wheels were up but our
airspeed was in the final-approach zone. Our ship had a nice loud horn for
this predicament, so every once in a while the confusion was compounded by
a blast that the Bull of Bashan would have been proud of. Believe me, it was
pandemonium. One night, one of our guys won a big stuffed panda at a local
fair. He tied it to the cockpit overhead on our next flight and it became our
mascot. From there on it was only a short step to our ship's name. Jake's flying
ability improved and by the time we went overseas he was holding formation
like a two-tour vet.

We got clobbered by flak over Brunswick and never got back our beloved
Panda-monium. Jake, God bless his soul, was killed, as was the co-pilot, one waist
gunner and the tail gunner. Jake probably knocked a piece off the gatehouse on
his way through the pearly gates.[26]

Section Eight, piloted by 2nd Lieutenant George Williamson, twenty-three,
of Columbus, Ohio, had just dropped its load of destruction on their target in
northern Germany when five Me 109s swooped down on the Fort in repeated
attacks. They came in madly, guns chattering continually, shooting red balls of
fire and rockets. A sudden explosion rocked the ship. A rocket had exploded near
the right wing, tore a hole about a foot and a half wide and started to blow the
wing up so it appeared like a balloon. More explosions rocked the ship, 20 mm
shells from the enemy aircraft cannon. The first shell exploded in the tail section
of the plane and barely missed the tail gunner, S/Sgt Donald Degen, twenty-one, of
Washington, DC. Another shell entered the plane through the left waist window,
exploded and seared the eyebrows and moustache off the left waist gunner,
Sergeant George T. Kruithoff of Grand Rapids, Michigan. These explosions were
lucky ones. No one was hurt, but the next shell counted. It exploded in the midst of

a group of incendiary grenades on the floor of the radio compartment. The radio operator, S/Sgt George W. Alvanos of Blacksburg, Virginia, pitched to the floor. He was a bloody mess. Shrapnel had peppered his body, his arms, his legs, his neck and his face. The radio compartment caught on fire. It was a roaring inferno of yellow flame. Several incendiary grenades had been touched off by the explosion. Although wounded he started to tear the burning floor and the lining around the radio room out with his bloody and burned hands. The engineer, S/Sgt Walter J. Honoik, twenty-two, of Omaha, Nebraska, rushed in and joined the wounded radio operator in fighting the flames. Their clothes were on fire. The co-pilot, 2nd Lieutenant Otis Stogsdill, twenty-three, of Cerro Gordo, Illinois, pushed his way to the burning compartment, threw some blankets around the flaming incendiary grenades, heaved them out of the top radio hatch and all proceeded to stamp out the fire, ripping the radio room apart in the process. How Alvenos managed to assist in stamping out the furious fire, with his body torn apart by shrapnel, his wounds bleeding profusely, his hands blistered from the effects of the fire-fighting and the intense pain of these wounds, is a saga of strength and courage. Yet there was only one thought in his mind, one thought in the minds of all the crew; to get their badly battered Fort home safely. They landed at Deopham Green, burned, torn apart and bloody. They had accomplished their purpose. They had bombed their target and brought their Fort home.[27]

On Friday 3 March the 401st flew their thirtieth mission, to Wilhelmshaven. Cologne was bombed the next day, one B-17 crash-landing on return. *Bonnie Donnie*, flown by Lieutenant Donald A. Currie, landed on its belly in a crash-landing at Deenethorpe. Thanks to Currie's superb pilotage, none of the crew was hurt. The crash-landing was made on the concrete runway of the base and was occasioned when flak over the Ruhr damaged Currie's landing gear so severely that he was unable to get his wheels down. Spectators who lined the field and roads surrounding the base as the Fortress circled and re-circled overhead saw the aeroplane come in at a speed of over 100 mph, level out say about 6 feet above the concrete and then hit, tail first. The second the tail hit the runway, Currie brought the nose of the plane down and then cut his switches. The sparks that flew from the crashing plane as steel met concrete practically enveloped *Bonnie Donnie* and onlookers thought it had burst into flames. The illusion of explosion, coupled with the ear-rending noise made by the giant fuselage grinding into the runway, led spectators to abandon any hope of a rescue. The impact was heard 2 miles away. Fears for the crew and plane lasted only a second. The Fortress came to rest on its belly and as crash trucks and ambulances sped to the scene,

Currie and his crew emerged from the hatches, shaken but unhurt. Currie had landed his plane flawlessly. Fellow pilots were referring to it a day later as a 'dream landing'. Damage to the aircraft was moderate. Ordinarily he would have set the plane down on the soft turf that fringes the runway but recent rains and snows had so mired the ground that a glide landing would have been impossible. As a safety measure, Currie had jettisoned his ball turret prior to landing. This piece of caution undoubtedly saved the day; the turret would probably have broken the B-17 in half at the point of impact. Colonel Harold W. Bowman, the CO, congratulated him on his achievement.[28]

Despite the losses during 'Big Week' of 226 8th Air Force bombers, Spaatz and Doolittle believed that the USSTAF had dealt the German aircraft industry a really severe blow. However, although the 8th had flown some 3,300 bomber sorties and had dropped 6,000 tons of bombs, the destruction was not as great as at first thought. Luftwaffe Gruppes were certainly deprived of many replacement aircraft and fighter production was halved the following month but it had cost the USSTAF 400 bombers and 4,000 casualties. Furthermore, although the small high-explosive bombs destroyed factories, the machine tools, lathes and jigs were left virtually untouched beneath the wreckage. It was only a matter of time before this equipment was recovered from the wrecked plants and put into use again. Nonetheless, Doolittle and his staff officers now felt sufficiently confident to strike at Berlin on 3 March. After all it was the biggest prize in the Third Reich.

By now 'BJ' Keirsted's crew were veteran fliers and, as Larry Goldstein noted, 'not many crews made it to this point. We added new crews and new aircraft to our depleted forces. We had two missions to go; would we make it?'

CHAPTER 3

The Bloody Hundredth and 'Big-B'

Still the Luftwaffe came in. About six 109s came in on our squadron and we were quite busy for a few minutes. One went by me smoking. Gidel or the bombardier must have hit him. I got in a burst at him. From then on they were with us all the way to the target and part way out. The group behind us got three 109s in just a few minutes. They got one B-17; we saw three chutes coming out. All our guns were going at once. We believed that our bombs fell short of our target, a ball bearing plant on the outskirts of the city. At the target the flak was accurate and heavy and there were rockets also. In fact they threw up everything but the kitchen sink! There were all kinds of fighters – theirs and ours. There were some great dogfights going on. We got back in a hurry due to a tail wind. Escort was good coming back.

Sergeant John Kettman, Berlin raid, 6 March 1944.

There wasn't any mention of it but I think we were all aware one particular raid would come up. It finally happened at our 3 March briefing.

"This morning gentlemen, your target is Berlin."

"No! Let the RAF take care of it, they're doing OK."

"It's better to bomb it at night."

"They'll scrub it."

'That was some of the conversation that ran through the briefing room at Snetterton Heath,' recalled Ernest Richardson.

Some crews stomped their feet in protest, others just groaned and there was lots of swearing. The S-2 officer tried to seem nonchalant; he had to know everyone hated the thought of going there. No one laughed at his jokes that morning. There was plenty of tension in the air. After briefing it seemed to me there were longer lines in front of the religious personnel than usual but it may have been my imagination.

At Seething, Wallace Patterson was having trouble writing up his diary on Friday 3 March. His fingers were sore from the freezing cold temperatures he had endured at altitude. For some inexplicable reason the leader had taken Al Northrup's crew and the others up to 26,000 feet, though the clouds were at only 12,000. The needle on the outside air temperature gauge, which could only register up to 60° below zero, stopped there but it was estimated that the maximum temperature was 67° below. The boys in the rear of the plane complained about the cold. They would have to be treated for frostbite when they landed. Back at Seething, Patterson tried to thaw out and he struggled to get his words about the 'fiasco' down on paper. When briefing officers had pulled back the curtains to reveal red tapes reaching like groping fingers all the way to 'Big-B', whistles and groans had greeted the news. A raid on Berlin had been scheduled for 23 November 1943 but had been postponed because of bad weather.

'We were briefed at 0500 for Berlin,' wrote Patterson, painfully.

It was to be the first time the AAF had ever hit the Jerry capital and a feather in the cap of everyone to participate. The target actually was Oranienburg, a heavy bomber factory and airfield 14 miles from the centre of Berlin. The route over put us in Germany near Hamburg after a long over water hop and return was routed entirely over land, which was German-held. Fighter support would leave us at the German coast and pick us up again over two hours later, leaving us unsupported over the most hotly defended sectors of the Reich. We were scared to death but anxious to go to Berlin.

The city was ringed with anti-aircraft guns that could fire high explosive shells to a height of 45,000 feet, much higher than the ceiling of Liberators and Fortresses. Flak towers over 120 feet in height and six levels underground could fire a salvo of eight shells that would explode simultaneously, covering an area of 260 yards across. They could do it every ninety seconds. Any bomber caught in that pattern was kaput.

At Flixton the day started like any other. Thurman Spiva, a navigator in the 707th Squadron, was one of many who were awakened at 0400 hours and caught the 6 x 6 tarp-covered-truck to the Mess Hall.

After chow we went to the combat crew locker room to get into our flying gear. Briefing was scheduled for 0600 hours. When the curtain was pulled back the ribbon reached all the way to Berlin. There were gasps, low whistles, moans and groans as the crews realised where they were going. We knew one day the target would be 'Big-B', the capital of Nazi Germany.

It was snowing, but the weather officer said the weather would be better over the Continent. The target was the Heinkel Flugzeugwerke at Germandorf, sixteen miles north-east of Berlin, where He 177s were being built. The Friederichstrasse station in Berlin proper was to be the secondary target. All divisions of the 8th Air Force were to hit targets in the capital and its suburbs. It meant flying more than 1,000 miles. Twenty-six Liberators loaded with M-47s would be dispatched from Flixton. John Goss and the crew of *Hula Wahina II* in the Bungay Buckaroos' 704th Squadron were slated to lead a three-plane element flying to the left and below the Group lead plane. Goss was a native of Honolulu and was there when Pearl Harbor was bombed. In fact, it was the Japanese display of air power on 7 December that made him decide to join the Air Corps. At nineteen he was the first pilot of a new B-24 delivered to Lowry Field. Goss had crew chief John Minturn find an artist to paint a Polynesian hula wahine below his cockpit. It was a sort of a reminder of home and it was in the perfect position for him to stroke her okole while taxi-ing out to take-off.

At Rattlesden wake-up was at 0345 hours for the 340 crewmen. At briefing, in addition to the thirty-four crews from the Group, there were two PFF crews. When the target was announced there were gasps from 360 throats.

At Knettishall, 'BJ' Keirsted and his crew in the 388th prepared for what was their penultimate mission; one more and they could go home. Larry Goldstein wrote:

We were called out to a very early briefing. When we entered the briefing room the chaplains were very visible. This made us uneasy and we thought it must be something big. When the route and the target were explained to us there was not one man in the room who thought he would be sleeping in his own bed that night. At the revetment, while we waited to board our aircraft, all of us constantly watched for a flare shot from the control tower scrubbing the mission. It never came. As we waited for our chance for take-off I tuned to Radio Bremen which spoke in English. Here we were waiting to take off for a raid over Germany and Radio Bremen was saying, "American bombers are on their runways in England now, waiting to attack north-west Germany." How did they know?

Fellow radio operator Ernest Richardson was equally concerned. 'While waiting for take-off everyone was looking toward the tower for the red flares that would indicate the mission scrubbed. I don't think there was one person that wanted to go. Later when we were at 10,000 feet and headed out over the North Sea, we knew we had gone too far for the mission to be cancelled.'

Larry Goldstein continues:

We finally got into our take-off position and rolled down the runway. Take-off was at 0730 hours. Soon after forming, the group was off on its way. I sat at my radio with my headset tight on my ears waiting for the abort signal but it never came. We used a tricky route in to the target and were to bomb and get the hell out quickly. The weather was our friend. It turned bad and the mission was finally scrubbed after our target was socked in. I recorded the recall in my log and after many repeats I called to 'BJ' on intercom. One very sharp operator somewhere in the force acknowledged receipt of the recall even though he was not authorised to do so. Then over the VHF system someone in authority ordered a recall. Non acknowledgement of the recall could have been disastrous. We turned about and headed for home. As we were well over enemy territory and flew in and out of heavy flak we received credit for a mission. We brought our bombs back and returned okay despite a bad engine.

The three Divisions dispatched 748 bombers, who were escorted by 730 fighters from the 8th and 9th Air Forces. Three Fortresses in the 447th aborted over England due to mechanical problems. The rest of the formation went on at 26,500 feet toward Denmark. The weather began to thicken. En route, the contrails from the B-17s ahead were heavy. All of a sudden the Wing headed west. The 1st Combat Wing had decided to abort and just did a 180° to return on the same course that they had flown inbound and they flew through the 4th CBW. A 94th B-17 collided with a 91st ship. The debris damaged Lieutenant Francis R. Graham's aircraft in the 447th, causing it to go down. There were no survivors. Lieutenant Don E. Ralston's B-17 was also damaged and went down. Only three men were picked up.

In the 96th formation, the weather got so bad that crews could hardly see their wing men, or, as Ernest Richardson recalls, 'for that matter, any ships at all.'

It's a hell of a feeling flying through clouds that thick, especially when you know there are about 800 planes in the same vicinity. We were all tensed up.

"Let's try and go over it, everyone keep their eyes open." It was Gillespie. It was good hearing someone. We were climbing for about five minutes when we finally broke out into a small clearing. I wished it could have been a couple of minutes later because just as we broke through the clouds, off to our left, two B-17s came together head on. All it left was a big blotch of black smoke in the air; a grim reminder of the event. I didn't say anything about it over the interphone; I didn't want to make anyone any more jumpy than they already were. It was strange; almost everyone else saw it and didn't mention it for the same reason. It came up later after we landed back at our base during interrogation. We climbed to about 30,000 feet and never did make it over the clouds. The mission already had been cancelled. I heard someone say the temperature was 70 degrees below zero. Everyone had their heated suits turned up as far as they would go. I stood with my legs straddled because there seemed to be too many heating wires in the crotch, we almost froze. Finally we went down to just above the water and all my radio equipment turned white with frost. We worried all the way back to England as I'm sure many other crews did that day.

Wallace Patterson saw the B-17s returning.

Heavily loaded for the 1,400-mile trip, we just barely got off the ground and after forming, started across the North Sea. Our formation was very poor and all around, above and below us ships were aborting like mad. Our group practically disappeared and we tacked onto the 93rd for mutual protection. Every ship left long vapour trails, which were visible for miles. At Heligoland, where they started throwing flak at us, we met the B-17s coming out. That was queer because they were supposed to return by land.[1] Then the fighters had to leave us. We could see the smoke rising over the clouds from Hamburg, which was the B-17 target. Luck told us his turret was inoperative, leaving our rear unprotected. I think I was praying in a way and 'Rod' [2nd Lieutenant Rodney E. Webb, navigator] was muttering something about murder. About ten miles in front of us were the contrails of hundreds of Jerry fighters waiting for us. And just then we were recalled. We caught a little more flak on the way home. It is still undecided whether or not we'll get credit for a mission, because we threw no bombs. But we should. We all agree none of us would have come back if we had continued.

Thurman Spiva continues:

It was not a CAVU (ceiling and visibility unlimited) day. The clouds continued to build higher and higher over northern Germany. The twenty-six plane formation tried to get above them, but it was a losing battle. You barely saw your wingmen through the thickening clouds. A fully loaded B-24 at high altitude reached a point where you were just 'hanging on by your propellers.' It was not the most stable or the easiest aircraft to fly under such conditions. The day was cold and dry … a stinging, piercing cold. The needle on the outside temperature gauge read minus fifty or sixty degrees Centigrade. Then the recall for the entire Eighth Air Force was received. We headed back toward the North Sea. It was a relief to let down where it was a little warmer and have our first cigarette in over four hours. The crews were unhappy about the recall – we were within 150 miles of the target.

Aboard *Hula Wahine II* radio static interfered with communications so John Goss turned it off. The clouds were getting thicker in front of them. Not wanting to fly under a formation of planes inside a cloud system, he climbed above it, still flying to the left of the lead element. His wingmen, both new to the Squadron, kept hanging in with him, flying nice and tight. Other planes were dropping out of the formation. Then they hit the front. *Hula Wahine II* was bouncing and they could not see the tips of the wings. The Group was gone. The wingmen were gone. With maximum power and a full rich mix, and after what seemed like an eternity, they popped out of the clouds at 25,000 feet. It was not a recommended altitude for a B-24. Lo and behold, there were his two wingmen and puffs of flak.

Goss asked Calvin Hanlyn, the navigator, for a heading to Berlin. The first heading was more like the way to Sweden. Quickly corrected, they were on course to Berlin. The three-plane element was quite alone. In the distance they saw fighters with Me 109 profiles. They salvoed their bombs somewhere in Germany – thought it might have been Hanover. Starting to head into the clouds, they saw the planes they thought were 109s were P-51s. They wished they had been more attentive during the aircraft recognition class. Heading for home, they dropped lower and saw the cloud cover disappear as they left the enemy coast. After six hours and being listed as MIA, they touched down at Flixton. The ground was covered with snow, runways were clean. Goss taxied the *Hula Wahine* to the hardstand. The disappointed crew felt they had missed enduring fame as the first USAAF crew to bomb Berlin in daylight.

At Knettishall, when the Group landed and 'BJ' Keirsted's crew pulled into their revetment, a communications officer drove up in a jeep, confiscated Larry Goldstein's radio log and ordered him to report to a Group Communications meeting immediately. It seemed that the mission lead and deputy lead radio operators never heard or acknowledged the recall. Goldstein was on duty, recorded the recall and was not one of those reprimanded. That night he wrote in his diary, 'One more to go. God be good to me on the next one!'

At least Wallace Patterson could feel safe in the knowledge that they would have a day off on Saturday the 4th and so he decided to go to Norwich to get some tyres for his bicycle. However, 'Big-B' would be splashed all over the target maps at nearly all the bomber bases once again and Patterson was not alone in feeling disgruntled. 'Like hell we got a day off. At 0430 we were aroused to go fly, to Berlin again, this time over land.'

At Rattlesden crews were awakened at 0400 hours. As they walked toward the mess hall, their hands were in their pockets, shoulders hunched over and pulled together in an effort to ward off the damp cold. There was the noise of engines being run up. Isaac Doyle Shields, navigator on Lieutenant Hamp Morrison's crew, could see that the constellation Cassiopea was dimly in the north-east sky. Born in Calvert, Texas, 12 December 1922, his parents were of German, Welsh, and German-Dutch and Scots-Irish ancestry. Mathematics was his strong subject in school. The numbers involved in navigation intrigued Shields more than being a pilot and at his request he was classified navigator. He was awarded his Navigator Wings from the Advanced Navigation School at Hondo, Texas, on 16 September 1943 as a Second Lieutenant and was sent to Moses Lake, Washington, where he was assigned to Hamp Morrison's crew. Hamp was from Memphis, Tennessee. This was their first combat mission. After they had completed their breakfast of fresh eggs and bacon, they headed for the briefing room for the 0530 briefing. When the curtain was removed from the map there was a gasp. The target was 'Big-B' again.[2]

At Knettishall there was an extra early briefing. Larry Goldstein in 'BJ' Keirsted's crew, who were flying *Pegasus II*, the ship they had flown on the last four missions, again noticed that it was attended by all three chaplains: Jewish, Catholic and Protestant.

This gave added importance to the destination. The briefing was a duplicate of yesterday; back to Berlin for the first daylight raid of 'Big-B'. It was the worst possible news that the *Worry Wart* crew could hear. After briefing we hoped the mission would be scrubbed and we constantly watched the control tower for a red flare. It never came. We went through our pre-flight ritual as we always did, but this one had a special meaning.

Ernest Richardson recalls:

Everyone was hoping they would call off all future raids to Berlin, however, we weren't the ones making the decisions, so we again heard the S-2 officer say, "This morning gentlemen, your raid is to Berlin." After the cat calls, yelling and shuffling died down he went on to tell us about our route in and out, fighters, flak, how long we would be on oxygen etc. We were sure we would get there this time. No one liked the unnecessary route we were to take it seemed to cover half of Europe. We had heard the 8th Air Force was trying to force the Luftwaffe into the air so we could eliminate them. We felt sometimes it was the other way around.

When he got out to his ship, Wallace Patterson found that it was covered with snow and the turret was full of it, both vents being broken. He would have frozen to death in an hour.

It was snowing so heavily that we couldn't see a hundred feet and while some of the other ships tried to taxi out onto the runways, most pilots said they would have faced court martial rather than risk their crews on slippery runways with ceiling and visibility zero. Fortunately the mission was scrubbed at zero hour. It snowed over six inches in the last 24 hours.

There was no recall at the B-17 bases further south, as Larry Goldstein confirms. 'Take-off and assembly were normal but we were a little bit more on edge. Over France and into Germany we had flak and fighters but no damage or injuries.'

Well into the mission, Ernest Richardson was looking out his side window and off to his left the sky was black with bursts of flak.

Not being tuned in on interphone, I naturally thought it was Berlin, so I got my parachute, shoes and other essentials ready in case I had to bail out. I didn't think an aircraft could go through that flak without being hit. I'd just about given up on our chances of finishing twenty-five missions. (Short time later they changed the number you had to fly to thirty). To my surprise we veered to the right, away from the flak. Naturally I was happy, but I couldn't figure out why we weren't going where the flak was so heavy. I was certain it was Berlin. The next day the *Stars and Stripes* reported the 8th Air Force bombed north-west Germany. Also in the article it mentioned there was one group that managed to reach Berlin.

Larry Goldstein continues:

Just before we reached the target there was a recall of the formation for the second straight day. It was the best possible news that I could hear over my radio. The fact that we were going home was sweet music to our crew when I told them of the recall, but someone said, "Can we take our bombs home on our last mission?" We all said "no, let us unload on any target". As a crew we made a decision by vote over the intercom to drop our bomb load on some target. Keith picked out a railroad marshalling yard on the German-French border. We dropped out of formation to make our bomb run despite 'Ace' Conklin's warning that the formation was getting farther and farther away. We dropped back out of formation away from the protection of our fellow bomb group, probably the dumbest thing that we could do because any enemy fighter pilot that saw a lone bomber immediately saw this as a kill and that is exactly what happened. After 'bombs away' we climbed back towards the formation, now many miles ahead. Our bomb bay doors were closing and according to Kent Keith they were closed. My job was to check those doors visually. I did. They were open. Several more attempts to close them were futile so 'BJ' gave the order for Jack Kings to leave his top turret and hand crank them closed. We were at about 25,000 feet. I watched to make sure he did not pass out. Suddenly, there was a loud explosion. A Me 109 must have seen a straggling Fort and fired several 20 mm shells at us. 'BJ' and Conklin took evasive action by falling off to the right. This quick action by our pilots probably saved our plane and us from destruction. Every time we came out of the clouds the German fighter was there with a couple of shots across our nose. We levelled off in the clouds before taking a head count. No-one reported any battle damage or injury. Little did we know that we were severely damaged.

We finally broke out over France. Our navigator, Lieutenant Brejensky, was unable to plot a course and I was asked to get a heading. Our G-Box was out of order so I contacted the RAF distress channel for help. God bless them because they answered immediately in the clear with a course for England, but the Germans immediately jammed it. A friend of mine, Tech Sergeant Wallace Gross, was flying as the alternate radio operator. Normally he was radio man on Hulcher's crew but somehow he was one mission behind his crew and volunteered to fly the ball position. He was not eager to be there for the whole flight and was sitting on the radio room floor. He was a crackerjack radio man and immediately set up another frequency. Again I transmitted and again the receiver message was jammed. We began to panic but Wallace put in a third unit and we received a heading which I gave to the navigator and when we broke out of the cloud we were over the Channel. When I saw the White Cliffs of Dover it was the most beautiful sight that I could ever hope to see. At this moment I did not realise the importance of my radio work, I had been too scared at that moment, but my training had paid off.

The rest should have been routine – but it wasn't. We were probably the last aircraft to land. Everybody had seen us get hit and figured that we were lost. As we came over Knettishall our landing approach was normal until touchdown: no brakes. We went off the end of the runway and did a slow ground loop coming to a halt. The fire trucks all rushed to our aid but they were not needed. The medics wanted to know if the radio operator was hurt. When someone on our plane said I was okay one of the fireman pointed to a tremendous hole in the right side of the radio room. It was then that I realised that we had flown like that for some three hours. I was probably too scared to realise how dangerous it had been. Nevertheless, it was twenty-five and home. We walked away from the plane and said our own individual prayers of thanks. A few days later, 'BJ' came into our quarters and ordered us all to accompany him to the base chapel and there we really became one crew that was thankful for our completing our missions without a major injury.

Doyle Shields remembered his first mission very well:

East of Lille, on return, the No. 4 engine quit and then shortly thereafter the number 3 engine quit. With two engines out we could no longer keep up with the formation. I had been told in orientation that for the first ten missions, I would be worried more about self preservation than where I was. They were right! Now I had to set course for home. I thought we were near Lille and if I was right we should take a heading of 330° and as the British said, "You caun't miss it." We salvoed our bombs on some farmer's outhouse (A standard characterisation when we dropped our bombs away from the target) and threw out everything that was loose. Morrison was so busy trying to keep the airplane in the air with two dead engines on the same side, that when he got off course he didn't have time to explain that he had to go the long way back to the heading I had given him. I got on the interphone and shouted and repeated, "Three, Three, Zero." We kept losing altitude. Through a break in the clouds, we saw water below. We made ready to ditch. When we broke through the clouds, there were the beautiful White Cliffs of Dover and we were still flying. The English gave us a shot across our nose. That didn't stop us. Morrison spotted Eastchurch, a grass RAF fighter field on the Isle of Sheppey on the south side of the mouth of the Thames and made a safe landing. This is an example of what caused a lot of losses among new crews. When Morrison tried to pull the valve to release the fuel in the Tokyo tanks into the main tanks, the valve was frozen and the engines just ran out of fuel.[3]

Wallace Patterson decided to give Norwich a miss because, as he added cryptically, 'We shall probably have to fly again tomorrow', but Saunders' crew was stood down on 5 March. They went on pass while Patterson 'loafed'. Lieutenant Robert Martin's crew, who were supposed to leave on a three-day pass, joined twenty-eight other crews at the briefing. They would fly as a replacement for another crew and the pass would have to wait until after they returned from the mission.

Alvin Skaggs recalls:

When the mission map was exposed, the crews groaned. This time we had a good reason to groan because the ribbon marking the mission route ran all the way across France to the Spanish border. The target was Mont-De-Marson at the foot of the Pyrenees. It would be the Group's longest mission to date. As we reached the target area, clouds covered it so our Group didn't drop our bombs. On the return trip, our group leader decided to bomb Bordeaux [sic].[4] They fouled up the first run and had to make a second run to drop the bombs. Shortly after bombs away, we were jumped by about twenty Me 109s. Since the 448th was alone, the Germans pressed their attack very hard. They demonstrated a lot of courage in their efforts but not skill. Some of their tactics indicated that they were green pilots and consequently our formation was officially credited with shooting down ten Me 109s. Our formation came out of the encounter with only one aircraft shot down. [It was Martin's].[5] However, almost every plane in the formation took hits with a number of men wounded. Flying our right wing was Lieutenant John McCune's Crew 63 [in *Maid of Orleans*], which took over 200 hits, including two men wounded. It wasn't without reward because even though his hydraulic system was shot out and the tail gunner [Sergeant Willard Cobb] was wounded, he managed to shoot down one Me 109 and probably another. For his efforts, he received the DFC and the Purple Heart. Lieutenant William Ross's Crew 73 failed to return from the mission.[6]

Martin's crew were from Barracks 4, which was gaining something of an unlucky reputation at Seething. Crew 55 slept in their own beds in the hut that night but they had to leave *Squat 'N. Droppit* at a P-47 base on their return when they ran short of fuel.

American claims on 3 March that Berlin had been bombed had been quickly refuted by the Germans, who were well aware that any target not hit through bad weather would receive a visit in the near future or as the opportunity arose. To fill their pages, the Sunday newspapers made the most out of the first raid on Berlin. Combat personnel, meanwhile, wrote letters home. At Thorpe Abbotts on 5 March, Lieutenant Ralph Cotter, a bombardier, wrote to his mother.

> Well, today is Sunday and I am sitting in the club. We did not have a raid today but it was such a nice day we went up and practiced bombing all afternoon. I had a very good day. I guess that is why I feel so well. Oh, Mom, I want you to look carefully in the *Gazette* and the Boston papers, because they gave our crew a write-up over the St-Omer raid. It starts off about Lieutenant William Terry, my pilot and all our names are mentioned. Enclosed you will find a clipping on my sixteenth raid. Just think only nine more raids and then I will be home. It will take about a month or more after I finish my twenty-five missions but there is nothing to worry about. Well, Mom, everything is fine and I will say goodnight until tomorrow. Love, Ralph.[7]

At one base a co-pilot, whose nerve was stretched ever since his crew had been shot down in his absence, awoke one night screaming having dreamt that he had been shot through the heart. The next night he dreamed that he went to Berlin by air. On 6 March he went to pieces. The Flight Surgeon told him not to fly. The co-pilot was in such a very bad nervous state that he had to be grounded permanently after that. Finally he had to be moved out of the crew hut. He was getting on everyone's nerves with his morbid conversation and moping attitude. He had not slept in a bed since his first big jolt, preferring to sit up all night in a chair or at the club.

At Seething on Monday morning, 6 March, at 0400 hours the charge of quarters (CQ) awoke Bill McCullah as he fumbled for the name on Staff Sergeant Kenneth L. Dyer's bunk. Awakening Dyer, the CQ informed him he was the replacement radioman on another crew.[8] 'Kenneth told me he'd see me after the mission and I went back to sleep. It was the last time I saw him!'

At Tibenham, Lieutenant George H. Lymburn and his crew experienced the usual 4 a.m. awakening they had eleven times before, ate the usual breakfast and took the usual position in the briefing room. Lymburn had given up his job in a Massachusetts department store after the attack on Pearl Harbor and had been sent to Montgomery Field, Alabama, where he went through pilot training and after graduating, had joined the 445th cadre in Orlando, Florida. At the age of nineteen, he was checked out as a first pilot of the 'magnificent' B-24. Following training, his crew had arrived in England in November of 1943. Lymburn was upset because his usual aircraft, with the unusual name of *Sutzrobbishplutzm oymoysurake*, had been lost the day before. George did not know the meaning of the name; he only knew it was some sort of Polish expression that he liked the sound of. He and his crew were not flying that day so his ship had been assigned to Lieutenant Lester Elke, who had failed to return from the mission to Ludwigshafen, so Lymburn's crew were assigned *Little Milo* (formerly *God Bless Our Ship*). They hoped it would be a good omen, but the crew really felt ill-at-ease that they were to fly a replacement aircraft.

At Old Buckenham a GI orderly was sleepily making his way down the wet and muddy walk that led past a row of Nissen huts where combat crews in the 734th Squadron were sleeping. Already there were sounds of activity. One of the B-24s was being tested for a sour mag that dropped 100 rpm. It was supposed to be fixed at 50 rpm but some crew chief was off the ball and it got worse. The orderly opened the door of one of the huts, turned on the light and called, 'Lieutenant Cripe?'

'Huh,' came the sleepy answer.

'Breakfast at 3 o'clock, briefing at 4.' He left and went on to call other crews.

Lieutenant Hubert R. Cripe got up and shivered as the cold night struck him. He called his co-pilot, Russell 'Russ' Anderson, and his navigator, 2nd Lieutenant Homer W. 'Spike' Ballacqua. Now Cripe knew how his father felt when he called him and his brother on a cold winter morning, only more so. Cripe got them up with lots of grumbling and cuss words. They put on their helmets, oxygen masks, coveralls and parachute harness in a C-3 bag, dressed and went to breakfast of powdered eggs and hot cakes. Groups of men were grouped around the stove, speculating on the target. However, trucks were waiting to take the crews to briefing so they cut it short and loaded up. Immediately on arriving at the briefing room, they drew their electric suits and put them on. Then they went in to briefing.

At Knettishall, as 'BJ' Keirsted's crew lay comfortably in their beds at four in the morning, there was a call for briefing. Larry Goldstein wrote: 'It was a great thrill and some satisfaction to all of us to just turn over and go back to sleep.'

In another hut on the base, Lowell H. Watts pulled on his clothes in the inky
blackness of early morning.

Perhaps I should have had a premonition of disaster. If not then, maybe the
briefing should have left me anxious and worried. We were all set for our final
combat mission; the mission, which would relieve the strain of combat and
give us at least a month at home with our friends and families. How we looked
forward to going home again. That trip was almost within our grasp. Just a
few more combat hours, that was all. But those hours were to be spent deep on
Germany over a city the 8th had twice before tried to bomb without success.
Berlin – 'Big-B' – defended in full force by the Luftwaffe and hundreds of flak
guns manned by some of the best gunners on the European continent. On the
previous recalled missions to 'Big-B' a dog-leg route had been planned. There
would be no bluff on this mission. We were to fly straight in and straight out.
In addition to this grim prospect, we were to lead the low squadron of the low
group of the second section of our combat wing. In short, our squadron would
be the lowest and furthest back and therefore the most vulnerable spot in the
wing to aerial attack. As I walked out to the briefing room Major Goodman, our
squadron commander, gave me a pat on the back and said his good wishes. He
was assured that *Blitzin' Betsy* would be back on the line that evening and if not,
it would have cost plenty to bring her down.

At Rattlesden, the CQs had started their rounds at 0400 hours. Briefing for thirty
crews was at 0530 hours. Ed Leighty, waist gunner on Bill Greenwell's crew,
remembers: 'The Intelligence Officer pulled back the curtain over the wall map
and there was the route to the target marked out in wool. "Men," he said pointing
with a stick, "today you will bomb Berlin." I didn't know any men being there in
the room. I do know that there were a lot of frightened boys!'[9]

At Old Buckenham the far end of the briefing room was a large map of England
and the Continent. The room soon filled and Major Edward F. Hubbard directed
the route he put on the map. A hush settled over the room as two S-2 men thumb-
tacked a thin sheet of Plexiglas in such a way that a red crayon line on the sheet
disclosed the route. Groans went up over the room as the red line stopped at
BERLIN!

Hubbard demanded order and called the roll. Cripe was given another
bombardier as his own had pleurisy and was unable to go. Captain Foster was to
go with him but nobody woke him so he was given 2nd Lieutenant Maurice A.

Dinneen, the regular bombardier on Lieutenant Dean H. Hart's crew. Destiny had a queer twist for Falla and Fay and an entirely different one for Dinneen and two other members of Hart's crew.[10] Hubbard continued and assigned ships, told gas load, bomb load and call signs. S-2 took over then and the first words they said were: 'Gentlemen, OUR target for today is Berlin.' Then the officer described the target, an electrical plant on the south side of Berlin. He continued that if they were unable to get back to England, to head for Sweden. 'If you are forced down in Holland or Belgium your chances of contacting the underground are pretty good. However, no such luck in Germany. Good luck, gentlemen.'

Next came the weather officer, who described what kind of weather to expect. The briefing officers had been up all night preparing this mission and with a few final remarks Major Hubbard dismissed them. Back to the equipment room they went, drew parachutes (Cripe's was a new back pack) and the Mae Wests that were to prove the factor to cheat death. The equipment Cripe wore was long underwear, a blue bunny electric suit, coveralls, electric gloves and shoes, fleece lined boots, a helmet with oxygen mask attached, Mae West and finally the parachute. He left a short coat, pink pants, green shirt and his cap in his C-3 bag in the dressing room. Past experience had taught him to take along a winter jacket, as the electric suit might not work.

Thus equipped they went outside, loaded their equipment and themselves on a truck and went out to their hardstand. The gas truck had just finished topping off the tanks after pre-flight.

'You'll have 2,700 gallons of gas,' Major Hubbard had said and the crew chief was seeing that they had just that. Dawn had not come yet and the lights were on inside the Liberator. As he crawled into the bomb bay to put his equipment in the cockpit, Cripe noticed the bombs. 'Eggs for Jerry – ten of them – 600 pounders, too.'

'S-2 must have wanted the place bombed good,' thought Cripe. He rejoined the crew, who were checking the guns, ammo and turrets. He was tense and he and Russ Anderson walked away from the B-24 to have a last cigarette.

'She'll be a rough one today, huh?' said Russ Anderson.

'Yeah,' Cripe said, wondering if it would be like the mission two days before when they got as far as Heligoland and were forced back on account of weather. Well, he vowed, today would be different. 'They'd blast that place wide open,' he told himself.

Harry Cornell's crew returned to Chelveston from pass just in time to go on the Berlin raid. John Kettman wrote: 'Well we were finally going to the dreaded target. The last two days our group started out to Berlin and was recalled both times.'

Ernest Richardson recalls:

We were thinking that perhaps they would give up the idea of ever reaching the German capital. We found out differently because on 6 March we were again briefed that the target would be Berlin. This time the route was to take us directly in and out, although everyone was once again disgusted that we would be trying to go there again, the route did lift our morale a little. At least we wouldn't be going all over the continent to get there. By now everybody was sure the Germans knew the 8th was going to bomb Berlin, we expected a really rough raid. We weren't disappointed.

Lowell Watts walked under a faded white half moon through the pre-dawn darkness to the equipment room.

The stars seemed cold and unfriendly. We had arrived at that mental state where one more extra long, extra tough raid meant almost nothing to us. It was just another raid. As for myself at least, I had grown calloused to many of the dangers of combat. The tougher the raid now, the better I liked it. Sure, the fighters and flak brought out the sweat and a tinge of nervous energy, but the thought of actually being shot down seemed like something that just wouldn't happen. Still, there was one thing certain, no chances would be taken on this last mission. I was deadly serious in checking over every detail of our 'plane and equipment. The sun crawled up and peeked over the eastern horizon, casting a pink tinge on the fluffy, scattered clouds that seemed to forecast a clear day. Had we known, could we have seen a few hours into the future, we would have taken that pinkish tinge as a portent of the blood that was to be shed above those clouds. But then, it just looked like another day with better than average weather. Still, I could show plenty of confidence when I told Harry Allert, our crew chief, to expect a first-class buzz job over his tent when we got back.

Berlin was the third mission for 2nd Lieutenant Charles A. Melton's crew in *Paddlefoot* in the 458th at Horsham St Faith. Master Sergeant Glenn R. Matson recalls:

The 2nd Bomb Wing would lead with the 14th and 96th composite to follow six miles behind. The 20th Bomb Wing would follow six miles behind them, bringing up the rear of the three Bomb Divisions of the B-17s and B-24s to make a bomber stream of over ninety miles long. The bomber force consisted of 243 B-24s and 567 B-17s. Originally our target was to be the Heinkel aircraft factory at Oranienburg, North of Berlin. It was feared that we would have to fly through the heaviest of flak over Berlin to reach our target, so they switched our target Genshagen to hit the Daimler-Benz Motor Works. The bombers had to fly over 1,000 miles to the target and back. At take-off, visibility was below 1,800 feet and patches of fog, with complete cloud cover between 3,000 and 6,000 feet. About 10.30 we departed England and headed for the North Sea and across Holland. Thirteen of our thirty-three B-24s aborted or failed to make the mission. The remaining twenty bombers joined up with the 14th and 96th Bomb Wing to form a composite Wing. We picked up our first fighter escort, the 56th Fighter Group, somewhere over Holland. We were following the 3rd Division B-17s when they got off course between Enschede and Osnabrück. The B-24s and part of the B-17s saw the error and stayed on the planned route. Temperatures at altitude were near 60 below zero F. We were to stay below 21,000 feet to prevent contrails and make it harder for the German fighters to spot us.

The stream of 777 B-17s and 305 B-24s was 94 miles long. The five heavily escorted combat wings in the 1st Division, which was assigned the ball-bearing plant at Erkner in the south-eastern suburbs, formed the van, with the 3rd, which was led by Brigadier General Russell Wilson, who flew in an H2X-equipped B-17, being assigned the Robert Bosch Electrical Equipment factory at Klein Machnow, south-west of Berlin, filling in behind them. At Knettishall twelve B-17s of the 'B' Group took off, followed by twenty-one Fortresses of the 'A' Group. Lowell Watts continues:

Our take-off was perfect. We slid into our formation position without trouble, the rest of the squadron pulling up on us a few minutes later. Everything was working perfectly: engines, guns, interphone. Every man on the crew was feeling well and in good physical condition. We were all set for this final and greatest combat test. I wondered then if all this was a harbinger of a smooth mission or the calm before the storm. The question was to be answered very definitely within a very short time. While we were assembling the wing and division formations over Cambridge, the lead ship of our section of the wing aborted. Our group took over the wing lead. I felt better then; at least we weren't in the low group now. We crossed the English coastline and the gunners tested their .50 calibres. The Channel passed beneath us and then the Dutch coast dropped under the wings and fell away behind us.

At Old Buckenham, ten minutes before engine starting time, Lieutenant Hubert Cripe's crew had a final pep talk and boarded the Liberator. Russ Anderson read through the checklist and the engineer started the Put-Put. The clock on the instrument panel had come to engine starting time as Anderson snapped on the switches and said, 'Starting No. 3.' The starting motor gave a low whine and increased. 'Mesh No. 3.'

'Meshing 3,' came the answer and the big prop started slowly turning. The 1,200 hp engines coughed, caught, blew out a cloud of blue smoke and burst into life. In such a manner the other three engines were started. After satisfying themselves that the engines were thoroughly warm, they waited for taxiing time. Already the lead bomber had taxied past their hardstand and the others were following in order. Cripe's crew were flying off Lieutenant Robert B. Witzel's wing and when Cripe saw him begin to move he released the brakes, increased the rpm and slowly made their way to the taxi strip. By the time they had taxied halfway to the end of the active runway, the lead plane was taking off. He was airborne before the end of the runway and other B-24s followed in order. They all showed evidence of their heavy load – 6,000 lbs of bombs plus 2,700 gallons of gas plus ten men and ammunition for ten machine guns; a total of nearly 35 tons. They stopped at the run up area and went through the take-off check list: '20° flap, Hi rpm (2,700), manifold pressure, 47 inches of mercury.' They taxied to the opposite side of the runway Witzel used to escape his prop wash and held their brakes awaiting the green light from control. 'Hatches closed, cowl flaps closed, auto rich, brakes set and 25° mercury.'

There was the green light and then came the white knuckles. Brakes released and they were rolling – throttles wide open and 4,800 Pratt & Whitney Horses bellowed their song.

Full military power – they got 49° mercury maximum from the ram effect. Tech Sergeant Mack Garrett, the replacement engineer, stood between the two pilots like Cool Hand Luke. He called calmly the air speed. '60–65–70–80. Come on baby, come on.' They were already past half the runway length. '90–95 – she's getting lighter – keep that nose wheel down, don't let her fly off yet. 100–105 – back pressure on the wheel – 110–120 and we're in the air just over the end of the runway.'

'Gear up! Gear up!' Cripe screamed. Why did it seem that he was the only white knuckled guy aboard?

Anderson calmly answered, 'Gear coming up,' and the massive gear swung out and upward. The brakes were used to stop the spin of the wheels or they would be just like a gyro. 'Yeah, we sure got a load of baggage', thought Cripe. 'We could scarcely climb but we were gaining.' Five minutes of full maximum military power was the limit and Anderson lowered manifold pressure and rpm and milked up the flaps. Their speed increased and they started their climb. They had to start a climbing turn almost as soon as the wheels were up. If not, they would be miles away from the formation. They started turning almost as soon as their wheels were off the runway. By turning inside of Witzel they soon caught up with him and assumed their position off his right wing. He had already assumed his position in the action and the plane that took off behind Cripe's got into position off his left wing.

Cripe's section got into a semblance of a formation and closed up. Lieutenant Elmer B. Crockett of Grafton, Virginia, leading the section of twelve ships, led them up to the first section. Cripe's position was No. 2 in the hi-right element – the Purple Heart element. After the 453rd had formed, they started looking for the other two groups – the 389th and 445th – in their wing. After much manoeuvring in banks, rolling in prop wash and racing engines, the entire division was formed. Planes seemed to be everywhere. This was a maximum effort – 730 B-17s and B-24s and 801 P-38, P-47 and P-51 escort fighters – every plane that would fly was up. Far ahead were the B-17s. They started earlier. High above were more B-17s. Time was marching on. The Air Force was formed and there was work to do. The Air Force started climbing. As the shores of England moved by underneath his left wing Cripe thought, 'Well, here's No. 8.'

Once again the Liberators brought up the rear. Their target was the Daimler-Benz works at Genshagen, 20 miles south of Berlin. This was the most important aero-engine plant in Germany, turning out more than a thousand engines per month. One of the Liberators on the raid was *Reddy Teddy*, a B-24J in the 328th Squadron in the 'Travelling Circus' at Hardwick, which was named for the pilot, 1st Lieutenant Glenn E. Tedford, by his crew. After the fourth mission the crew had decided to stay together and fly every mission. This was because Sergeant W. D. Wahrheit, the tail gunner, was killed after being put on another crew that never returned from the mission. Tedford's crew had started out for Berlin on 2 March. It was the coldest weather the young pilot from Wichita Falls, Texas, had flown in, with an outside air temperature hovering around 62° below zero. Missions to Frankfurt and France followed and on 6 March *Reddy Teddy* took off at 0905 for the mission to Berlin. Glenn E. Tedford's brother, Clois, was a gunner's mate in the US Navy in the South Pacific. It is hard to distinguish who had the most dangerous assignment but the first mass daylight attack on Berlin was as bad as it could get in the ETO.

Enemy fighters could hardly miss the column of bombers heading for Berlin. Jafü 4 had directed some fighters against a formation of B-26 Marauders en route to Poix but had decided not to send any fighters to the north. Instead, Jafü ordered part of II./JG 26 to fly east just in case the heavies turned for Frankfurt or targets in southern Germany. The bombers maintained their course and so all three Gruppen were told to wait on their bases until the direction of the bombers' return flight could be determined. The bombers, meanwhile, sailed over the Zuider Zee and were almost over the German border when the storm broke. Over the Dummer Lake, the fighters concentrated on the leading 1st Division groups and the 91st, 92nd and 381st were given a thorough going-over. The 'Fireball Outfit' was met by head-on attacks and one Bf 109, which did not pull out in time, crashed into 2nd Lieutenant Roy E. Graves' B-17 and the combined wreckage fell on 2nd Lieutenant Eugene H. Whalen's Fortress. All three fell to earth.[11]

Next it was the turn of the 3rd Division groups to feel the weight of the enemy attacks. The leading 385th at the head of the 4th Combat Wing came in for persistent fighter attacks. Brigadier-General Russell Wilson was flying in an H2X radar-equipped Fortress flown by Major Fred A. Rabbo, whose crew included Medal of Honor recipient Lieutenant John C. Morgan. Just as the formation approached the Berlin area, the flak guns opened up and bracketed the group. General Wilson's aircraft was badly hit but continued on the bomb run with one engine on fire. Rabbo gave the order to bail out when the bomber began losing altitude but before the dozen crew could put on their parachutes, the aircraft exploded, killing eight of them. Incredibly Morgan survived, being somersaulted out of the aircraft with his parachute pack under his arm. He managed to put it on after several attempts and was saved from possible injury when a tree broke his fall. In England Morgan's fiancée, 2nd Lieutenant Helene Lieb, a nurse from Minneapolis, waited anxiously for news.[12]

In the 447th formation, 2nd Lieutenant Bryce B. Smith's left inboard engine supercharger was wrecked and shell splinters punctured two tanks, causing fuel to run into the wing and flow out the trailing edge. He aborted the mission and headed for home. At 1240 hours, north of Hannover and Brunswick, the stream began to turn to the south-east in order to go south of Berlin, where the targets were located. An 88 mm anti-aircraft shell hit *Dotie Jane*, piloted by Lieutenant Socolofsky in the 708th Squadron. The tail gunner, Lyman Enrich, tells the story:

> The shell blew the hatch above the radio compartment. This sucked the radioman, Alton Moore, out, taking nine bombs and most of the fuselage in this area. The

shell cut a wing spar causing both wings to drop down. There was no intercom or hydraulic power. There was no way for Socolofsky to know the condition of the crew men. He managed to keep control of his airplane as he returned home.

Robert Benjamin was wounded in the right leg and buttocks. Lyman Enrich was wounded in the left buttocks and leg. Their wounds were extensive so they flew no more missions.

'Shortly after crossing the Zuider Zee, reports started coming in,' recalls Ernest Richardson.

"Fighters twelve o'clock. Our level."

"Fighters nine o'clock; keep your eyes peeled."

"Seventeen going down twelve o'clock, one, two, three, four, five … five chutes open."

"Fighters coming in twelve o'clock." That followed by a burst of machine gun fire from our plane.

"Take him ball-turret. He's yours." More gun fire sounded.

We had enemy fighters all the way to the target. It was a mixture of fighters, bombers and parachutes going down as far as you could see. Of all the raids we had been on this was undoubtedly the worst.

The unprotected 13th Combat Wing, comprising the 95th and Hundredth and 390th Bomb Groups, caught the full venom of the enemy fighter attacks. In thirty minutes the enemy shot down twenty-three Fortresses in the 13th Wing or damaged them so badly that they were forced to ditch or crash-land on the Continent. It was another black day for the Hundredth, which had set out with thirty-six ships led by Major Albert 'Bucky' Elton, six ships having aborted, leaving thirty to carry on. The Group lost the entire high squadron (350th) of ten B-17s and the Bloody Hundredth lost fifteen B-17s in all. Robert J. Shoens, pilot of *Our Gal Sal* in the 351st Squadron, which flew lead, recalls:

I was part of 'Fireball Yellow'. It was a spectacular day, so clear it seemed we could almost see Berlin from over England. Somewhere over eastern France we suddenly realised that we hadn't seen our fighter escort for several minutes. We had been without escort for about 20 minutes, which meant that a relay had not caught up with us. (The German fighters had engaged them somewhere behind us, knowing it would leave us without fighter escort.) The reason wasn't long in coming. Ahead of us, probably ten miles, there appeared to be a swarm of bees; actually German fighters. Guesses ran as much as 200. They were coming right at us and in a few seconds they were going through us. On that pass they shot down the entire high squadron of ten 'planes.

At 1159 – almost High Noon – six Forts of the high squadron were set on fire, trailing long sheets of flame from their engines. As the fighters attacked again, all six peeled out of formation while two others were obviously in trouble. This attack, which took place over Haseluenne, a small German town 12 miles northeast of Lingen, had barely lasted a minute. The high squadron lead was hit directly in the windshield of the cockpit by a fighter, which came out of the sun. The nose was shot away and Captain David Miner and his co-pilot, George Kinsella, were killed. The bombardier was thrown from the nose without a chute. The ball turret gunner was also killed. The rest of the crew, who were on their twenty-fifth mission, bailed out and they were taken prisoner. The bomb load aboard 2nd Lieutenant Zeb Kendall's B-17 exploded, killing all ten crew instantly. 2nd Lieutenant Sherwin Barton piloted the aircraft flying on the right of Kendall's ship. All ten men bailed out of the blazing plane and were taken prisoners of war. *Ronnie R*, piloted by Lieutenant Dean M. Radtke, had two engines knocked out and a fire in the bomb bay. All of the crew except the ball turret gunner, who was killed by a 20 mm burst, bailed out. *Terry and the Pirates*, piloted by William Terry, was hit hard and went down. Lieutenant Ralph Cotter bailed out without a chute. The tail broke off and the control cables snapped back, trapping the gunners. James Aitken, the engineer, lost a leg below the calf to a 20 mm shell and was thrown out by Terry and another crewmember just before the plane exploded and hit the ground. Only Aitken and the navigator and ball turret gunner survived. The remains of the Fortress came down near Quakenbrück. The tail section, containing the body of gunner Carl Hampton, was found some distance away.

Barricks Bag, piloted by 1st Lieutenant Samuel L. Barrick and co-piloted by 2nd Lieutenant Ira Munn, had two engines knocked out and, with other damage, rapidly lost altitude. Unable to catch up, the bombs were jettisoned and they headed for neutral Sweden. After crossing the coast they could not find a suitable field at Ystad in which they could land but Swedish fighters led them to Bulltofta airfield near Malmö. *Barricks Bag*'s left leg collapsed when it touched the ground but the crew were uninjured. Lieutenant George W. Brannan, pilot of *Lucky Lee*, ordered the crew to bail out after the right wing and two engines caught fire. The co-pilot and the navigator were killed and the radio operator was badly wounded and died later in a prison camp. The survivors were taken prisoner of war after several were machine-gunned as they floated down. Six men in Merril Rish's *Spirit of 44* bailed out when the plane was suddenly engulfed in flames. Seconds later the fuselage broke in two near the radio room, to explode, throwing the top turret gunner and one waist gunner clear. The navigator was also blown out of the gaping hole but recovered to pull his ripcord. The pilot and co-pilot were killed, as were the tail gunner and ball turret gunner. The rest of the crew were taken prisoner of war. Such was the intensity of the fire aboard *Going Jessie*, flown by Robert Koper, that only three men were able to bail out before the ship exploded. The rest, including Koper and the radio operator, were killed. *The Pride Of The Century*, the low squadron lead, flown by Coy Montgomery's crew because their B-17, a new ship, was out of commission after the last raid on Berlin, crashed at Colnrade. Montgomery was killed. The rest of the crew, including five replacements, bailed out and were taken prisoner. After the success of their previous mission Robert Connaway, co-pilot, had felt sure that they would make it back in good shape. This was in spite of the plane, formerly known as *Torchy 2nd*, then *Hot Spit* and then *Miss Carriage*, which he described as 'just about the oldest on the field – definitely a wreck of two crash landings'.[13]

These losses had a profound effect on the crews that remained, as Bob Shoens recalls.

When an airplane went down you had to shut out the fact that it took men with it. On this raid it became most difficult because so many were lost. One loss in particular was an example of this. Flying off the right wing of our airplane was the crew from our own barracks. Suddenly, during one of the fighter passes, their entire wing was on fire. In the next instant there was nothing there. The fighters made two more passes and when it was over *Our Gal Sal* was alone. The last airplane from the group that I had seen flying was Captain Jack Swartout in the 351st Squadron lead flying in *Nelson King*, piloted by Lieutenant Frank Lauro. He was struggling along with about six feet missing from his vertical stabiliser and was the only other airplane from the squadron who came back with us.

Nelson King had collided with a Fw 190 in the initial attack. With only a spar securing what was left of the rudder, it kept swinging from side to side and the plane peeled out and turned for home. Edward Handorf and his crew, flying as the Deputy Group lead in *Kind A Ruff*, took their position. Having survived the fighter attacks, they bombed the target and headed home also, but near Diepholz a

Bf 109 attacked at 1 o'clock low and sprayed the front of the Fortress with 20 mm cannon fire, setting the wing tanks on fire. *Kind A Ruff* went down. Only two men got out before the aircraft exploded. Right waist gunner John Willsey, who was on his ninth mission, stepped through the open bomb bay doors and while still in the prop wash, the Fortress exploded, blowing the tail gunner Fair Lawrence clear. Willsey delayed opening his chute until going through the last layers of cloud at about 10,000 feet. He and Lawrence landed about 60 yards apart. Lawrence had a broken leg and Willsey was free for just three hours before some German civilians with shotguns captured him.[14]

Robert J. Shoens continues:

We saw another group ahead of us, so we caught up with it. The airplanes had an 'A' in a square on the tail, so they were from the 94th. We flew on to Berlin with them and dropped our bombs. The flak was heavy but over Berlin the sky was black. The target was on the south-east side of Berlin. For reasons we couldn't figure out, the group we were with chose to turn to the left and go over Berlin. Since we were not part of the group we decided to turn to the right and get out of the flak. When we did that, a German battery of four guns started tracking. They fired about forty rounds before we got out of range. None of them came close because of the evasive action we had taken. Higher up and ahead of us we saw another group, so we climbed and caught up with it. It was also from our wing, having a 'Square J' on its tails [390th]. We flew the rest of the way home with them without further incident. It was a beautiful day still and with a chance to relax we began to wonder what had happened to our group. It couldn't be that we were the only survivors of 'Fireball Yellow'.

In thirty minutes the enemy pilots had shot down twenty-three Fortresses in the 13th Wing, or had damaged them so badly that they were forced to ditch or crash-land on the Continent. Worst hit had been the Bloody Hundredth, which struggling back in a ragged formation and came limping home to Thorpe Abbotts at about 4 o'clock in the afternoon, having lost fifteen B-17s over Germany. Ten had formed part of the Low Box of the 13th Combat Wing. They were joined by *Half and Half, The Bigass Bird II, Buffalo Gal, Rubber Check* and one other B-17. Lieutenant-Colonel John M. Bennett, the acting CO, noted that every other one of the fifteen ships that came home fired red flares, signifying wounded aboard. 'Just exactly 50 per cent of our force, which entered Germany, had been shot down…'[15]

Of 812 bombers that set out, 672 of these attacked their primary or secondary targets in the Berlin area. None of the aircraft in the 1st Bomb Division hit the primary target at Erkner. The B-17s dropped their bombs on the Kopenick and Weissensee districts of the capital. The 3rd Division also missed the primary target and bombed the Steglitz and Zehlendorf districts. Only the B-24s of the 2nd Division released some of their bombs on their primary target; the rest of the attack fell on secondary targets in and around 'Big-B'.

Ernest Richardson continues:

As we neared Berlin the sky was the blackest I'd ever seen with flak bursts. At most targets the flak was right around our altitude, here at Berlin it was quite a ways above and below us and tremendously heavy at our altitude, which was about 23,000 feet. We made history, it being the first time in daylight that Berlin was bombed with the full force of the 8th Air Force. Both sides paid a heavy price.

Captain Ed Curry, a bombardier in the 401st, recalled:

I'd been to Oschersleben and the Ruhr but I'd never seen flak as heavy as they had over Berlin. It wasn't just the odd black puff; it was completely dense; not just at one altitude but high and low. There was a saying that you see the smoke only after the explosion; but we actually saw the red of the explosions. One shell burst near us and we had chunks of shell tear through the radio room and the bomb bay.

At 12,000 feet Hubert Cripe and Russ Anderson put on their oxygen masks and at 15,000 feet Cripe ordered the crew to put theirs on. It was going to be a long raid and a long time on oxygen so he told them to 'save all you can!'

The choppy, cold North Sea was beneath them now. They seemed to be standing still but the air speed indicator read 165. After what seemed hours the coast of Holland came into sight. Enemy occupied territory! Little did Cripe know that he would be on Dutch soil in a very few hours.

Mack Garrett had finished transferring gas out of the Tokyo tanks and was back at his top turret, searching the sky for enemy fighters. High above were many single contrails. Fighters! Maybe they were their own? Sure enough, as they got closer the wing and tail positively identified them as P-47s. If any enemy fighters were present, they kept away from the bombers while they had fighter protection.

They were well inland now and Spike Ballacqua called up and said that they would be over the German border in seven minutes. 'Well, so far, so good', thought Cripe. 'No flak yet.'

The gunners were keeping a line of talk going over the interphone. For himself, Cripe was comfortable. 'Electric suit OK. Oxygen mask OK. Plane OK except that No. 3 was getting pretty warm.'

Suddenly, out of nowhere dark smudges of black smoke appeared in the group ahead.

'Flak!'

'Hope they leave us alone,' thought Cripe.

He did not see any apparent damage but by then they were in it. It was not too accurate though and they flew on unhindered. Their route took them out of most of the flak areas and they flew on, occasionally seeing light flak and many of their own fighters, which had changed to P-38s. 'We'll change again before the target to P-51s,' thought Cripe. They were well over Germany by now and Spike Ballacqua called again to tell him that they would change course for the IP in 15 minutes. 'Well, so far this had to be a milk run.' Cripe would have been 'plumb happy' only they were 250 miles inside Germany.

They changed course for the IP all right but ten minutes later Witzel suddenly pulled out of the formation. Cripe well knew that being out of formation 100 miles from Berlin was like 'slitting your own throat' but he followed him. He was definitely in trouble. And sure enough – he feathered No. 3. What was Cripe to do? 'Why didn't the dumb fool try to stay with the formation? But no, he was going home.' He knew he had to catch the formation or 'his goose would be cooked'. He gave the B-24 full throttle and caught his group just after they had passed the IP but he got the wrong section! Cripe was in the first one and his own was behind. Well, he'd stay 'here'.

Ahead of them was the target. 'Berlin, here we come – Jerry had the welcome mat turned upside down and inside the door.' Over the target was the most concentrated flak barrage Cripe had ever seen. It was almost a solid black cloud, with red bursts of exploding shells. They could see it 50 miles off and it filled Cripe with dread. Right then he preferred fighters to flak.

They kept approaching the target, the lead plane using the bombsight and making corrections. Bomb bays were open and they were going to drop their 'eggs' when the lead plane did. Suddenly they were in the flak. It was everywhere. When you could hear it, it was too close – and Cripe heard plenty. Spent pieces of flak bounced off their ship like 'BBs'. A burst directly to one side rocked the ship. 'Boy, a hit in our bomb bay and we've had it,' thought Cripe. 'There go the bombs!' Instantly the bombardier hit his bomb release. 'They're off'. After what seemed ages they were out of the flak and the bomb bays closed. Their section wasn't without damage. Whoever was flying No. 2 on Stock had a bad gas leak in the bomb bay. Flak got a gas line or tank. It was Elmer Crockett. Cripe learned that he ran out of gas and ditched.[16]

Little Milo, flown by George H. Lymburn, had taken its position in the formation, climbed to 22,000 feet, and approached Berlin from the south. Helpless, Lymburn had witnessed the destruction of the Hundredth group in front of him. Now the 445th headed towards the centre of Berlin on the bomb run. 'Wham!' Almost immediately, a cluster of flak bursts caused the ship to break into flames. One shell exploded under the wing and drilled a hole right through it. Another burst above the B-24, showering it with red-hot shrapnel and hitting Sergeant Downey, the top turret gunner, on the head. Fortunately, Downey was wearing a flak helmet, which saved him from a serious injury. Another shell tore into the tail section, damaging the controls and causing the rudder to flutter. The final shell burst directly in the bomb bay, starting a fire. The damaged wing was losing fuel, which ignited to form a stream of flame from the wing back to the tail section. Downey swung his top turret to face forwards and saw the trailing edge of the wing melting in the intense heat. Lymburn ordered the crew to bail out. He would try to hold the Liberator steady while they exited the aircraft but the controls were shot up and it was no easy task. Once the crew were gone, he left the flight deck and made his way to the bomb bay to bail out but once there he could see the ground one minute and the sky the next. At this moment he lost his nerve and found that he could not jump, so he made his way back to the cockpit and hoped that he could put the Liberator down somewhere. 'I picked out a green field,' recalls Lymburn, 'crash landed and was astonished to realise that the tail gunner, Frank Cittadino, had come down in the back of the plane. We were captured and spent the rest of the war in a German prisoner of war camp at Stalag Luft I, Barth.' The only casualty was the bombardier, who was dragged by his chute into a large tree stump and he was killed on impact.

The 458th had taken a course south-east after passing between Brandenburg and Magdeburg to the Initial Point to start the bomb run and had then swung north into the wind to the target. 'The worst flak hit us as we approached Oranienburg,' recalled Glenn R. Matson.

There may have been kids firing those 88 mm flak guns, but they were good. It was bad enough riding that flak road in and out of Berlin, but as we arrived at the IP we were on a collision course with a B-17 Group on their bomb run. Our Group leader, who was a lieutenant-colonel, had to abort our bomb run, change course and close bomb bay doors and set up for another run. Again we were off our target and he turned us 360° over Berlin instead of away from it. That put us in almost constant flak for over thirty minutes. He wasn't satisfied with our other two runs; he wanted to hit the rail station and yards, not just 'Big-B'. We were flying in the lower left three-plane element in the position of Purple Heart corner. The guy leading our element took us under the main Group formation. By now our bomb bay doors were open again and we were in a very precarious situation. We didn't like looking up at those open loaded bomb bays directly above us. Melton decided to leave the element and slid back up in the formation where we belonged. Our element leader and the other wing man were two of our five losses that day. We feared at the time that our own Group's bombs fell on them. It was on this third bomb run that our navigator, 2nd Lieutenant Charles C. Weinum, stuck his head up in the navigator's dome in front of the pilots and thumbed his nose at them. He noticed a dog fight and got down inside to get a better view through the side window. After he had left, a chunk of flak made a hole through the dome about the size of a fist. If his head had been there; Pow! No head. He stuck his head up there again, saw a flak hole and got the surprise of his life.

We had to divert to an alternate target. By then we had heavy cloud cover and ended up dropping our bombs near Potsdam. With the target no longer visible, we had to resort to PFF and the results were very poor. Shortly after leaving the target area, we were attacked by two Fw 190s without causing any damage. Our Group had been badly shot up by flak, one aircraft lost over the target. This was *Ford's Follies*, flown by 2nd Lieutenant Guy C. Rogers, who crashed west of Berlin; eight men were killed and two bailed out when the plane exploded. The next to go down was Captain Jack Bogusch's crew. Four men were killed and six survived the crash and were taken prisoner. Then 2nd Lieutenant Thayer Hopkins' crew crashed. All ten men survived and were taken prisoner.

Next to crash was 2nd Lieutenant Beverly Ballard's crew. Three were killed and nine men taken prisoner. The ball turret gunner, Sergeant Victor W. Kruger, evaded capture for fourteen months when the Dutch Resistance found him and hid him out until the British troops rescued him in April 1945. 2nd Lieutenant Jesse McMains' crew was shot down by a Me 110 and crashed near Ueltzen, Germany. Two were killed and eight taken prisoner. As for our crew, *Paddlefoot* experienced a bit of flak damage, but no one on the crew was injured and our

1. Larry 'Goldie' Goldstein at Wendover Air Gunnery School, Utah, in July 1943 – the only air gunnery school without aerial gunner (no flying). (Larry Goldstein)

2. B-24D 41-23707 *Second Chance* in the 93rd Bomb Group at Hardwick, which FTR on 7 December 1943. (Via Hardwick Aviation Museum)

3. B-17F-75-DL 42-3522 *Gremlin's Delite*, which was assigned to the 482nd Bomb Group at Alconbury on 7 September 1943 before being transferred to the 337th Bomb Squadron, 96th Bomb Group, on the same day. It then served with the 533rd Bomb Squadron in the 381st Bomb Group at Ridgewell before returning to the USA, at Okmulgee, on 9 July 1944. *Gremlin's Delite* was scrapped at RFC Walnut Ridge on 8 December 1945. (USAF)

4. Combat crews in the 401st Bomb Group at Deenethorpe enjoying 'Java' and 'Stinkers' at debriefing following the raid on 20 December 1943. (USAF)

5. Christmas party at Horham, Suffolk, home of the 95th Bomb Group, Christmas 1943. (USAF)

6. B-17F-10-BO 41-24484 *Bad Egg* was assigned to the 401st Bomb Squadron in the 91st Bomb Group at Bassingbourn. On return from Cognac on 31 December 1943, Hilary Evers and his co-pilot, Paul McDuffee, were diverted to Great Dunmow and then Andrews Field because of bad weather. They hit a jeep and killed Corporal Gillies, the driver, on landing. Badly damaged, *Bad Egg* was declared salvage and taken to 2 SAD, where the front half joined B-17G-5-BO 42-31229 and was assigned to the 390th Bomb Group, retaining the name *Bad Egg*. The 'new' aircraft FTR on 9 September 1944 when it was put down at A-22 on the Continent and was later salvaged, on 14 November. (USAF)

7. B-17G-15-BO 42-31414 in the 615th Bomb Squadron, 401st Bomb Group, which was on a ferry trip from Little Staughton to Deenethorpe on 27 January 1944 when Leon Van Sycle, the co-pilot, was at the controls and came down on the wrong runway, but pilot Mitch Woods retracted the landing gear instead of lowering the flaps and the aircraft crashed. The aircraft was salvaged by 2 SAD at Little Staughton on 30 January. (USAF)

8. Officers in the 381st Bomb Group relaxing in the 'O Club' at Ridgewell in January 1944. (USAF)

9. Red Cross Club show at the 379th Bomb Group base at Kimbolton on 11 January 1944. (USAF)

10. B-17 42-31034 *Bonnie Donnie*, which was assigned to the 612th Bomb Squadron in the 401st Bomb Group at Deenethorpe on 8 November 1943. It is pictured here after crashing on 22 January 1944. It was repaired but went MIA with Lieutenant George E. West's crew on the mission to Cologne on 28 May 1944 after being hit by flak and crashed at Krensitz, 9 miles north-east of Leipzig. Seven of the crew were taken into captivity. George West, Hugh Russell and Mike Lefkin were KIA. Doug McKinnon, Lloyd Nutter, Tom Montgomery, Francis Russell, Bob Andrus, John Womble and Alf Morini were taken prisoner. (USAF)

11. Lieutenant John C. Stolz and crew in the 381st Bomb Group after bombing Frankfurt on 4 February 1944.

12. B-17F-55-BO 42-29524 *Meat Hound* in the 303rd Bomb Group, which was assigned to the 423rd Bomb Squadron, 306th Bomb Group, at Thurleigh on 2 March 1943 before being transferred to the 358th Bomb Squadron, 303rd Bomb Group, at Molesworth on 30 July 1943. On the raid on Oschersleben on 26 January 1944 the aircraft was hit by enemy aircraft over Durgerdam and the pilot, Lieutenant Jack W. Watson, bailed the crew out over the Ijsselmeer and returned alone. Navigator John Leverton, engineer top turret gunner Sam Rowland, waist gunner Gene Stewart and tail gunner Roman Kosinski were taken prisoner. Bombardier Vance Colvin, radio operator Harry Romaine, ball turret gunner Fred Booth and waist gunner Bill Fussner all drowned in the Ijsselmeer. Co-pilot Clayton David evaded. Jack Watson brought *Meat Hound* home to crash land at Metfield in Suffolk. (USAF)

13. James Stewart (second from left, front row), executive officer on the staff of Brigadier-General Edward 'Ted' Timberlake, commanding 2nd Wing Headquarters (centre, front row). On 22 March 1944 Stewart flew his twelfth combat mission, leading the 2nd Bomb Wing in an attack on Berlin. On 30 March he was sent to RAF Old Buckenham to become group operations officer of the 453rd Bombardment Group, a new B-24 unit that had just lost both its commander and operations officer on missions. Stewart flew as command pilot in the lead B-24 on several missions deep into Nazi-occupied Europe. As a staff officer, Stewart was assigned to the 453rd 'for the duration' and thus not subject to a quota of missions of a combat tour. He nevertheless assigned himself as a combat crewman on the group's missions until his promotion to lieutenant-colonel on 3 June and reassignment on 1 July 1944 to the 2nd Bomb Wing, assigned as executive officer to Brigadier-General Edward J. Timberlake. His mission tally while assigned to the 445th and 453rd Bomb Groups was twenty missions. Stewart continued to fly with the pathfinder squadron of the 389th Bomb Group, with his two former groups and with groups of the 20th Combat Bomb Wing. He received a second award of the DFC for actions in combat and was awarded the Croix de Guerre. He also received the Air Medal with three oak leaf clusters. Stewart served in a number of staff positions in the 2nd and 20th Bomb Wings between July 1944 and the end of the war in Europe and was promoted to full colonel on 29 March 1945. On 10 May 1945 he succeeded to command of the 2nd Bomb Wing, a position he held until 15 June. James Stewart died at his home in Beverly Hills on 2 July 1997. He was eighty-nine.

14. B-17G-30-BO 42-31779 was assigned to the 524th Bomb Squadron, 379th Bomb Group, at Kimbolton on 6 February 1944 and suffered bomb damage on 27 August 1944 on the mission to Esbjerg, Denmark, and crash landed. The aircraft was salvaged the next day. (USAF)

15. B-17 42-39782 *Pistol Packin' Mama* in the 526th Bomb Squadron, 379th Bomb Group, went MIA with 2nd Lieutenant Herbert W. Rossberg and crew on the raid on Frankfurt on 8 February 1944 when it crashed at Amy airfield, 4 miles south-west of Roye in France. Herb Rossberg, Jim Dougherty and Alby Paplaskas were KIA. The co-pilot Matt Bauer, ball turret gunner Ed Dugan, waist gunner Thurman Smotherman and tail gunner Fred Brown were taken prisoner. Navigator John Cupsick, engineer-top turret gunner Chas Atkinson and radio operator George Bennett evaded. (USAF)

16. B-17F-75-BO 42-29832 *Our Mom* with Lieutenant Robert E. Miller and crew in the 534th Bomb Squadron, 381st Bomb Group, at Ridgewell on 24 February 1944. The aircraft was first assigned to the 364th Bomb Squadron, 305th Bomb Group, at Chelveston on 18 May 1943 and was named *Spirit Of A Nation*. Transferred to the 534th Bomb Squadron, 381st Bomb Group, at Ridgewell on 22 August 1943 and renamed *Our Mom*, this Fortress was then assigned to AFSC on 5 April 1944 and returned to the USA, seeing service at Tinker, Memphis, Tinker again, and finally RFC Arledge Field on 23 November 1944. (USAF)

17. B-17s in the 457th Bomb Group flying through heavy flak on the mission to Schweinfurt on 24 February 1944. (USAF)

18. B-17s of the 337th Bomb Squadron, 96th Bomb Group, at Snetterton Heath in formation. AW-M is B-17F-55-DL 42-3519 *Pee Wee II*, which was first assigned to the 339th Bomb Squadron [QJ-M] and was transferred to the RAF on 26 March 1944. B-17G-1-VE 42-39814 AW-S in the 337th Bomb Squadron FTR on 21 February 1944 on the mission to Brunswick with 2nd Lieutenant Alver R. Smith's crew, the aircraft crashing at Gross-Munzel, near Kolenfeld, 5 miles south of Wunstorf. Smith, bombardier Ernie Martin, ball turret gunner Frank Morales, waist gunner Dan Kricks and tail gunner Bob Means were KIA. Co-pilot Jim Lynn, navigator Bernie Moynahan, engineer top turret gunner Loyal Messler, radio operator Harry Angus and waist gunner Bill Ford were taken into captivity. B-17F-115-BO 42-30659 AW-K was salvaged on 29 May 1945. (USAF)

19. B-17F-20-DL 42-3040 *Miss Quachita* in the 323rd Bomb Squadron, 91st Bomb Group, at Bassingbourn which went MIA with 2nd Lieutenant Spencer K. Osterberg's crew on 22 February 1944 when it was shot down by Major Heinz Bär and crash landed near Bexten, north of Lingen, on the mission to Gütersloh. Osterberg and seven crew members were taken into captivity and two were killed. (USAF)

20. B-17F-l5-BO 41-24490 *Jack the Ripper* in the 324th Bomb Squadron, 91st Bomb Group, went MIA on 22 February 1944 with the loss of 1st Lieutenant James I. Considine's crew. It was the last of the original 91st Bomb Group aircraft to be lost. (USAF)

21. B-17F-10-BO 41-24487 *Eager Beaver* in the 368th 'Eager Beavers' Bomb Squadron, 306th Bomb Group at Thurleigh, was the longest-serving B-17F in VIIIth BC, September 1942 – October 1943. It was transferred to AF Service Command on 1 May 1944 and returned to the ZOI in July 1944. It went to the Williamsport Technical Institute at Patterson Field, Ohio, on 20 June 1945. (USAF)

22. B-17-20-VE 42-97622 *Paper Dollie* in the 303rd Bomb Group was assigned to the 457th Bomb Group at Glatton on 10 February 1944 before being transferred to the 358th Bomb Squadron, 303rd Bomb Group, at Molesworth on 23 February. On 23 July 1944 it suffered bomb damage on the raid on Creil. Flight Officer Cecil M. Miller and Bill Zweck were KIA. John Peterson, Saul Cooper, Jack Severson, Earl Sheets, Bill Wilson, Jim Pierce and Karl Calson returned and the Fortress was crash landed at Bishop's Waltham, Hants, and was salvaged by 2 SAD on 25 July. (USAF)

23. B-17F-75-BO 42-29889 *Rocky* in the 525th Bomb Squadron, 379th Bomb Group, at Kimbolton caught fire on 24 February 1944 while under ground crew maintenance. (USAF)

24. A burial at Madingley Cemetery near Cambridge. Today, in this beautiful and inspirational setting in the shade of tulip trees, liquidambars and American oaks, lie 3,811 American servicemen who gave their lives in the Second World War. The 472-foot-long Wall of the Missing is inscribed with the names of 5,125 who have no known grave. (Via Peter Worby)

25. A formation of B-24J Liberators in the 706th Bomb Squadron, 446th Bomb Group, en route to the Messerschmitt Bf 110 plant at Gotha, 420 miles due east of the White Cliffs of Dover, on 24 February 1944. Intelligence described Gotha as 'the most valuable single target in the enemy fighter complex'. B-24J-95-CO 42-100360/ B *Luck and Stuff* and Lieutenant Weems D. Jones' crew FTR on 29 April 1944. It crashed at Luckenwalde, Germany, killing three crew while seven crew survived and were taken prisoner. (USAF)

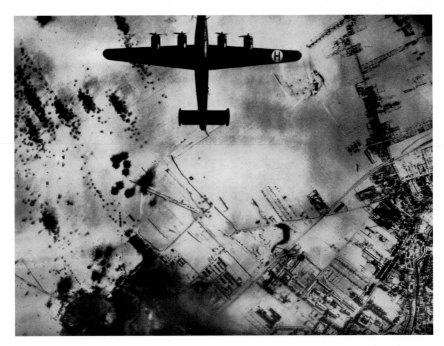

26. A 446th Bomb Group Liberator at Bungay (Flixton) over the Gotha plant on 24 February 1944. (USAF)

27. Colonel Myron Keilman (right) in the 392nd Bomb Group receives the Distinguished Flying Cross from General Leon Johnson, CO, 14th Combat Bombardment Wing. (Keilman)

28. B-17F-120-BO 42-30800 *Cock O' The Walk* was assigned to the 563rd Bomb Squadron, 388th Bomb Group, at Knettishall on 3 September 1943. It FTR from the mission to Brunswick on 29 February with a 452nd Bomb Group crew after suffering a flak hit in the cockpit and crashing near the Luther factory at Bienrode, 4 miles north of Brunswick. The pilot 2nd Lieutenant Jake S. Colvin, co-pilot Dick West, ball turret gunner Andy Saari and waist gunner John Clayton were KIA. Navigator Allen Johnson, bombardier M. E. Glass, engineer-top turret gunner Ray Rottler, radio operator Allen Rose, waist gunner Bill Mack and tail gunner Grady Justice were taken prisoner. (USAF)

29. The first crew to drop American bombs on Berlin on Saturday 4 March 1944 was this PFF crew of a 482nd Bomb Group B-17 captained by 1st Lieutenant William V. Owen of Columbus, Ohio (kneeling, left). By favour of his position in the nose of the Fortress, bombardier Lieutenant Marshall J. Thixton of Corsicana, California (kneeling, second from left), took the honour of being the first to reach the German capital in an American bomber. Kneeling, second from right, is the navigator, 2nd Lieutenant Albert J. Englehardt of Chicago, Illinois, and at right is the co-pilot, 2nd Lieutenant Frank L. McAllister of Omak, Washington. Standing, left to right, are: Tech Sergeant Donald E. White, engineer, of North Bennington, Vermont; Staff Sergeant Harlin R. Sours, rear gunner of Luray, Virginia; Staff Sergeant Edmund R. Aken, radio operator, of Elkville, Illinois; Staff Sergeant George E. Moffat, ball turret gunner of Grosse Point, Michigan; Staff Sergeant John J. O'Neil Junior, waist gunner, of Malden, Massachusetts and Staff Sergeant Ellsworth A. Beans, of Pittsburgh, Pennsylvania, waist gunner. (USAF)

30. 1st Lieutenant William V. Owen and Lieutenant Marshall J. Thixton, pilot and bombardier of the 482nd Bomb Group Pathfinder Fortress, on 4 March 1944. (USAF)

31. The news is announced to the crews of the 351st Bomb Group at Polebrook on 6 March that the 'target for today' is Berlin! (USAF)

32. B-24J-95-CO 42-100353 in the 703rd Bomb Squadron, 445th Bomb Group at Tibenham, which crash-landed in a field at Fressingfield, Suffolk returning from the raid on Berlin on 8 March 1944 and was salvaged on 13 March. (USAF)

33. B-17G-20-BO 42-31488 was delivered to Cheyenne on 8 November 1943 and was operated at Great Falls, Kearney, Romulus and Bangor up to 5 December 1943 before being assigned overseas and joining the 614th Bomb Squadron, 401st Bomb Group, at Deenethorpe on 2 January 1944. *Shade Ruff* went MIA on the mission to Berlin on 8 March 1944 when it crashed at Teglingen Sluice, 2 miles south-east of Meppen. Pilot 2nd Lieutenant Dale A. Peterson, co-pilot George Morse, navigator Harley Honeberger, bombardier Bob Greed, engineer top turret gunner Bob Del Giorno, radio operator John Kuntz, ball turret gunner Art Newell, waist gunner Joe Jay and tail gunner Howard Kneese were taken into captivity. The other waist gunner, Frank Bailey, was also taken prisoner but he died of exhaustion near Neubrandenburg on 27 April 1945 while marching from the Russian advance. (USAF)

34. A reporter interviews Ray L. Sears (later lieutenant-colonel, CO of the 735th Bomb Squadron, MIA 29 April 1944) and co-pilot Jim Kotapish in the 453rd Bomb Group at Old Buckenham, Norfolk, on their return from Berlin in the *Reluctant Dragon* on 8 March 1944. 'On this clear day there were aircraft as far ahead and as far back as the eye could see. A mass of 1,200 plus bombers and fighters that somehow made the sweating out of the bomb run a little more endurable.' The 453rd lost four B-24s on the 6 March Berlin raid and one on 8 March. (Jim Kotapish Collection)

35. B-17G-100-BO 42-30340 *Screamin' Red Ass* was assigned to the 563rd Bomb Squadron, 388th Bomb Group, at Knettishall on 26 June 1943. It went MIA on the mission to Berlin on 8 March 1944 with 2nd Lieutenant Allan O. Amman and crew, crashing at Neu-Ummendorf, near Eisleben, 19 miles west of Magdeburg. Amman, co-pilot Don Wollard, navigators Bill Pierson and Ralph Diederich, engineer-top turret gunner Bob Carter, radio operator Joe McGonagle, ball turret gunner Boyd Iverson, waist gunner Harlie Sands and tail gunner Frank Metzler were KIA. Waist gunner Harry Quick was taken into captivity. (USAF)

36. Crew of B-17G-15-DL 42-37886 *Blitzin' Betsy* in the 388th Bomb Group, which was assigned to the 562nd Bomb Squadron at Knettishall, Suffolk, on 25 October 1943. This aircraft and crew were shot down on the mission to Berlin on 6 March 1944, causing a mid-air collision with 42-40054 in the 562nd Bomb Squadron and crashing near Zwartemeer, near Emmen in Holland. Back row, left to right: 1st Lieutenant Lowell H. Watts, pilot; 2nd Lieutenant Robert M. Kennedy, co-pilot; 2nd Lieutenant Emmett J. Murphy, bombardier; 2nd Lieutenant Edward J. Kelley, navigator. Crouching, left to right: Tech. Sergeant J. B. Ramsey, top turret; Staff Sergeant Ray E. Hess (KIA 6 March 1944), right waist; Tech Sergeant Ivan Finkle, radio operator; Staff Sergeant Robert H. Sweeney (KIA) ball gunner; Staff Sergeant Harold A. Brassfield (KIA), tail gunner; Staff Sergeant Don W. Taylor (KIA), left waist gunner. B-17G-10-VE 42-40054, piloted by Captain Paul Brown, crashed at Schoonberkerveld, south-east of Emmen. Brown, bombardier Rolland Gill, engineer top turret gunner Roy Joyce, waist gunner Elbert Moyer and tail gunner Bill Mocario were taken prisoner. Co-pilot Captain George Job, navigator John DuPrey, ball turret gunner Edwin Pfanner, waist gunner Walter Reed and observer Lieutenant Joe Lechowski were killed. Radio operator John Blatz died in hospital from injuries and severe burns on 18 March. (Watts)

37. B-17s of the 390th Bomb Group at Framlingham on the mission to Berlin on 9 March 1944. B-17G-15-DL 42-37806 *Stark's Ark* was assigned to the 571st Bomb Squadron on 15 October 1943. It went MIA with Henry Holmes' crew on the mission to Magdeburg on 28 May 1944 when No. 2 and No. 3 engines were hit and the left wing was set on fire. The Fortress was last seen in a vertical drive, crashing at Walternienburg, 17 miles south-east of Magdeburg. Nine men bailed out and were taken prisoner. The radio operator, Forrest Knight, was KIA.

38. B-17G-10-VE 42-39967 *Mary Kay*, which was assigned to the 324th Bomb Squadron, 91st Bomb Group, at Bassingbourn on 25 January 1944. It went MIA with Lieutenant Harry L. Theophilos and his crew on the mission to Oberpfaffenhofen on 18 March 1944 when a flak hit caused the Fortress to drop out of formation. Enemy aircraft then struck and *Mary Kay* crashed on the shore of Lake Constance, near Bregenz, Switzerland. Theophilos, co-pilot John DeLavore, navigator John Herr (whose parachute failed and was never found in the lake) and tail gunner Chas Jochmann were KIA. Bombardier Joe Pletta, engineer-top turret gunner Joachin Vizinho, radio operator Jim Norris, ball turret gunner Elden Newman and waist gunners Marion Porter and Chas Perry were taken into captivity. (USAF)

39. B-17F-70-BO 42-29751 was assigned to the 96th Bomb Group at Grafton Underwood on 19 April 1943 before being transferred to the 534th Bomb Squadron in the 381st Bomb Group at Ridgewell on 7 December that same year and it acquired the name *Mis-Abortion*, which was later changed to *STUFF!* The B-17 survived twenty-one missions but stalled on take-off at the start of a test flight on 31 March 1944 and crashed at Wood Barns Farm, Belchamp St Paul, a couple of miles from base. The pilot of the aircraft was Wayne Schomburg but Captain Paul Stull, an engineering officer, who occupied the co-pilot's seat, is believed to have been at the controls. They were killed, as were Don Carr and Chas Carter, radio operator Melvin Wilson and ground crew member Alby McLain. (USAF)

40. Luftwaffenhelfer 'Opi' Dahms (left), Friedrich Kowalke (centre) and A. Prüfer (right) manning their flak battery. (Kowalke)

41. Colonel Albert Shower, CO, 467th Bomb Group, the only 8th Air Force commanding officer to retain command of his bomb group throughout the whole of hostilities in England in the Second World War. (USAF)

42. Lieutenant Abe Dolim, a Hawaiian-born radio operator who flew two tours in the 94th Bomb Group at Bury St Edmunds (Rougham). (Dolim)

43. The crew of B-24J-50-CO 42-73497 *Vadie Raye* in the 715th Bomb Squadron, 448th Bomb Group, April 1944. Standing, left to right: 2nd Lieutenant Andy H. Hau; 1st Lieutenant Elbert F. Lozes, bombardier; Captain Alvin D. Skaggs, pilot; 1st Lieutenant Donald C. Todt, navigator; Lieutenant B. F. 'Max' Baer, co-pilot. Kneeling: Master Sergeant George Glevanik, top turret gunner: Staff Sergeant Ray K. Lee, left waist gunner; Staff Sergeant Francis 'Frank' X. Sheehan, right waist gunner; Technical Sergeant Stanley C. Filopowicz, radio operator; Staff Sergeant Eugene Gaskins, nose gunner; Staff Sergeant William F. Jackson, tail-gunner (KIA 5 September 1944). (Sheehan)

44. B-17G-80-DL 42-37722 was assigned to the 401st Bomb Group at Deenethorpe on 21 January 1944. It caught fire on the base seven days later and was salvaged by 2 SAD on 30 January 1944. (USAF)

45. B-17G-1-BO 42-31083 *Tenny Belle*, which was assigned to the 525th Bomb Squadron, 379th Bomb Group, at Kimbolton on 19 October 1943. It suffered bomb damage on the mission to Sorau on 11 April 1944 and crash landed at Fen Farm, Stow Bardolph, Suffolk. John Daly, co-pilot Bob Koerber, S/Sgt Carl Christianson, engineer-top turret gunner Adriel Langendoerfer, radio operator Omer Young, ball turret gunner Harvey Tuber and waist gunners Frank Hearne and John McCallum and tail gunner Howard Polizzo were killed in the crash. Navigator Bill Evans bailed out safely. The aircraft was salvaged the following day. (USAF)

46. On 11 April 1944, General Dwight D. Eisenhower christened B-17G-40-BO 42-97061 *General Ike* with a bottle of Mississippi river water at Bassingbourn. Major James McPartlin in the 401st Bomb Squadron was responsible for the naming of *General Ike*, which flew its first operational mission on 13 April 1944, two days after it was christened. On 29 May 1944 *General Ike* led the 91st Bomb Group to Poznan, Poland, on the longest daylight raid of the war up to that time. *Ike* completed seventy-five combat missions, returned to the USA in June 1945 and was broken up for scrap. (USAF)

47. B-17G-25-DL 42-38004 *Old Man Tucker*, which was assigned to the 534th Bomb Squadron, 381st Bomb Group, at Ridgewell on 6 January 1944. On 19 April 1944, on the mission to Eschwage, flak set fire to the wing and the Fortress crashed at Rohrsburg, north-west of Frettenrode. Lieutenant Bob Rayburn, pilot; Maynard Craft, co-pilot; and Don Peterson, radio operator were KIA. Navigator Loren Morse, bombardier Ralph Simons, engineer-top turret gunner Bill Purser, ball turret gunner John Bristow, waist gunner De Forest Main, and tail gunner Gerald Gerber were taken prisoner. (USAF)

48. B-17G-50-BO 42-102453 was delivered to Cheyenne on 4 March 1944 and was subsequently operated at Kearney and Grenier Field before being assigned overseas and joining the 358th Bomb Squadron, 303rd Bomb Group, at Molesworth on 30 April 1944 and being named *Princess Pat*. The aircraft was salvaged by 2 SAD on 26 July 1944. (USAF)

49. B-17G-45-BO 42-97315, which was assigned to the 532nd Bomb Squadron, 381st Bomb Group, at Ridgewell on 6 April 1944. On 5 May 1944 it was taken on a mechanical test by Captain Doug Winters, Lieutenant Jim Turner, Lieutenant Julian O'Neal and Sergeant Hessle Buck and lost No. 3 and No. 4 engines before crash landing at Larkins Farm, Twinstead, near Halstead and catching fire. The four crew were uninjured. (USAF)

50. B-17G-55-BO 42-102700 *I'll Get By* in the 95th Bomb Group. This aircraft was assigned to the 412th Bomb Squadron, 95th Bomb Group, at Horham on 4 May 1944. It went MIA on the mission to Paris on 2 August 1944 with Captain Bob Baber and his crew when it crashed at Lisieux, France. Babe, co-pilot Jasper Kaylor, navigator Ray Dallas, bombardier Frank Sohm, engineer-top turret gunner Oscar Walrod, radio operator Bill Hill and Captain Elmer Bockman, the mission pilot, were KIA. Ball turret gunner Don Phillips, waist gunner Barney Lipkin and tail gunner Walt Collyer were taken into captivity. (USAF)

51. B-24D-1-CO *Bomerang* in the 328th Bomb Squadron, 93rd Bomb Group, at Hardwick which returned to the ZOI (Zone of the Interior; USA) in May 1944. Here, hardened British 8th Army veterans, the 'Desert Rats', recently returned to Britain, renew acquaintances with the bomber that supported the British offensive campaign at Tripoli, Sfax, Sousse, Tunis, Bizerte, Messina, Palermo and Cetrone. The British saw plenty of *Bomerang* and the other Liberators in the Mediterranean skies as Rommel's Afrika Korps were driven back into Italy. *Bomerang*, one of the Liberators originally brought to England by the 8th Air Force, completed fifty-three combat missions over Germany, France, Norway, the Low Countries, North Africa, the Middle East, the Ploesti oilfields and Austria. Having been away to war for eighteen months, *Bomerang* was saying goodbye to the ETO, gathering up a crew of air and ground heroes and taking them back to the USA. Left to right: Private George Read of London; Private Bernard Birch of Watford; Private Thomas Burchow MM of London; Private Harry Alger of New York City (in US flying jacket); Private Frederick Hopkins of Fulham and Lieutenant David Hodson of Minchin, Hampton, an 8th Army platoon leader. (USAF)

52. 'Chick's Crew' in the 360th Bomb Squadron, 303rd Bomb Group. Standing: Lieutenant Anthony 'Chick' J. Cecchini, pilot (WIA 11 May 1944); Lieutenant Stan Fisher, co-pilot; Edward 'Jasper' Veigel, navigator (who, when asked by the pilot in the US on the crew's first cross-country flight what town it was below, had replied Jasper, Texas. It was the port of Beaumont!); Theodore McDevitt, bombardier. Kneeling: Cliff 'Bachy' Bachman, flight engineer, who completed fifty-two combat missions; Clarence 'Alvin' Cogdell; George Kepics, ball-turret gunner; Robert J. 'Chunk' O'Hearn, waist gunner; Ben Smith Jr, radio operator (WIA 11 May 1944); Ward Hudson, tail gunner (WIA 11 May 1944). (Ben Smith).

54. B-24H-CF-5 Liberator 41-29387 *SNAFU Snark* in the 785th Bomb Squadron, 466th Bomb Group, at Attlebridge, Norfolk. 'SNAFU' stood for 'Situation Normal – All Fouled Up'. This aircraft failed to return when it landed on the Continent on 8 September 1944 and was salvaged on 11 November. (USAF)

Opposite below: 53. Bombs fall from the bomb bays of B-17G-35-DL 42-107091 9Z-D *Forbidden Fruit* in the 728th Bomb Squadron, 452nd Bomb Group, on Schwerte, Germany, on 31 May 1944. This Fortress was assigned to the Group at Deopham Green on 12 March 1944; on 20 May 1944 *Forbidden Fruit* suffered bomb damage on the mission to Liège and Brussels. The crew consisted of Captain Ed Skurka and Joe Knoll the pilot; co-pilot H. S. Kronowski; navigator D. E. Newton; bombardier H. F. Martin; engineer-top turret gunner Norman Burton; radio operator Dave Bittner; ball turret gunner Norman Hess; and waist gunners Chas Hickman and John Choprias, who returned safely. The tail gunner, John Tinker, was KIA when a flak burst took off part of the tail plane. *Forbidden Fruit* limped home to land at Rattlesden in Suffolk, but with controls damaged it ran on into a meadow, clipped a crash truck and fatally injured a ground crew member. (USAF)

55. Lieutenant Herman C. Mitchell, a pilot in the 93rd Bomb Group at Hardwick, on leave in Trafalgar Square in London in 1944.

56. B-17 landing back at base. (USAF)

57. Liberators bombing their target on the Continent. (USAF)

58. B-17 Fortress peeling off for landing. (USAF)

59. B-17 Flying Fortress crew. (USAF)

return to England was uneventful. This was a very costly mission for the Eighth Air Force as well as the 458th, which alone lost five bombers and three returned with minor battle damage – the most ever for one mission throughout the remainder of the war. Approximately one out of every ten bombers was lost on this mission, the greatest on any separate mission for the Eighth Air Force. We knew we had been on a big one. Yes it was a big one – 'BIG-B.'

The crew of *Reddy Teddy* in the 93rd formation had crossed the enemy coast at 22,000 feet at 1121 and at 1213 they encountered flak for the first time on the flight. About an hour later, Me 109s and 110s and Fw 190s and Stukas appeared in the sky but they sailed though and began the bomb run at just after 1330 hours. Tedford recalls,

There was very heavy flak by extra heavy guns and rockets. As we began the bomb run flak was brutal from 88 mm guns and we guessed 150 mm guns because of the size of the bursts. Two engines were out leaving Berlin. I feathered one prop for good and feathered the other off and on and was able to transfer gas to the engine giving us some power. Our altitude dropped from 22,000 feet to 20,000 feet and Ken Keene, co pilot, called in escort fighters to drive off the Me 109s attacking us. Finally we were at 18,000 feet, out of formation and on our own. We could have gone to Sweden or Switzerland. If we went to either we would lose our crew. On the crew's advice we brought *Reddy Teddy* home. We crossed the Dutch coast at 14,500 feet at 1516 and landed at Hardwick at 1600 hours. After this experience we were sent to southern England for rest (two weeks). Our plane had the two engines replaced.[17]

The weather was considerably better than the past few days and Thurman Spiva in the 'Bungay Buckaroos' had the feeling that they would make it all the way to Berlin this time. But the young navigator was proved wrong.

The take-off, climbing into formation and departing the English coast were routine. We were a little behind schedule at departure, but were back on schedule by the time we crossed the Dutch coast near the Zuider Zee. Every minute it took to make up lost time cut into the scanty fuel reserve. We could see the black patches of flak ahead in the Dummer Lake areas. The First and Third Divisions preceded us. Our turn at the target came just after Noon and was followed by scattered enemy fighter attacks. Fortunately, most made only single passes through the formation and there were no losses. At the bomber stream breakup point north of Magdeburg, the 446th made a turn to the right. Berlin was abeam to the left just about fifty miles away. You could see the Third Division ahead as they made their turn at the IP. They headed almost due north toward their target at Kleinmennow. The air around their formation was filled with vapour trails as the battle reached a climax. Then the bombers entered the flak area around the target. The 446th had seen flak many times, but few times could compare with the sight before the Group. Whistling shrapnel burst into coloured balls of purple, orange, green and gold. Shrapnel hitting the planes sounded like hail on a tin roof. Being the last Division in the bomber stream, the Group looked into a great black sea of smoke as it turned at the IP and headed toward Genshagen. It was a sobering sight. Flak was dreaded more than enemy fighters. You could shoot back at fighters; there was nothing you could do about anti-aircraft fire. Maybe take evasive action and drop chaff to attempt to foul up their radar. You just had to sit there and let them shoot at you. Many times we were told at briefings that most of our losses would come from fighter attacks. The losses from anti-aircraft fire were estimated to be less than 1 per cent. All that information meant little when you had to penetrate a flak area like that defending Berlin.

As we levelled out after the IP turn, our troubles began. The prop on our No. 2 engine ran away. The pilot reached for the throttle to cut it back. Unfortunately, this was our first mission in the latest model B-24. The throttles were ganged together on a bar to make it easier for the pilots to fly in formation. By the time our pilot had the power reduced on the engine, it had blown a cylinder. One dead engine and worse, the propeller had failed to feather. The plane began to shudder from nose to tail.

It was apparent, with the vibrations, that we were not to get much farther unless the situation could be corrected. The pilot worked feverishly to feather the prop. The crew readied themselves for possible bail out. There couldn't possibly be a worse place to bailout. We were over the edge of Berlin, and it was the Eighth Air Force's first full raid over the German capital. If forced to hit the silk, it would have been a very warm reception when we hit the ground. Finally, after what seemed like an eternity, the pilot, by using the starter on the dead engine, turned it enough to feather the propeller and we settled down to normal flight. Although all this took only a few minutes, when it was over we had dropped 12,500 feet and found ourselves alone in the sky. We could see the tail end of our formation miles ahead as it approached the target. Simple arithmetic told us we could not regain altitude and rejoin our formation by the time they reached the target. It was also obvious we were having to use high power settings and were burning a lot of fuel just to carry our full load of bombs. The pilot decided to head north and drop our bombs on the first target of opportunity and hope to rejoin the formation as it made its homeward turn north-east of Berlin. Our bombardier, Adrian Perrault, soon found a small railroad marshalling yard and he salvoed our twelve 500-pounders there. When we arrived at the turning point, we found the formation, which had been briefed to descend 2,000 feet by the time they reached that point, was still at bombing altitude of 21,000 to 22,500 feet. When contacted they told us they were going to remain at that altitude. Our fuel calculations showed if we climbed to their altitude and joined the formation with only three engines we would run out of fuel before we reached the British coast. We decided to remain at our present altitude and try to keep up with the formation and stretch our fuel as far as possible.

We soon found the formation was leaving us. It was a lonely feeling as we were still about 400 miles from home. Fortunately, everything went well until we reached the Wittingen area. Our right waist gunner reported enemy fighters. Two Me 110s came in level from 9 o'clock. Their first pass was not pressed home closely as they passed underneath and turned to our rear. They were joined by two more Me 110s and lined up for another pass from 9 o'clock. This time they came in pairs. I looked out the right side of the aircraft as they came barrelling in and wondered how we could possibly escape major damage with four of them pressing home the attack. The Luftwaffe pilots were bad shots. A crew check after their pass revealed only two nicks in one of the props. The tail gunner reported one of the Me 110s was trailing smoke indicating at least one of them had been hit. Only a minute or so passed when two Me 109s were coming in from one o'clock high. They came in head-on and passed under the right wing as they attacked. We were now a sitting duck and knew they would continue the attack until we were shot down. We had watched this drama played out too many times not to know what the outcome would be. The lone cripple always lost. Crews that were lucky had enough time to bail out before the fatal blow was delivered. The unlucky crews went down with the plane as it blew up or went into its final spin. Our pilot contacted our own fighter escort and requested assistance. It was our lucky day. The Me 109s were still in their descending turn below us as two P-47s came out of nowhere and attacked them. Above us were two other P-47s flying an 'S' pattern back and forth to stay down near our speed. We were passed from one escorting fighter group to another. They covered us until we departed the enemy coast. Two P-38s joined us about half-way across the North Sea.

They stayed with us until we saw the English coast. We were about forty minutes behind everyone else as we landed. There was so little fuel in the tanks that it was almost impossible to measure it. Everyone had given us up for lost. We owed our lives to the courageous fighter pilots who stayed with us that day.[18]

At Old Buckenham there was no word of Elmer Crockett's or Hubert Cripe's Liberators. Just after Crockett had gone down, Cripe and his crew were 'very glad' that they were through the flak and damage and were going home. The only apparent damage that he could see was 'a tiny flak hole the size of a dime just in front of the windscreen'. Immediately after releasing the bomb load, he noticed that the manifold temperatures started lowering, 'a good sign as they could close the cowl flaps'. The formation was 'pretty ragged' but it got better as they started letting down to 14,000 feet, the altitude on the return leg.

Cripe tried to get into a position but was chased out by other Liberators so rather than 'brush wings' he let them have it until he finally got on the left wing of *Shack Rabbit*, flown by Lieutenant Patrick D. Tobin Jr, who had one engine feathered. They did not know then but it was a mistake, as he started lagging behind. Flak was negligible and neither Russ Anderson nor Cripe saw enemy fighters. He thought that 'things were going too well'. Sporadic conversations were coming over the interphone so he let Anderson fly and he tuned in the radio to fighter-bomber frequency. Enemy fighters were around. As the waves were full of frantic calls to fighters to come to their aid, Cripe glanced around. Their formation was quite a ways ahead of them and Cripe knew that they were 'letting themselves wide open for attack!'

They were in the Dummer Lake area, where lots of enemy fighters were concentrated. Should he leave Tobin, chance getting to the formation, or try to give the stricken Tobin what protection they could? 'The Jerries settled that question,' Cripe was to recall. One minute all was 'tranquil', the next he heard an explosion in his ship!

They were under attack and they had been hit. Almost immediately, he saw a large gaping hole appear in the trailing edge of Tobin's left wing as a 20 mm shell exploded. The attack was from the rear. Cripe jerked his head to the left and looked out the side window. There was one of their attackers! He could see that he was making a 'graceful left bank' and the black crosses on the wing were 'plainly visible'.

He thought, 'Why don't Albert Edgett and Tom Keefe, the waist gunners, get him? He was a sitting duck!' Cripe got on the radio and called for fighters. A cool

Texas drawl said, 'Don't get excited, sonny, poppa's coming.' Almost immediately two P-47s appeared and chased the Bf 109. Cripe did not look to see if they got him as 'more pressing business was at hand'.

Cripe realised that Tobin had evidently 'had it'. A figure appeared in his waist window and bailed out.[19] Then Cripe's engineer called from the top turret and said that they were on fire, left wing. Cripe looked out. Sure enough, flame was coming out of a 20 mm hole that had punctured the tanks. He knew that if Mack Garrett had not left about 20 gallons of gas in there when he transferred, the fumes would have exploded, undoubtedly blowing Cripe's wing off. However, just now the gas was burning. Cripe thought, 'Should we or shouldn't we bail now?' It looked bad. 'Maybe we can slip out the flames,' he thought. They tried but to no avail.

Meanwhile, they were nearing the Dutch border. Cripe's decision was try to ditch in the North Sea. He knew 'that was a bad one'. Trying to ditch a twenty-four was bad enough without it being on fire. William S. Chappell Jr, the radio operator, as soon as he heard Cripe's decision, began sending 'SOS' on his radio. The cockpit was filled with gas fumes so Cripe cracked the bomb bay doors. Anderson took off his oxygen mask and suggested smoking a cigarette, 'as they probably wouldn't get any for a while'. Cripe ordered him not to and to get ready to bail out. Over the interphone he ordered the crew to stand by to bail out, as they might not reach the North Sea.

Then he started losing altitude. At 10,000 feet they entered a cloud and the flames mounted higher. He knew that they were not going to make it! He unfastened his belt, took off his mask and clamped down on the alarm bell, the signal to bail out.

Spike Ballacqua's face appeared in the astrodome. He grinned, waved and vanished. Dinneen had bailed out before him through the nose wheel door. Russ Anderson climbed out of his seat and went back to the bomb bay. Cripe tried putting the ship on automatic pilot but it would not work.

'To hell with it,' he thought, 'I'm leaving.'

He crawled out, walked through the radio room and saw Anderson on the catwalk, fastening his Mae West. Cripe thought everyone had left. He and Anderson shook hands and the co-pilot jumped. Cripe saw his hand on his ripcord and with 'just a little bit of fear' he stepped off the catwalk, 'into two miles of space'. His first sensation was a 170 mph slipstream hitting him and – 'quiet'. He felt no sensation of falling. His last glimpse of the B-24 was 'flame all over the left wing and fast getting to the fuselage'. He must have been on his back when he saw the B-24. He grabbed for the ring and yanked. Instantly there came a loud report as the nylon caught the wind, followed by a hard jerk that he hardly noticed, then – silence. He didn't even seem to be falling; instead he seemed to be going up! He was in a cloud bank and did not get to see the ship crash. However, he heard it.

At Deopham Green men of the 452nd, two of whose aircraft were missing, recounted the raid to waiting newsmen. 'I saw smoke pouring up from the target,' recalled S/Sgt Zenas R. Cole, the ball turret gunner of *Junior*. 'They hit it right on the nose.' S/Sgt John G. Brown, right waist gunner of *Sunrise Serenade*, claimed that, 'We really set Berlin on fire and it will almost take the entire Atlantic Ocean to put it out.' T/Sgt Larry A. Zaccardi retorted, 'Berlin will have a heck of a lot of rebuilding after this raid.' Some of the other groups experienced 'walls of bursting metal'. About nine of our planes received major flak damage. 'It was like a solid blanket,' stated 2nd Lieutenant Robert O. Lloyd, co-pilot of *Sleepy Time Gal*. S/Sgt Andrew M. Vanover, a gunner on *Tangerine*, told how he shot down a Fw 190. 'I opened fire at him while he swooped down on us. Part of the engine blew off and fell towards earth and hit the ground. He had broken into five pieces before he hit the ground and the pilot never did manage to get out.' 2nd Lieutenant Robert C. Schimmel brought back his battered ship all alone to England from Berlin after he ordered his entire crew to bail out when he thought it the only way they could survive.

The 388th was missing seven Fortresses. One of them was *Shack Rabbits*, flown by 2nd Lieutenant Augustine B. Christiani. Ray Newmark, the bombardier, recalls the events of the day he would never forget.

We got to Berlin and could see our checkpoints on the river. We were around 24,000 feet and ready. Suddenly, we were told to circle Berlin again. We had already survived the flak. We almost decided to abort. We made a very sharp turn out of the area and headed for the secondary target. We were scared. We did not want any more flying over Berlin. As soon as we relieved ourselves of our bomb load we headed back to base. We dodged some flak and there were no fighters. It seemed we were living under the wings of angels because other groups were getting picked up and strafed. When our lead navigator radioed that up ahead was the Zuider Zee and we could see it, we started a turn and began to relax. Off came our oxygen masks and we started eating our Mars bars. All of a sudden, at about 2 o'clock high, I saw some specks in the distance. "Here come the P-51s. It's about time," I said. A few seconds later someone said, "Hey they're flashing their lights at us." Someone else said, "They're not lights: they're shooting at us!" Sure enough they were the yellow-nosed kids from Abbeville.

Those German pilots were terrific. They came through our group and we closed in as tight as we could possibly get. I shot at one that came across our nose from around 3 o'clock. I led him and saw him blow up. Then I ran my guns to another one which was coming in at 2 o'clock but I forgot to release my finger on the trigger and my guns froze. The formation at this time had really spread out and we wound up as tail-end Charlie. All of a sudden I got hit in my left forearm by a 30-30, a 20-mm armour piercing incendiary (API) and another 30-30 simultaneously. (We knew they were firings APIs because we could see them going through the airplanes and exploding elsewhere instead of on impact. It was lucky for me because the API went right through my arm and exploded in the No. 1 and 2 engines. One of the 30-30s bounced off my flak helmet and the other bounced off my flak suit. The impact of all three knocked me clear all the way back to the hatch underneath the pilot's seat.

As I lay there looking up I could see that the plane was a blazing inferno. Tech Sergeant S. Ciaccio, the engineer, was screaming in his top turret. He was on fire from head to foot. There was no way of saving that boy. I did not see Christiani or Farrington, the co-pilot. I yelled to Lieutenant Levy, the navigator, to get me an oxygen mask; I was starting to lose consciousness. Mine was knocked off by the impact and shredded. Luckily, the extra mask was lying near the escape hatch. He slapped it on me, plugged into the oxygen system and revived me. The next thing I know, I said, "Get my 'chute." My chest pack was completely shredded. Luckily, the extra 'chute was available to be snapped on. Levy said, "I'm going to pull the hatch door and get you out of here." I said, "OK, providing you follow me." He pulled the release and shoved me out at around 20,000 feet. As I left the door, suddenly it became quiet. I passed out momentarily. I revived and realised that I had to pull the ripcord on my parachute. I reached over and could not find my left arm, I thought, "Oh my God; my arm's been blown off." I pulled at my flight suit and there was my arm but it was dangling.

I could do nothing with it so I picked it up and put the thumb in between my teeth so that it would remain there if and when I pulled the ripcord the impact wouldn't snap off my arm. I passed out again. The next time I revived I was face down and floating like a falling leaf. I was at about 2,000 feet and the ground was rushing up to me. I just did not have the strength to pull the ripcord. I said, "God, give me the strength," and with one big yank I pulled the ripcord. The 'chute popped open and I bit my thumb so hard I killed all the nerves, permanently.

I landed in a field that had just been ploughed. It was as soft as a feather bed. I was a young twenty-two-year-old and like most of us, didn't have much religion in those days. But suddenly I believed that there was something or someone looking out for me. I tried to remove the parachute and harness from my body when a farmer and his two children came up to me. They spoke to me in what appeared to be German but I realised it had to be Dutch. I needed to get out of the harness and also get some morphine because I was in a heck of a lot of pain. I unzipped my first aid kit attached to my harness and reached inside for the morphine sachet. I broke it open with my teeth and was about to inject it into my arm when the farmer grabbed it and threw it away. He said, "No. No! Do not commit suicide! We will help you." It seems as though the Germans had indoctrinated those people to believe that American flyers would rather commit suicide rather than be captured, which was wrong. So there I was without anything to kill the pain.

I looked down to unhook my harness and realised that my right leg parachute harness had not been fastened but I was still alive with nothing wrong with my crotch. It was a miracle because I had always been told if the harness was not tightly fastened it could pull you apart. All these wonderful things were beginning to dawn on me. Who am I to deserve all this? I shouldn't be here; I should be dead.

The farmer marched me to his house. His daughter was crying because I must have looked like the man from Mars, covered in grease and blood. The farmer sent his twelve-year-old son to get a doctor in Zwolle who was helping downed Allied airmen. The farmer's wife made me some porridge and tried to clean and console me. She used my white silk scarf to make a sling for my arm. It eased the pain a little. About four hours later near dusk the boy returned. He was crying bitterly. The doctor had been executed in the town square by the Gestapo.

The farmer could get me back to England via the Underground but it would take at least a week and probably I would not make it because of my wounds. Alternatively, I could be turned in so I could get immediate medical attention under the terms of the Geneva Convention. It would save my life. I decided I would become a PoW.

I gave him my .45 pistol. He turned it on me as if he had just captured me and marched me up to the road from his house. It wasn't very long before a black car with two men dressed in black with hats on came along. As luck would have it, they were the goddamned Gestapo. They thanked the farmer, took the gun and put me into the car to take me to town. I was thrown into jail, interrogated, beaten and my wounded arm kicked time and again. I told them I didn't know anything and cussed them. The more I cussed them the worse it got. Thank God I passed out. The pain was excruciating.

Next morning the Luftwaffe came to get me and drove me to an airfield where the 109s that shot down were based. A lot of captured Americans were there. So too was Hermann Goering himself! He was up on a stage in front of us and the whole squadron of Luftwaffe pilots. Over the loudspeaker he lauded us. "Only the flyers are heroes in this war," he said, "I salute you." He broke out the champagne and passed round glasses. We all had to drink a toast with him. The irony of it all. He told us that the wounded would be sent to hospital and the others would be sent to a PoW camp. Christiani, Levy and the two waist gunners were the only survivors from my crew. They were shipped off to PoW camps. I was put in a truck with four other fellers, on top of a bunch of dead bodies. In early June four of us left hospital on crutches and were moved to Dulag Luft and then PoW camp.

Back at Knettishall, *Little Willie*, flown by Flight Officer Bernard M. Dopko, and *Blitzin' Betsy* were among the missing. So too were Monty Givens' crew, who shared the same Nissen hut as Watts. 'Dopko's crew were our room-mates,' recalls Larry Goldstein, who was lying on his bunk when someone in the barracks said, 'Dopko's crew went down today on their first mission.'

Replacement crews always had brand new equipment plus Dopko's had a much cherished item; custom-made leather boots from Africa that they had picked up on the way over to England. There was a mad scramble as twenty-five men reached for the brand new equipment and the leather boots. Later that evening after chow one of our barrack members said, "Guess who I saw having late chow – Dopko's crew." They had made it back home on the deck, had landed at another base and had been trucked over. We were embarrassed. Each of us who had taken some piece of equipment attempted to put it back. Unfortunately, we could not remember where all of the items went so they were just piled on one bed. When Dopko's crew walked into the barracks, the quiet was astounding. Although one of Dopko's crew complained to the CO, nothing ever came of it. It seems this was an accepted way of life. (Three days later Dopko's crew did go down. We didn't have the heart to do what we had done once before.)[20]

Harry Allert, *Blitzin' Betsy*'s crew chief, had waited in vain for the first-class buzz job over his tent that he had been promised by Lowell Watts. *Blitzin' Betsy* had been attacked by fighters and three of the crew bailed out before their Fortress exploded, blowing Lowell Watts and two others clear of the aircraft. They pulled their ripcords on their parachutes and landed safely, to be taken into captivity. Four of the crew were found dead in or near the wreckage of their plane.

The first American air raid on Berlin had certainly flushed the Luftwaffe just as Doolittle had hoped it would. The Luftwaffe flew 528 fighter sorties against the bombers, of which about 370 made contact with the enemy. Aerial gunners and the fighter pilots claimed more than 170 German fighters destroyed[21] but the Americans had lost sixty-nine bombers – a loss rate of 10 per cent – the highest number lost by the 8th in a single day. Six more were salvaged after landing. Sixty bombers returned with severe damage and 336, including 121 in the 3rd Division, had lesser damage. The 1st Division lost eighteen B-17s, the 2nd sixteen B-24s and the 3rd, thirty-five B-17s. Apart from *Barrick's Bag*, three other missing bombers had landed in Sweden. *Hello Natural* in the 448th, which was forced to seek refuge at Bulltofta, was the first of nineteen Liberators in the group that would be forced to land in Sweden during the war, the highest total of all the B-24 groups.[22] *A Good Ship & Happy Ship* in the 388th was put down at Rinkaby, where the guns in the ball turret ploughed into the ground, acting as emergency brakes. *Liberty Lady* in the 306th was belly landed on an island in the Baltic and was set on fire by the crew, who were convinced that they had landed in German-occupied territory. It was not until they arrived by boat at the Swedish mainland that they discovered that they were in Sweden![23]

Four groups suffered more than half of the total bomber losses: the 91st lost six B-17s, the 95th eight and the 388th six in rapid succession. A seventh was lost when a crippled B-17 flying on autopilot after it had been abandoned by the crew ran into it and both Fortresses went down. The Bloody Hundredth had again suffered unmercifully at the hands of the Luftwaffe, as Robert Shoens, pilot of *Our Gal Sal* recalls.

> When we got home we found that we were one of only five B-17s to return to Thorpe Abbotts. We had lost 15 airplanes. To say the least, we were upset, as was everyone on the base. Lieutenant Colonel Ollen 'Ollie' Turner, the 351st Squadron Commander met us as we parked the airplane. He was in tears. Most of the losses had been from his squadron. It was hard to take but this was what we had been trained for.

When Hubert Cripe floated out of the cloud, he looked below. 'Water.' It was the Zuider Zee and a piece of wreckage was still burning on the surface. He looked up and counted the chutes. All he could see were seven, including his own. He would never know what happened to the other three. On the water were objects he took to be fishing boats. The surface was smooth so he could not tell how far from the water he was. The leg strap of his chute was hurting him but it had just skinned his leg.

'Probably too loose.'

Suddenly the water seemed close and he tried to unfasten his chute and slip out but he was too late. He hit the water with a splash. 'Boy was it cold!' He went under and came up 'blubbering'. Treading water, he tried to unfasten his chute but he could not get hold of the snaps. Then he tried to jerk the cord to inflate his Mae West. He missed. He tried again and missed. Cripe recalled that 'God must have heard my silent prayer' because on his next try he got it and yanked. Instantly, the tiny cylinder filled with carbon dioxide inflated one side of the Mae West and kept his head above water. He rested. Then he unfastened his chute, which was tangled around one leg.

Russ Anderson had landed about 100 yards from him and he was 'about all in, too'. One of the fishing boats had pulled alongside him and taken him on board by the time he had swum to the side of the boat. The Dutchmen on the boat hauled Cripe aboard, 'a dripping, cold, half drowned man who was very thankful to be alive'. Russ Anderson and Cripe shook hands and 'almost bawled to each other'. The fishermen were very kind and while they were stripping off their wet clothes they asked, 'Drink?'

'Nothing bashful about them.' They said 'Yes', expecting maybe some Schnapps but no, 'it was water!'

'They only had about half the Zuider Zee inside them and the fishermen wanted to know if they wanted water!' The fishermen finished taking their clothes off and put the pilots to bed. Cripe thought that they would have been very helpful in getting them back to England but a German harbour patrol launch pulled alongside and took them on board. In the cabin was Spike Bellacqua, one of only three survivors of Crew 44.[24]

Ernest Richardson concludes:

Landing back at the base, we saw a large group of people standing around watching us come in. The first people I saw after the engines were shut down were two radio mechanics that pulled up in a Jeep. Our ship must have been the first one they hit. They looked excited. "How's your radio equipment?"

"Swell." I no more than got that out when they were asking how the raid went. How much flak? How many fighters? Was it rough? You had the feeling everyone was sweating out the 96th Bomb Group that day.

As for the results of the raid, the majority of the bombs fell on a 5-mile stretch of the suburbs, due mainly to overcast, creating huge fires and destroying the gas, power and telephone services. Oslo Radio, which was German controlled, regarded it 'as a catastrophe ...' Even the Berlin News Agencies admitted that 'several hundred bombers had reached the city, despite intensive flak and unceasing fighter attacks'. Air Chief Marshal Arthur Harris of the RAF sent a message to his opposite number, Carl Spaatz at High Wycombe: 'Heartiest congratulations on first US bombing of Berlin. It is more than a year since they were attacked in daylight but now they have no safety there day or night. All Germany learns the same lesson.'

The 8th was stood down on 7 March. Philip H. Meistrich, one of the replacements who joined the 453rd at Old Buckenham, remembers that:

On the way up we listened in on Radio Berlin and heard the charming voice of 'Axis Sally', of whom later we were to hear a lot more. She invited all Americans up to Stalag Luft, where the beds were soft and the sheets are clean and she'd be there. The food was also good, she said. When she had finished, her friend, a renegade American newspaperman, speaking to his "fellow Americans", attacked the Plutocratic-Juder-Bolshevik President of the US. When this jerk was finished we switched to the BBC, where a charming female voice, sounding 'veddy-veddy' British, announced a programme of choice swing music, which was very enjoyable. All good things must come to an end and her programme did. Then the BBC reporter came through with a very depressing report about the 68 US bombers, which failed to return after a raid on Berlin. Gulp! And we were on our way to the 8th Air Force. Yipe!

Ernest Richardson recalls:

After interrogation, Steve Condur told us we were on pass and that we could take off immediately. I asked him where he was going and it wasn't long before we were waiting for a train to London. Dressing before we left, we kidded with the new crew that had taken Dickert's crew's place about being sure to hit the target, etc. Take care of yourself and we would see them when we got back. When Condur and I arrived in London our first impression wasn't very nice, fog was floating around everything and it was quiet, blacked out and very gloomy. We ran into an Englishman and asked him how to get to the Red Cross club. He gave us all kinds of directions ending with "You can't miss it". We couldn't make heads or tails out of what he said, but it made us laugh. Although we had a common language and it was our bond, we found that it was a barrier. We didn't understand it when they said 'keep your pecker up'. It meant keep your spirits up. 'Knock him up' meant to wake him up in the morning. When we did find the Red Cross club it was full, so we just curled up and slept in chairs we found in the lobby.

The next morning was bright and clear, so we were sure where the bombers would be going. Now that they knew they could go to Berlin, they wouldn't spare the horses, or should I say planes? Around nine o'clock the bombers started passing overhead, there wasn't much doubt in our minds as to where they might be going. We were happy not to be with them. Condur and I spent most of the morning trying to find enough to eat and a place to spend the night. I think we hit every restaurant in and around Piccadilly Circus. It had the largest Red Cross club in England. Around Piccadilly, a person could acquire almost anything, black market or otherwise. American soldiers, the English said were over paid, so anyone who had anything to sell usually brought it there. This also included ladies of the evening. Condur and I looked it all over. A lot of it was kind of disgusting but we realised England had been at war a long time. We wondered what it was like before the war. Our two day pass went by real fast. Before we knew it we were on our way back to the base. The train was crowded so we had to stand. Looking out the window we saw places the Germans had bombed and were still bombing. Some of it looked rather recent. At other times we saw ruins from the '41 Blitz; places beyond repair. It wasn't a very nice sight. Later, as we moved away from London, we saw some Spitfires zoom by. We also saw some B-26s forming for an afternoon raid. All in all, it wasn't the sort of things that would raise your spirits. It would be another two weeks before we would get another pass; a lot could happen in that time.

On 6 February 1944, 2nd Lieutenant Glenn Folsom and his crew were assigned to the 66th Squadron at Shipdham. After a period of training and practice missions and flights, they flew their first combat mission on 2 March, followed by a second on the 5th. When the mission slated for Tuesday 7 March was scrubbed, several crews, including Folsom's, were given practice flights to sharpen their skills. This crew did not carry a full complement and flew with only seven men – a bombardier and two gunners were apparently not needed on this flight. During this training flight, a P-47 pilot for reasons known only to him apparently began simulated attacks on Folsom's ship. Somehow, either due to his manoeuvres, or he over-shot, or perhaps prop wash caused him momentary control loss. The result was a collision that tore off one wing of the B-24. Staff Sergeant Raymond McNamara stated that when he looked up he saw the B-24 fly on for a few moments, he saw one of the wings tear off and then the plane winged over and crashed and burned. The P-47 also spun down, partially disintegrating, and crashed. There were no survivors from either aircraft. The tail gunner, Sergeant Hazen E. Hawkes, from Drummond, Idaho, had married Margaret shortly before leaving for overseas. He had always wanted a little blond girl. 'Look at that doll baby blond,' he would say as they strolled hand in hand down Latimer Street, walked quickly to the bus stop in Harlingen, or ducked their heads against the wind in Casper. And after Margaret had looked jealously about, he would chuckle teasingly and point with his chin, 'See that babe, right over there?' And Margaret would see the child. 'That's what we'll have, a little blond girl. When I get back.' Margaret never thought to ask how he expected a black Irishman and a brown-eyed red-head to produce a blond. She was just happy that he had such a positive attitude about coming back.

And now here we are – my brand new blond daughter, as close to you and me as we can get. It's very peaceful here. There's a busy quiet: The water spray whirring; the lawnmower droning. With my back to a headstone, my recently slimmed body cross-legged in the summer grass, the fragrance of flowers is in my nostrils; an uncertain honeybee is circling my head, while my baby sleeps in my lap.

I had faced the fact you might not return. It paced beside me as I followed you from camp to camp and when you were really gone the endless miles of land and sea away, it moved in and lived with me, leaned over my shoulder to peer at the mail and departed only when it could say, "See, I told you so."

Months later when the lieutenant with the young face brought your body back I behaved as I had promised myself I would, careful not to snap at anyone. I conducted myself like a proper mourning widow even if some of your disapproving relatives didn't think a proper widow would be there on the arm of her second husband and six months gone with child. I behaved, that is, until one of your second or third cousins from down Thermopolis way sniffled and forced your courageously dry-eyed mother to agree for the nth time as she stood there with her arm around my thickening waist that yes, it was nice you were buried where there was such a wonderful view of the Tetons and that's right, you had certainly loved those beautiful mountains.

"I most certainly hope he isn't down there, in that God-awful hole," I said before I could catch myself. The very idea gave me nauseating claustrophobia. I took a deep breath to control my queasiness, avoided looking at your mother. Understanding, patient, she deserved the Gold Star she wore proudly. My child stirred and mixed me up further: You gone, me here, carrying another's child – I buried my face in my hands and burst into tears, Jake helped me to our car and drove me home.

You'll like Jake. Really, you will. He thinks like you. Physically, you are exact opposites. You: Lanky, dark. Him: Short, sturdy, fair. He came back from the Pacific area. When he talked about it infrequently, I saw how he would look as an old man. Women grow up fast in wartime, too. You were gone and I was twenty-one, then twenty-two, twenty-three, well on my way to fading into an undistinguished twilight like a tragic maiden of the south keeping hopeless vigil for the sweetheart who had ridden off to the war between the states. "As long as there's anybody left on earth who loves me, I'll not be dead," you said once. It was night, almost our last night together, something we suspected but did not know for sure. There in the darkness we spoke haltingly of God, His plans and our beliefs. Haltingly, for such things did not come glibly to our tongues. Like so many of our agnostic generation we were reticent about speaking familiarly, lovingly of God and His Beloved Son as our Victorian forefathers had been about the details of sex. I clung to your words and heard impatiently all the good intentioned bromides and clichés designed to rouse me to living again, from your mother's insistent "Life must go on, darling," to Jake's patient, "Time heals all wounds."

I can't explain the change exactly. I know when it came. One day I was a fading young widow dedicated to anachronistic black. The next day I was ready to live again and declared myself by going out and buying a scarlet dress. For, you see, it was my twenty-fourth birthday and I had looked in my mirror. Then I had put the usual fresh flower, a pink peony this day, before your picture and really looked at you, not at my memories.

"Why, you are only twenty-one," I said aloud. "You'll always be twenty-one. For all eternity." I sat down slowly. I had made a momentous discovery: I would never be twenty-one again.

It's time to go now. The bee has found the yellow roses I brought. I can see Jake's and my '39 Chevy coming from town – your mother is driving it. She didn't say a word at the hospital when I asked to come here before going home with my baby.

I can't be twenty-one forever, or even twenty-six, like Jake. But I have managed that doll baby blond. You would consider it the more important achievement.

You and Jake. For along with my five-day-old daughter, I am carrying another War Department telegram. The words are the same, but the name is not yours – this war.[25]

CHAPTER 4

Death or Glory?

The left waist gunner, Norm Willig, was laying on the floor and Robert Hampton, in the ball, was not moving. Fire was streaming past the waist window. The right outboard engine was feathered. Another fire was between Daniel Jones in the nose turret and me in the tail turret. He was screaming, "Help me Pappy, get me out Pappy." Things were happening so fast, I was only reacting to the flames, when enemy fighters came in from all directions putting round after round into our ship. I screamed over the intercom to Lieutenant Dallas Books, "Bank left and head for Switzerland!" His response: "Hang on, we'll be OK." Again, the fighters came through what was left of the formation. The oxygen system failed and I became light headed. Our ship was streaming flames and slowing down, not able to keep up now, as more rounds came smashing through the ship. On the intercom I heard the co pilot, Captain John Slowik, screaming and cursing the German fighters as more rounds came through *Old Glory*. The ship started to pitch and dive, then the oxygen tank next to my head exploded, blowing me out the waist window. I awoke to find myself falling and instinctively pulled the ripcord. Pieces of the plane were falling around me, but I didn't see my ship, or my crew, or my friends, ever again.

S/Sgt Chester C. Strickler, tail gunner, *Old Glory*, 579th Squadron, 392nd Bomb Group, flown by 1st Lieutenant Dallas O. Books, which was damaged by flak at the target at Friedrichshafen, 18 March 1944.[1]

On Wednesday 8 March Dick Ghere, a gunner on Lieutenant Charles R. 'Chuck' McKeny's crew in the 'Bungay Buckaroos', was awakened early. And then it was breakfast and on to briefing, where it was announced that the primary target was Berlin (PFF) with the secondary, the VKF ball-bearing plant at Erkner, in the suburbs 5 miles south-east of 'Big-B'. Crews were told that 600 bombers would be flying the third raid on the German capital in a week. The 3rd Division would lead the 8th to Erkner, east of Berlin, the 1st Division flying in the middle, with the 2nd again bringing up the rear. McKeny wanted to ask Lieutenant Herbert F. Bohnet Jr to let them fly *Shif'lus Skonk!* but *The Princess* was ready to go and McKeny's crew took off one minute before time for last take-off. Dick Ghere had quite a time with the Consolidated turret. It was comparatively new to him and 'breezy ... b-r-r-r'. He adds:

'Rich' disliked the nose also. It had a Norden sight. Anyway we caught the formation and headed for Berlin. Hit flak at Osnabrück and Hanover. As we neared the target we saw *Shif'lus Skonk!* leave the formation, losing altitude and going far to the right. Three 109s jumped them and in a few minutes *Shif'lus Skonk!* was flaming. Four chutes came out. The plane exploded and another chute came out and then another chute opened from the pieces after that. That was a great blow to our crew. Our very close friends, lieutenants Bohnet, Charles Zimmer, Herschel Carter and Robert Gilbreath and their crew members were MIA.[2] We hit for home and about forty-five minutes out of the target area, three 190s surprised us out of the sun. They bore in very close – VERY close, made one pass and knocked down Merriman on our right wing. No chutes seen. A third crew was lost; Clifton Helfer never returned to base.[3]

Lieutenant Franklin L. Betz, a navigator in the 379th at Kimbolton and part of the 1st Division force, was flying his first mission this day.

Promptly at 0915 hours the lead plane took off. Taxiing behind a line of Fortresses that one after the other soared into the grey sky, the pilot, Captain Douglas H. Buskey, swung our plane on to the runway as the B-17 before us started on its way into the 'wild blue yonder'. The four 1,200 hp Wright Cyclone engines roared and our heavy bomb-laden plane shuddered as Buskey pushed the throttles forward. Bobbing gently, it rolled down the runway with increasing speed, the ride becoming smooth as the massive bulk lifted gracefully above the Huntingdonshire farmland. Climbing steadily, one by one each of the eighteen planes slipped into its designated place of the group formation; six in the lead squadron and six each in the high and low squadrons. Wide-eyed, my heart racing from excitement (or was it apprehension from the realisation that I'd soon be departing the friendly shores of Britain?), I was awed at the magnificent sight of the vast air armada stretching for miles in precise formations against the frosty blue sky. The palms of my hands were moist when we headed over the English Channel and I noted in my log, altitude, 20,000 feet, time, 11.06, ground speed, 170 knots.

Scattered flak greeted us at the Dutch coast a few miles north of Ijmuiden. Happily though, the fighter planes we saw were identified as our 'little friends', P-51 Mustangs. On we droned, due east, and the Dummer Lake in western Germany loomed ahead. Suddenly, black splotches darkened the sky around us a few miles north of the lake. Flak! The concussion from exploding shells rocked the plane. Fragments of flying steel tore through its aluminium skin. The oil line of number one engine was cut and, gushing like a geyser, the oil covered the cowling and adjoining wing surface, quickly congealing on the metal in the minus 30 degree temperature. Promptly, Buskey feathered number one engine as he called over the intercom, "Number two engine's only pulling half power." We were flying on two and a half engines! Fortunately, none of the crew was hit. We learned upon our return to Kimbolton that flak had damaged the vital induction pipe of the turbo-supercharger, reducing the engine's thrust.

"Pilot to navigator, what's the estimated flying time to the target?"

Consulting my map and log I applied pertinent data to my E-6B computer and made a calculation.

"Navigator to pilot," I replied. "It's approximately two hours flying time at our present ground speed."

The plane rocked gently. "Bandits at 2 o'clock high," the engineer called. Warily, I watched the two 109s, as yet out of gunfire range, while I manned the right nose gun. Flying high and ahead of us, suddenly they peeled off into a screaming dive, the front edge of their wings from which the tips of machine-gun barrels protruded, lighting up like firecrackers when they fired. In a flash they were way below us and out of range. Lucky! All the Fortresses in the formation continued droning determinedly toward Berlin. If any of them had been hit by the 109 gunfire, none had gotten it fatally this time.

"Pilot to crew. Despite the flak damage to two engines, the plane's flying well. We'll continue to the target in formation instead of dropping out and trying to get back to England alone. It could be tough going."

Breathing heavily from the excitement of my first major encounter with flak and fighters, I slid on to the seat by the navigator's worktable to make entries in the log. Peering through the window over the worktable I saw twin-engined

P-38 fighters engaging enemy fighters, keeping them away from the bomber formations. A reassuring sight. High above the peaceful-looking German countryside we flew, in tight formation. Our course to the IP took us far enough south of Berlin to avoid the formidable anti-aircraft defences. A lump rose in my throat when we turned onto the IP for the thirteen-mile run to the target. Five miles above the ball-bearing factory the Germans had the sky enveloped in a murderous box barrage of flak and the air was filled with black puffs of exploding shells and unseen fragments of deadly steel.

The formation flew in a straight and unwavering line to the target. There was no turning back, no evasive action. The lead bombardiers were busily aiming their Norden bombsights on the target and the lethal loads of bombs would drop automatically from the bomb bays when the cross hairs in the exquisite bombsight centred on the buildings far below. At that moment, bombardiers in other planes of the group would release their bombs by flipping a toggle switch and the destructive explosives would hurtle toward the doomed factory. Ahead of us, planes in precise group formation entered the pall of smoke from bursting flak. Suddenly, a brilliant ball of orange lit up the sky. Hit by flak, a bomber exploded! No 'chutes were seen. Off to the right, one of the splendid aircraft, out of control, spun lazily to its destruction. It reminded me of a seed pod drifting from a tree. One, two, three 'chutes emerged from the plane, as it disappeared into a cottony cloud. Sweat from my brow trickled into my eyes.

The plane rocked from the concussion of bursting shells as we entered the envelope of fire.

"Bomb bay doors open," the engineer called.

"Bombs away!" cried the bombardier. The plane lifted perceptibly when the tons of bombs dropped from her belly. Ahead of us, bombers emerging from the flak barrage in ragged formation were attempting to close up for maximum protection against the Luftwaffe fighters circling above us. As we pulled away from the target area, the plane perforated by flak but the fliers unscathed, Buskey said, "We've got to get the bomb bay doors closed quickly. There's too much drag and with only two and a half engines, I may not be able to keep up with the formation."

Closing the massive bomb bay doors was no easy job. The engineer had to crank them shut since the electrical system which powered the motor that normally closed them was out. In a cramped space 25,000 feet above Germany, temperature way below freezing, wearing a weighty fleece-lined flight suit, gloves, flak vest and helmet, an oxygen mask with the hose dangling like an elephant's trunk and hooked into the life support system, wires from his throat mike and earphones to contend with, plus a parachute strapped on his back, all helped to make it an interminable task.

"Pilot to crew. Someone help the engineer close the doors."

"Yes Sir," the right waist gunner volunteered. This meant he had to disconnect from the plane's oxygen system and hook on to a walk-around bottle that provided about eight minutes of the life-giving element, a routine any time a crewman left his position to go elsewhere in the plane. The walk-around bottle was an aluminium cylinder 6 or 8 inches in diameter and about 30 inches long. Really cumbersome. To get to the engineer and help him, in his bulky flight gear, the waist gunner had to shuffle through the radio operator's compartment, then into the bomb bay, balancing precariously on a narrow catwalk, squeeze between V-shaped bomb racks, the bomb bay doors below him only partly closed, until he reached the engineer's station behind the cockpit.

Buskey continued to do a magnificent job of flying the disabled aircraft and managed somehow to stay in formation. The engineer, Sergeant George Thomas, was slowly and laboriously cranking the bomb bay doors closed. Those of us on the guns were warily watching the enemy fighters in the distance, who fortunately, didn't attack. Sergeant Thomas said, "Engineer to pilot. I see the waist gunner on the catwalk. He's stuck between the bomb racks. He can't move." Sergeant Louis J. Kyler, the radio operator, closest to the helpless waist gunner, attempted to extricate him but his oxygen bottle fell through the partly opened doors and he had to go back to his position and hook into the plane's oxygen system. Private Willis Volkeming, the left waist gunner, on his twelfth mission, the only experienced combat crewman aboard, came forward and tried unsuccessfully to rescue his buddy, who had fainted from lack of oxygen. Somehow he had freed himself but unfortunately he had toppled off the catwalk and dropped part of the way through the bomb bay doors that were nearly closed.

The radio operator came back again and tried once more to save his pal but to no avail. He had to go back to his position for much needed oxygen.

"Radio operator to pilot. We can't get the waist gunner out of the bomb bay. He's unconscious. You'll have to hit the deck if he's to live."

"Pilot to crew," Buskey called, his voice faltering. "If I leave the formation and try to go it alone at 10,000 feet or lower, where we don't need oxygen, we may not make it back to England. German fighters will jump us. It means losing one with the hope that the rest of us will get back."

The waning winter sun of late afternoon shone warmly through the transparent nose of the battle-scarred B-17 as we approached our airbase. The red flare fired from the plane by the engineer alerted the ground personnel that we had a casualty aboard and the tower gave the pilot priority to land. The plane dropped smoothly to the concrete runway and the tyres screeching on touchdown sounded like a whining protest against the terrible ordeal the plane and its crew had endured. Buskey taxied the splendid Fortress to its dispersal area. The medics removed the dead body of the right waist gunner and took him away. I dropped to the ground from the plane's nose hatch, sombre and weary after more than eight hours in the plane. I realised the hardening of a naive airman to combat in the crucible of war had begun.

Seventeen-year-old Friedrich J. Kowalke, a Luftwaffenhelfer (schoolboy),[4] had joined the flak school on reaching his sixteenth birthday in February 1943. He now manned one of the thirteen batteries in the old Hanse town of Magdeburg, south of Berlin, and had the opportunity to track many B-17 boxes in the bomber stream on the Berlin penetration of 8 March, as he recalls:

The B-17s were clearly visible against high cirrus overcast, flying outside of our flak battery range [tracking was performed by the four-metre-base optical rangefinder]. Our time was far after twelve o'clock. The most northern flak batteries of Magdeburg had fired all their ammunition against the bomber stream. Thus it was clear geographically that the bomber stream's penetration leg ran along the Midland Channel from west to east. One B-17 was seen making interrupted loops, thereby shooting some salvos of flares, and spinning down at last. I have learned that this was the fate of *Holy Terror III*, a B-17 in the 100th Group.[5]

When looking towards Berlin with our rangefinder about one hour after our first penetration observations, we discovered a large bomber stream approaching, which meant that it was on its withdrawal leg, moving from east to west. At first many B-17 boxes were seen. Later on, B-24 boxes appeared too, making up the rear. This armada avoided the flak zone of Magdeburg to some degree, flying a west-north-west course, well timed by repeated placing of marker bombs or corresponding flares. Some Me 109s were seen making head-on attacks on one of the B-17 boxes. The last observation I made that day was a single B-17 circling to the ground defended by a P-38. One or more Me 109s were in the neighbourhood. Then dusk came…

More than 460 bombers bombed Erkner with 'good results' (while seventy-five others bombed targets of opportunity) but once again the price was high. The leading 3rd Bomb Division encountered fierce opposition and lost thirty-six Fortresses, including sixteen in the 45th Combat Wing. Curtis E. LeMay, the 3rd Division Commander, singled out the Wing for special praise.

> The crews of the 45th Combat Wing delivered a punishing blow today to the morale of all Germany. In successfully putting bombs on the enemy's capital and his vital plants they furthered the war effort more than any of us can adequately evaluate. At the present writing, the major part of the hurt to the Third Division forces fell on the gallant crews of the 96th, 388th and 452nd Bomb Groups. The spirit and fight these units displayed made it easier on the other wings who wanted to share the brunt of the battle with them. Convey to all officers and men who participated, my deep admiration for the courage and determination with which they pushed the air attack into the heart of the enemy's territory and blasted Berlin.

At Deopham Green, where the 452nd was missing five Forts, returning crews put on a brave front for the newsmen. 'We gave them hell,' commented Sergeant Fred C. Fuller, radio operator of the *The Hard Way*. 'It was excellent bombing all over and I saw fires burning madly away in every section. 'Those fires sure toasted Hitler's bun,' Staff Sergeant Elmer A. Parsons, right waist gunner on *Lucky Lady*, remarked. 'Our bombs fell directly on the factory and the entire area was covered. It was a good job well done. While flying away all we could see was black smoke spiralling up in the sky.' Sergeant Roland Clark, ball turret gunner on *Dog Breath*, claimed that 'all those fires made Berlin a madhouse. Visibility was extremely good and we blasted away a portion of "Beer Hall Berlin". The residents on Wilhelmstrasse are looking for new quarters today.' Staff Sergeant Fred B. Hern, right waist gunner on *Dog Breath*, celebrated his birthday by probably destroying a Fw 190. 'It was a swell present from the German Air Force,' commented the happy Sergeant.[6]

'God really created something when he made mother earth, but Boeing really created something too when they made the Flying Fortress,' in the opinion of twenty-five-year-old 1st Lieutenant Harold G. Fulmer, pilot of *Mon Tête Rouge II* in the 452nd, upon his return from the aerial assault against Berlin. The Visalia, California, pilot sacrificed his crew in order to prevent the loosening up of the formation that he was leading. Just north of the target, a flak burst hit the number three engine, puncturing the oil cooler. Fulmer tried to feather the propeller but couldn't for the oil had leaked out. The engine started to vibrate the ship and caused the plane to lose speed. At this time, recalled Fulmer, 'Fw 190s and Me 109s hit us.' Fulmer had one of two choices to make: he could remain at the head of the squadron, slowing it up and scattering it, thereby placing it at the mercy of the German fighters, or else he could peel off from the formation and fly through the Luftwaffe horde alone to an almost certain end. He chose the latter. 'I dived out of the formation,' continued Fulmer, 'trying to make it appear as if I was out of control, so that the fighters wouldn't come after us. I aimed for the clouds below us.' In the dive, Fulmer's entire crew stayed at their positions even though the plane was tearing through space at an excessive speed, well above the safety limit, for the distance of 15,000 feet. The well-constructed plane held up. He had hidden in the clouds and then ice began to form on the wings. The de-icer system had been shot up by the flak, making it necessary to come out of the clouds occasionally to shake the ice off. It was while doing this that they spotted enemy fighters twice and luckily lost them in the clouds. *Mon Tete Rouge II* arrived home safely, landing at Deopham Green in good condition and with all lives saved. It was a testimony to a sound leader, an excellent pilot and a perfect Flying Fortress.[7]

The worst hit group in the 3rd Division during the series of Berlin missions had been the Bloody Hundredth. In the first American operation to Berlin, on 4 March, the 'Bloody Hundredth' had won through to the target with the 95th while all the others had turned back. Raids on the capital that week cost the group seventeen aircraft.[8]

'The base looked good; it was our home,' recalls Ernest Richardson.

We were kind of glad to be back after our leave in London. We walked into our hut expecting to hear some weird tales of aerial combat from the new crew. Both days we were away was flying weather. What we walked into was supply picking up their personal belongings.

My God! Not again, remembering the last time we saw the same scene.

"Yeah," ventured 'Fletch', who had gotten back a couple of hours ahead of us. "They got shot down today. No one is quite sure just what happened to them. I heard both pilots were shot up and the engineer was trying to fly the plane. Everyone in the formation was trying to get away from them. They were all over the sky. Their plane finally pulled out of the formation and blew up, no one saw any chutes."

Berg and Chris Christiansen came in while supply was still there. No one was saying anything. We were standing around sort of dumbfounded. "That's it, I quit. I've got two kids." It was Berg. He'd often threatened to quit but we didn't pay any attention to him. That day, I was sure he was serious, by now we all had faith in him and hated the thought of him dropping out. Reliability is very important at 25,000 feet.

"My folks would never forgive me if I quit." It was Jack Fletcher. I thought the remark was uncalled for and told him so. I figured if I ever decided to quit, I wouldn't care much what anyone thought, you know, 'better a live coward than a dead hero'.

A short time after this happened we were moved to the 339th Squadron. The 413th went into path finding – a plane that was equipped with radar so they could bomb through the clouds. (Never could figure how that could be done). At the 339th we met another crew. They had one member who was nineteen years old who always yelled "I'm too young to die" every time they woke us for a raid. He was only saying what most of us thought. I was twenty-two at the time. We had more raids than they did so they couldn't scare us with wild tales of combat. They told us the crew we were replacing had been shot down a day or two before we moved in. We weren't crazy about taking over someone else's bed so soon. I for one thought it would have been better if they would have kept their mouths shut. We were all superstitious as hell and didn't need anything else to worry about. Our next raids were mixed, some to France as well as Germany. Berg made everyone of them. We were glad he didn't quit.

At Rattlesden on Thursday 9 March the day began at 0330 hours. Doyle Shields says:

Those beds were so warm. It was a jolt to hit the cold floor, as was the cold air between the huts and the latrines. After our fresh eggs breakfast, we were in the briefing room at 0550 hours. After Colonel Harris had made his opening remarks, we learned it was 'Big-B' again. Our weatherman prepared us for a $^{10}/_{10}$ undercast at the target, the Brandenburg Gate at the centre of Berlin. The intervalometres were set for maximum distance between bombs. We were to start releasing our 500 lb GP bombs, incendiaries and leaflets at the edge of the city to be sure that we hit the Gate. When one man asked if this was indiscriminate bombing, he was ignored. This was one of the very few times we could have been accused of indiscriminate bombing.[9]

Three hundred and thirty-nine B-17s were in the armada bombing Berlin but $^{10}/_{10}$ cloud prevented visual bombing and there was a black cloud of flak over the city.

The 158 B-24s bombed three secondary targets in the Brunswick, Hannover and Nienburg areas. The Luftwaffe was conspicuous by its absence but six B-17s and two B-24s were victims to flak.

Al Saunders' crew in the 448th was one of eighteen B-24 crews that were assigned a He 177 factory at Brandenburg, as Wallace Patterson wrote.

Above the dense overcast the weather was clear and not too cold. We were carrying fifty 100 lb incendiaries. Over Hanover we ran into the worst flak any of us has ever seen. It was very accurate and I heard a big piece hit the ship. Directly in front of us, Everett Musselman flying *Baby Shoes* took a hit on his No. 2 engine and eventually fell out of formation. He hasn't been heard from yet.[10] We were late getting to the target and then stayed around for hours it seemed, dodging flak and waiting for the Pathfinder to drop its flares. It never did and eventually we headed for home. All the way back until we reached Holland, planes were dropping their bombs. We got rid of ours and dodged flak all the way to the enemy coast. We landed awfully hard and Al told me when we parked that we had had to feather two engines to keep enough gas to land with the other two. We barely made it to the hardstand. There was a flak hole six inches from my feet but didn't come in. Next day was a stand-down so Bill Trunnell and I decided on the spur of the moment to take off for London. While there we got a dog – a Chow puppy, a bitch, which the boys named 'G.P.' (General Purpose).

E. Z. Duzit in the 66th Squadron in the 44th BG, which had been hit by four bursts of flak just as the bombs were released, landed back at Shipdham at around 1730 hours and buried its nose in the earth near the runway. One of the flak bursts had torn off the left leg of 1st Lieutenant Kenneth G. Jewell, the bluff, plain-speaking Pennsylvanian pilot with Indian blood coursing through his veins, at the knee and it struck him in his face. One engine was destroyed. Lieutenant Harold L. Koontz, the co-pilot, who was on his first mission, was dragged unconscious from the flight deck. It seemed that he could not stand the sight of blood and he had vomited into his oxygen mask and passed out. Lieutenant Arthur Sakowski, the navigator, had told Jewell to get out of his seat and he would patch him up but when he tried to get up he found that he could not. Sakowski, an ex-football player and very strong, picked him up and laid him on the deck. He cut the pant-leg off and it was a mess. Only the bicep muscle of Jewell's left leg was there. Sakowski had nothing to splint it so he put sulphur on it and gave Jewell two shots of morphine and then tore the bottom of the seat from the parachute to get the jungle knife. He then began to saw and hack at the remains of Jewell's leg but the blade was too dull. The next time Jewell awakened the co-pilot was in his seat and the Liberator was over the English Channel. Jewell put the B-24 under control and passed out. When he awoke they were above the balloon barrage in Norwich. When they saw the airfield, someone shot red flares and the two pilots got *E. Z. Duzit* down. Jewell was declared dead upon arrival at the base hospital but the following afternoon he came round. His sides hurt so badly that he forgot about his leg. He had not emptied his bladder for thirty hours and he filled three urinal ducts. Jewell threw back the sheets and he had no left leg! He got furious, flung himself out of bed, tore off the bandages and started bleeding again. He could not accept the fact. He was young, had a good career, a beautiful wife and here he was to be a helpless cripple for the rest of his life.[11]

In the co-pilot's seat of a 'Fightin' Bitin' Squadron Fortress, weaving its way through the intense and accurate flak barrage much in the manner of a broken field runner, sat 2nd Lieutenant Robert C. Fife, Jr., Newark, New Jersey. They had dropped their bombs and were turning off the target, their traffic pattern leading them over the heart of the 'Big-B'. Running into an especially heavy concentration of flak, the pilot, 1st Lieutenant Frank A. Warner, Linden, New Jersey, asked Fife to hand him his flak helmet from under the seat. Fife, who had been dividing his time between watching the instrument panel and the flak bursts, was unaccustomed to the darkness of the interior of the plane. While reaching for the helmet his fingers touched what he thought was its strap and he pulled. It stuck slightly; so he pulled sharply. It came out and he found himself holding the red handle of a parachute rip-cord. At this instant, the ship was hit by flak and Fife realised his mishap had left his pilot without a chute. He didn't tell Warner what had happened, because he was having enough trouble with the flak and fighters.

'When I saw the chute open, I had the hell scared out of me,' said Fife. 'I climbed out of my seat and stood by ready to aid in case of trouble. I couldn't call for an extra 'chute because there weren't any. As soon as we got out of the flak I leaned down and switched my chute for the opened one.'

Fife then leaned back and prayed that nothing would happen. It was a long jump, to make without a 'chute. He didn't tell Warner what had happened until they were well over the Channel on the way home. Fife grinned, 'It was a hell of a place to be without a parachute.'

Smaller-scale raids on targets in France and Germany followed the early March Berlin strikes. On Saturday 11 March PFF techniques were used by 121 B-17s to bomb Münster, and by thirty-four Liberators to attack a No Ball site at Wizernes. V-1 targets were again bombed 12–13 March.

Early on Wednesday 15 March only 330 bomber crews in the 3rd Division were put on mission alert. Celesta B. 'Red' Harper in the 350th Squadron in the Hundredth, who on the mission to Berlin on 6 March had daringly evaded enemy fighters by putting *Buffalo Gal* into an almost vertical dive to 5,000 feet at 270 mph, recalls:

We were awakened with the usual fanfare of noise and confusion. Lieutenant Herbert Devore and the other three of his crew officers dressed out in full class 'A' uniform – pinks, blouse, tie and brass – the whole works – just as though they were headed out to a dance. We joked with them about it and Herb said, "This is our last tour mission and we're going to finish up in style." At that time twenty-five missions constituted a tour of duty and that was to be their twenty-fifth. We were briefed that morning to hit a Messerschmitt plane factory at Brunswick. The Waggum aircraft plant nearby was introduced as a secondary target in case we were weathered out of the primary target. Secondary targets were designed to keep us from making the trip for naught. Our Group formation for this mission consisted of twenty-one aircraft. Six ship lead – nine ship high and six low elements – stacked into the sun. Departure was at 0640 hours. Our Group made assembly at 2,400 feet over the base at 0700 hours. We flew the low Group position that morning in the 13th Combat Wing with the 390th in the wing lead position and the 95th in the high Group position.

Herb Devore was flying Group lead pilot with Captain Roland Knight as command pilot in the right seat and the crew's regular co-pilot, Martin Tashjian, was in tail gun position as formation observer. I was flying on Herb's left wing and Frank Malooly was on his right wing. We had climbed to an altitude of 24,000 feet, which was about 2,000 feet above an overcast. We had good fighter support. Our little friends were thick as fleas on a dog, thank goodness. We reached the target IP at 1154 hours and the flak was intense in the target area.

I was flying in close to the lead ship as we approached the target to ensure a good bomb pattern. Our bomb load for the mission consisted of ten 100 lb GP bombs and twenty-three 100 lb magnesium incendiary bombs. Our bomb bay doors were open and we were about ten seconds from bombs away when I suddenly saw the entire cockpit area of Herb's plane fill with red smoke and fire and I saw his body slump over against the control column. The plane nosed down slightly as it started down. I had my co-pilot take over so I could watch our Group lead plane going down. The plane started burning and pieces of the smoking Number 3 engine cowling started to fly loose as the bomber went into a flat spin about 1,000 feet above the cloud layer. Just as they reached the undercast, the aircraft exploded and the fiery mass disappeared into the clouds below. I saw no parachutes before the explosion. Devore had apparently received a direct flak hit that set off his flares and incendiaries and the plane really just melted down.

Burton Joseph, Devore's navigator adds:

Just past the IP we took a direct hit from what I believe to have been an 88 mm flak shell, which was what started all the red fire and smoke. The shell exploded in the hatchway directly below the cockpit and probably ruptured the oxygen tanks and ignited the fuel transfer system. There was a blinding flash of flame behind me and I knew we were 'done'. After a moment's hesitation, I ripped off my flak vest, which in turn pulled off my oxygen mask. I then hooked my parachute to the chest harness I was wearing, turned and dived out the already open escape hatch. I was immediately behind Harry 'Shorty' Longhi, our top turret gunner/flight engineer. Captain Bob Peel, who was flying with us just for that mission as lead bombardier, exited behind me. The other seven members of the crew, including the command pilot, perished. I delayed pulling the ripcord until I was fairly close to the solid undercast, figuring that the cloud height would allow sufficient time for the chute to open before landing. This prevented my passing out for lack of oxygen at the higher altitude and possibly saved me from becoming the object of further German target practice. I guess that I probably fell free for 20,000 feet. The chute opened just as I broke through the cloud cover, perhaps 2,000 feet above the ground. Beneath me stretched a vast sea of flames. Our incendiary raid on the target city of Braunschweig was highly successful! However to my dismay, I had left a burning plane only to land in the still smouldering ruins of a burned-out house! I had been burned about the face and hit by shrapnel while still in the plane. Now, I was burned again, about the hands and head, upon landing. On leaving the burned out house, I was confronted with a new situation. An angry group of German civilians was moving toward me. You can well imagine their feelings, with many of their homes destroyed by Luftgangsters such as myself. Fortunately, a Wehrmacht sentry stationed at a nearby air raid shelter got to me before the mob of civilians. He had to hold them off with his rifle and in so doing, undoubtedly saved my life. This mob would most certainly have torn me apart had they gotten to me first.[12]

At Rattlesden on Thursday 16 March the wake-up hour was 0300 hours for the 0430 briefing. It was hard to get up so early. 'One thing good about mission mornings,' recalled Doyle Shields, 'we had a very good breakfast with fresh eggs. As we walked to briefing we emitted a vapour as our warm breath hit the cold air. The intelligence officer removed the black curtain from the mission map. Our target was deep in southern Germany; an aircraft plant at Augsburg. We were to have plenty of company; 501 B-17s from the First and Third Divisions.'[13]

Harry Cornell's crew would return to Augsburg, as John Kettman, who was flying his fifteenth mission, recalls:

Our primary target was an airfield about four miles from Munich but we had to bomb with the Pathfinder, so Augsburg was our secondary. It was a pretty smooth trip. We didn't see one enemy fighter. The escort was spotty but good and we had plenty of cover over the target. At the target the flak was light and there were a couple of rockets. Coming back we caught a lot of flak at Amiens France. We got a few holes in the ship, one was two feet from Leo Hartman, navigator. P-47s were with us all the way back. We didn't lose any ships from the group. Darius Logan's mask kept coming lose and he kept falling asleep, until I finally found out what the trouble was and I tightened up his mask.

The 447th reached their bombing altitude of 19,000 feet as they crossed the coast of the Netherlands. Doyle Shields continues:

Shortly after going into Germany, the Luftwaffe hit us with Messerschmitt Bf 109s and FW 190s. They came at us wave after wave. They came in from the front with guns blazing and rolled over on their back as they slipped under us. They were armoured on their bellies. Our escort missed their rendezvous with us. The German fighters did a lot of damage to the group behind us. Near the target about 75 Ju 88s and Me 210s joined the fray. There were 30 Bf 109s in another group. Elwin Kreps saw one Me 210 going down and saw three bail out of a Ju 88. Lieutenant Wesley C. Huckins, 711th Squadron, was seen to going down.[14] The fact that Colonel Harris stressed tight formations kept us from being hit as bad as some groups. Harris would always tell the wingmen to, "Put your wing in the lead plane's waist window." The flak was heavy over the target, so we were not bothered by German fighters, but after we left the target they were on us again. Bombs were dropped using PFF so results were not observed. As we neared the North Sea our escort was good and remainder of the mission was uneventful.[15]

1st Lieutenant Robert 'Bob' Meyer in the 550th Squadron in the 385th at Great Ashfield in Suffolk had volunteered to replace the pilot of *Lonesome Polecat*, who was unable to take part in the day's mission.

We crossed the German border and I looked down at the low group and they were getting the hell pounded out of them. The rocket-launching planes had sneaked up behind them and were launching rockets into the formation. I looked up and there were six Focke Wulf 190s coming in from the front; one for each of the low squadron. The one that had a bead on me could not miss. I slammed the throttles forward, pulled the stick back, kicked the left rudder and went way up in an arc, out of formation. Instead of hitting us he tore up the bottom of the plane, ripped the low part of the nose, the ball turret as well and the engine. I looked back at the formation and two of the planes were already down and another one was falling back.

With the damaged number four engine windmilling, the aircraft could not keep up with the formation. Removing his parachute so that he could climb into the bomb bay, the engineer was able to crank the doors down and salvo the bombs. However, after the bombs were released, the doors wouldn't close. With the nose off, the bomb bay open and just three engines, the aircraft could only manage 100 mph. Meyer decided to head for Spain, knowing that he would have to fly over Switzerland – but as he crossed the border two Bf 109s moved in. Bob takes up the story:

They rocked their wings and we could see the white Swiss crosses. They wanted to take us down to an airfield but to get there we had to go over a mountain pass. I could not keep the altitude because we had been burning the engines really hot. We barely got over the top, with the propeller kicking up the snow. We had one more small pass to fly through but we could not make it. So we bailed the crew out. I was going to land the plane between two roads, which was fine, except that everybody was running into the street and waving. I looked ahead and there was a church spire, how the hell was I going to raise the wing over that? I leaned on the rudder and by a miracle something raised the wing. As I went over the top of the church I looked directly into the sun and at a lake below which was just like a mirror. I had no idea how near I was to the surface, so I let the left wing down a bit more. When it started to cut a little trail in the water I pulled everything over, cut the engines and sat her down on the lake – a perfect three-point landing with the nose up a little bit. I thought that was really beautiful. Just like in a boat. But then the water came pouring in through the bomb bay and the tail started dropping down, followed by the nose. I pulled the co-pilot's window open to climb out and to crawl to the top of the plane. When I jumped down on the wing, the plane suddenly lurched forward and went down. I popped open my Mae West. The water was icy cold. I'd never been so cold in my life…

Robert Meyer was rescued by two young brothers, Werner and Norbert Henggeler, who rowed out to him. As a reward, he gave them his fur-lined boots but these were later confiscated by the police, much to the boys' disappointment. The American was brought ashore and given a hero's welcome as he was marched through the village of Zug. At the local police station he changed into dry clothing and Florence Iten, a young translator, tried to question him, but without much success. Bob was reunited with his crew later that day and learned that the navigator, Robert Williams, had been killed when his parachute failed to open. S/Sgt Charles Page, the ball turret gunner, had been hit by shrapnel and suffered a deep wound in his buttocks and bombardier T/Sgt Carl Larson, who was being treated in the same hospital at Baar, had three Swiss bullets removed from his legs. Those members of the crew fit enough to travel were transferred to Dübendorf, where they joined the crews of the four B-17s and three B-24s that landed there that day.[16]

The 2nd Division went south and west to hit aircraft plants in Friedrichshafen, the important railway junction on the north shore of Lake Constance (Bodensee), opposite Switzerland. Friedrichshafen was the centre of Dornier aircraft production and the birthplace of airships including the *Graf Zeppelin* and *Hindenburg*. Thirty B-24s in the 93rd were dispatched to Friedrichshafen and two Liberators were forced to put down in Switzerland. 2nd Lieutenant Secar J. Harris of Mobile, Alabama, flying 42-100116, was last seen heading south-west after leaving the target. Harris crash-landed at Diepoldsau on the Swiss border and he and six of his crew were rounded up by the Germans and taken into captivity. Two other members reached Switzerland and were interned. *Big Noise*, flown by Lieutenant Richard J. Pettit, who had been the pilot of the ill-fated *Heavenly Daze* in January, was seen tagged onto the 'Bungay Buckaroos' formation. Flak-damaged, Pettit headed for Switzerland and landed safely at Dübendorf.

Twenty-three bombers failed to return to their bases.

At Seething on Friday 17 March, Wallace Patterson noted that they had fresh eggs and doughnuts and pineapple juice and bacon for breakfast. 'It was very foggy out; so we were briefed for two missions. No. 1 was an aerodrome just outside of

Augsburg, with Munich as the secondary target. No. 2 was Frankfurt. Both were scrubbed however; so we came back five hours after we had been awakened and had another breakfast.'

The 490th was returning from a raid on Bittefeld when they encountered cirrus clouds, which forced them to fly on instruments for thirty minutes. The Fortresses moved into tighter formation. Suddenly, a squadron in the 385th cut through the clouds into the 490th formation and caused one of the 490th ships to veer upwards. In no time at all it collided with another 490th B-17, flown by Lieutenant Robert H. Tennenberg. The radio room in the lower Fortress took the full force of the collision and the aircraft broke in two. In Tennenberg's Fortress, Chester A. Deptula, the navigator, dragged John Gann, the stunned nose gunner, from the shattered nose to the radio operator's compartment. Despite a smashed engine, another partly disabled, a wing tip bent, the front of the nose knocked off and the pilot's front view window broken, Tennenberg kept her airborne and managed to reach Belgium, where he made a successful crash landing. The crewmen stepped out unhurt and surveyed the damage. Among the wreckage was the mutilated torso of a man later identified as the radio operator from the Fortress which had collided with them. He had been forced through the shattered Plexiglas nose of Tennenberg's aircraft on impact.

On Saturday 18 March B-17 crews were able to sleep a little longer and the CQs did not start their rounds until 0515 hours. Briefing was at 0515 hours. Intelligence advised that the target for the 3rd Divison was the centre of Munich, and for 284 1st Division Forts an aircraft plant at Oberpfaffenhofen and air depots at Lechfeld and Landsberg. All told, 679 bombers were to bomb aircraft plant and airfields in south-west Germany and the Dornier works at Friedrichshafen, the target for the Liberators in the 2nd Bomb Division.

Starting at 1000 hours, twenty-eight B-24s began taking off from Wendling. Four returned early with mechanical problems, leaving the remaining aircraft to continue over France. Lieutenant Gerald M. Dalton's crew in *Amblin' Oakie*, a Gotha veteran, got caught in prop wash and collided with *Late Date II*, flown by Lieutenant Ellsworth F. Anderson, slicing off the tail and its turret. Both aircraft collided again as they went down and exploded in sheets of flame before crashing.[17] As the bombers neared Friedrichshafen, the leading 'Flying Eightballs' at the head of the 14th Wing made an unscheduled 360° turn. The leading element in the 392nd bombed the target but the second block, disconcerted by the manoeuvres ahead, chose to attack the rail yards at Stockach instead. The Liberators became strung out and heavy flak dispersed the formation to such an extent that many

B-24s flew over Swiss territory on the opposite side of Lake Constance and drew fire from the Swiss guns. The Liberators were running nine minutes late for their rendezvous with P-38 fighter escorts, which was missed and the 14th Wing was left to fend for itself against an estimated seventy-five single-engined enemy fighters. They attacked in line abreast, five and six at a time, and harried the Liberators for over 100 miles. Captain Myron Keilman in the 392nd formation recalls that: 'The lead ship had an engine shot out on the bomb run; then persistent fighter attacks worked the group over all the way to Strasbourg. A 20 mm shell blinded the lead navigator.' Even when P-38s came to the rescue, the German pilots continued to press home their attacks. The 392nd was decimated, losing fifteen Liberators. The 44th lost eight B-24s.[18]

On only his fourth mission, Colonel Joseph Miller, the 453rd CO, led the 2nd Combat Wing in *Little Bryan* flown by Captain Stock in the 733rd Squadron. Jim Kotapish, co-pilot aboard *Reluctant Dragon*, flying below the lead ship recalls:

Our astute group navigator [Captain Joseph O'Reilly] had led the group over the harbour and everyone was waiting for us. The first flak burst hit the bomb bay of the lead ship and immediately burst into flames. All I could think of was, "Please God, don't blow up right now or we'll get the whole 'plane in our nose." It didn't; it banked right in a low spiral and several men bailed out of the 'plane, which was streaming flames from the bottom and the waist windows. The second burst hit our left wing. While I heeled over to follow the deputy leader out to sea, Ray Sears, pilot, was busying himself with No. 2 engine, which had taken the brunt of the burst. I followed the flight of the lead 'plane as long as I could but it fell behind. The early parachutists were swept out across the lake and drowned before the speedboats could pick them up.[19]

Next day the bombers carried out 'milk runs' to V-1 sites in northern France. While 172 heavies unloaded their bombs over the No Ball sites, Bill Rose in the 92nd completed his twenty-fifth and final mission to Frankfurt. 'As we entered the flight pattern over Podington,' he remembers, 'we broke away and buzzed the field. Then we partied until our papers came through.'[20]

Meanwhile, a replacement had to be found for Colonel Miller at Old Buckenham and Ramsey D. Potts, who late in 1943 had become the Wing chief of staff at 2nd Combat Wing headquarters, received a message on 19 March to report to 2nd Bomb Division headquarters at Ketteringham Hall near Norwich. Potts, who had gone from squadron commander to group Operations Officer and was responsible for planning missions, assigning crews, deciding what squadrons flew in what order and running training missions for the entire group, had helped with the 453rd Bomb Group's orientation and battle training. He recalled:

The 2nd Bomb Division was commanded by Major General Hodges, a salty, West Point type. When I entered his office, he told me he had two colonels from Washington on their way to take commands, but General Timberlake, who was my wing commanding officer, said he wanted me – not one of them – as the new group commander. This was beyond my wildest dreams. I looked at Timberlake, who was nonchalantly blowing on his finger-nails, looking up at the ceiling like nothing was happening. Hodges continued and told Timberlake I didn't have the experience and was not a West Point graduate. But then he asked me, "Do you think you can do the job?" I seized the moment and said "yes". He looked at Timberlake and said, "I'll give him six weeks."

I had a lot of trepidation because the squadron commanders were older than I was and many were West Pointers. I shuffled the structure of the group and asked for a new operations officer, somebody from the outside. Low and behold, they sent an officer from another group – a guy named Jimmy Stewart, the actor, became my operations officer. We hit it off very well, even though he was eight years older than I was. He was a wonderful addition to the group and had the same languid style as in his movies. Everyone loved him. We whipped that group into tip-top shape and it quickly became one of the best groups in the Air Force. But we weren't together long. Sometime later I became the Director of Bombing Operations for the 8th Air Force, a position I held until the end of the war.

Wallace Patterson finished a forty-eight-hour pass on the night of 19 March.

After holing up at the Norwich Red Cross for a while, I spent all day at Cambridge, by far the most beautiful part of England I have ever seen. I visited two of the oldest colleges, whose spacious lawns slope down to the river, whose banks are bordered with trees just coming into leaf and the first crocuses. The train trip was rather tiresome as most of Norfolk County is rather dull scenery but I had enough energy to go to a dance. As I was walking home there was an air raid. One Jerry was bracketed in searchlights but was not shot down. The bombs dropped mostly on the north-western outskirts of town, starting one big fire that was soon put out. Bill Trunnell the co-pilot, who stayed at Seething for the first day of the pass, flew co-pilot in another crew on a raid but got only fifty miles into enemy territory. It was another screwed-up raid and the group lost two planes. Jack Edwards, our CO, was killed. One section was left behind when most of the others were called back for weather and it caught very bad flak over the French coast. Al and Bill and I went to a Norwich cinema to see *North Star*.

On Monday 20 March, bad weather and malfunction of blind bombing equipment caused nearly 300 of the 445 bombers dispatched with 594 escorting fighters to abandon the mission to a propeller plant at Frankfurt. Only fifty-one B-17s bombed industry and transportation targets and another ninety-six attacked targets of opportunity including Bingen and the Mannheim and Mainz areas. At Seething 1st Lieutenant Meyers 'The Chief' Wahnee's crew in the 448th was on 'stand-by' for the raid on Frankfurt. In the event there happened to be an abort by one of the other Liberators scheduled for the mission and Meyers' crew were roused from Barracks 4 as the other aircraft were starting their engines.

'It was very cold and damp in the early morning light,' recalls co-pilot Stuart K. Barr, 'and we had to hustle to get our personal gear together and head for the plane.'

Barr had first met Meyers Wahnee at Boise, Idaho, in August 1943 when he received his wings and appointment as Flight Officer and had been shipped there for assignment to a combat unit for training. Orders had been issued assigning him and nine others to a crew assigned to the 714th Squadron under a 1st Lieutenant Wahnee, or 'The Chief', as he was called by all his fellow officers. At their first meeting Wahnee looked Barr straight in the eye, extended his hand to shake and said, 'I am Meyers Wahnee. You and I are going to see a lot of each other from now on.' He continued, 'I'm an Injun, a Comanche from Anadarko, Oklahoma.' Barr replied:

Well, I don't know what in the hell I am: Scots, Swiss and Airdale I think, from Pennsylvania. Plain people stock, raised in Florida. It was the Chief's job to train me and to that end he did a good job. After twenty hours in the B-24, he had checked me out, to the satisfaction of the Group Operations Officer, as a qualified pilot. I had never had a more exacting instructor in all my life. And too, I appreciated his honest interest in me and in my proficiency as his alternate, should the situation ever demand. The Chief and I were equally very proud of our crew after we had tasted the salt of combat in the skies over Europe. However, after several missions, our beautiful bird was rapidly becoming war weary. The Chief and I sat side by side in training, the long flight from the States and now through 150 hours of combat. We also spent our free time, between missions, together. We had become as close as brothers.

All the crew was assembled at *The Comanche* with the exception of the navigator, Dick Hager. The Chief decided to do this mission without the navigator and told them to take their positions for take-off. While taxiing to the end of the runway, a jeep with a navigator pulled alongside with the man to fill the crew vacancy. With twelve 500 lb General Purpose bombs in the bomb-bays, the war-weary *Comanche* took to the blue to catch up to the rest of the Group and fill the empty slot in the formation. Barr continues:

We made our rendezvous with the Group midway across the Channel and took our position in the formation. At 23,000 feet, the ground was clearly visible and the weather unusually clear. However, far ahead, the weather looked less inviting. The morning sun felt good coming into the cockpit until it was blocked by the oncoming clouds. The Group Leader had turned his formation onto the IP when an abort of the mission was called: So on this day, Frankfurt was spared 84 tons of high explosives. The return to our base in East Anglia was interrupted by anti-aircraft fire over northern France. A quartet of 155 mm rounds exploded near *The Comanche*, severely crippling her ability to stay aloft. We could feel the compression of the shells on our bodies and the plane seemed to ring from the blasts. To recover control of the plane, the bombs and other ordinance was released, the crew ordered to 'Bail Out', leaving the Chief and myself alone in the dying *Comanche*. A purple screen of 100/135 grade fuel clouded the inside of the plane and streamed down the instrument panel, windshield and the walls of the cockpit.

The following few moments seemed like an eternity to me. The Chief finally decided the plane was out of our control and we would have to abandon our gallant *Comanche*, with the chalk cliffs of the UK on the distant horizon. The Chief waved me to bail out. At my exit position on the catwalk in the bomb bay, I looked back into the cockpit to see that the Chief was following me. He was still in his seat, battling to control the plane. Was he injured? I asked myself and headed back into the cockpit to assist. At this moment I saw him release his safety belt and turn toward his exit. I could see in his face, he was unhappy to leave the *Comanche*, now a derelict mass of machinery, jumping around the sky over northern France, headed for its rendezvous with the earth and inevitable destruction. This was the last I was to see of the Chief until 1951. He was a PoW for the next 14 months until the invading forces of the American and British recaptured his prison camp.[21]

In the 401st, 2nd Lieutenant John A. Dunnaway's B-17 was shot down by enemy fighters after straying from the Wing formation and then attempting to rejoin it, 12 kilometres west of Rheims. Lieutenant T. J. Krol, the bombardier, was helped to evade by a French family, Monsieur and Madame Camille Simon. Sergeant J. W. Crowley, the right waist gunner, was severely wounded in the fighter attack. He was taken to hospital but died that night after an operation. While preparing to bail out, S/Sgt Frank Mastronardi, the radio operator, noticed that Sergeant Walt Rusch was trapped in his ball turret, its door jammed with empty 50 calibre shell casings from the fight with the 109s. Mastronardi and one of the waist gunners, Sergeant J. Katsaros, began clearing the casings as the plane lost altitude and when Mastronardi saw that Rusch was almost free he told Katsaros to bail out. But the hatch was still jammed. Finally he freed Rusch and because the ball turret gunner was blinded by the debris, he had to search for his chute. His parachute had been hit by machine gun fire but not damaged, although it had opened. Between them they gathered the open chute and Busch bailed out holding it in his arms and it opened successfully. Mastronardi then bailed out and landed safely.[22]

Ignoring his own wounds, the right waist gunner of the Fortress *Passionate Witch* in the 452nd shielded his fellow crewmen from heavy enemy gunfire during a wild ride back from Frankfurt in which the bomber was wrecked by 2,000 shell holes. Both waist gunners were hit by 20 mm bursts. The co-pilot, Lieutenant Ronald J. Casey of Pontiac, Michigan, said that while he was bandaging the left waist gunner, the right waist gunner 'stood over us to protect us although he was hit in the face and his whole leg was covered with blood from a bad leg wound'. 'He said his wounds weren't bad and he kept manning his gun at the same time,' said Casey. 'He wouldn't have bled so much had he lain on the floor, but he wouldn't.' Casey said that the left waist gunner, although he was wounded badly and would be hospitalised for a month, was concerned only over getting back to combat. 'There were wounds all over him,' said Casey. 'He had deep wounds in both legs, the right shoulder and a compound fracture of the right arm, yet he asked, "Lieutenant, when I'm better, can I come back on the crew?"'

A third hero was the other gunner. While blood dripping from his wounded back, he put out a fire in his ammunition box and went back to his guns. The pilot, Lieutenant Robert M. Cook of Hollywood, California, and Monroe, Washington, said eight German fighter planes attacked the Fortress, 'buzzing around us like Indians at a war dance'. The top turret gunner, Sergeant Gerald Poplett of Peoria, Illinois, and the navigator, Lieutenant John F. Osswaltof of River Forest, Illinois, blew up a Fw 190 apiece. As the Fortress hedge-hopped homeward on three engines, the gunners shot up a radio station, flak tower, a locomotive and tug boat. Over France they exchanged the 'V for victory' sign with peasants working in the fields only 100 feet below. The bomber survived two hot barrages of fire from flak emplacements and was almost knocked down by a geyser of water thrown up by a shell which burst right in front of her nose. 'Hitting that water was like crashing into a brick wall,' said the pilot. 'We were only 20 feet above the English Channel.' The *Passionate Witch* landed at a RAF airfield with its left aileron shot off, gas tank, bomb bay, tail, control cables, interphone and hydraulic system shot up. 'She looked like a piece of imported lace,' said Osswaltof.

Seven bombers in all were lost and eight fighters failed to return.

'Bo' Bottoms arrived back at Seething after a six-day furlough, missing his bill fold with all his money and everything in it. The Red Cross had loaned him £2 10*s* and he got back to Barracks 4 with 1*s* left in his pocket. Bottoms sure hated to lose it and he was even more distressed when he discovered that those in 'Chief' Wahnee's Crew 56 had not returned from the mission to Frankfurt. The curse of Barracks 4 had struck again. In April Bottoms and others in Crew 55 moved from Site 4 to Site 1 though no one knew why.

On Tuesday 21 March about 650 bombers raided the Berlin area, including the aircraft factories at Basdorf and Oranienburg.[23] Just over fifty B-24s bombed V-weapon launching installations at Watten in northern France. Next day 474 heavies, including the 466th Bomb Group, which made its bombing debut, were dispatched[24] to bomb aviation industry plants at Oranienburg and Basdorf. However, 8/10 to 10/10 cloud cover prevented an attack and the bombers hit the secondary target of 'Big-B' and other targets of opportunity. Berlin was John Kettman's seventeenth mission and his second trip to the 'big town'.

We went by way of the North Sea, going in and out through Germany and Holland. I flew in the ball turret the first hour and a half. Our escort picked us up around Denmark. We didn't see one enemy fighter all the way. Over the target there were all kinds of flak, all of it a little off to our right. We caught more flak on the way home. It was a long ride as usual. Just before the IP Lieutenant Eldred Wipple turned back and headed for Sweden. We prayed that he made it. Hawkins, who lived in my barracks, was on the crew. One of their engines was out.[25]

In the 'Travelling Circus', Lieutenant Herman C. 'Mitch' Mitchell's crew flew their fifth mission this day in *Sweater Gal*. The pin-up on the nose had previously been unclad and she had the risqué title of *Buck-Fifty Job* before orders were received to cover her up and change the name! Charles E. Clague Jr, bombardier, recalled that they were on oxygen for six hours and the temperature was -45°. The twenty-one-year-old bombardier, who had been yanked out of college near Cleveland in 1943 and inducted into the Air Corps, also said that it was 'the most screwed up mission he hoped to be on'. The tail turret was out, there were oil leaks in three engines, five electric suits were out and the fifty-two 100-lb M-47 incendiary bombs would not release electrically. To cap it all, en route to the target the navigator, twenty-three-year-old 2nd Lieutenant Howard 'Howie' W. Mesnard, developed anoxia. Howie was a student at Purdue University at the time of Pearl Harbor. Almost immediately, he enlisted in the Air Corps, and applied for and was accepted into pilot training at Maxwell Field, Alabama.

One of Howie's assigned roommates was twenty-one-year-old Herman C. Mitchell, a tall, gentle, friendly guy with a soft Virginia drawl. After several weeks for processing, Mitch and Howie were sent to Albany, Georgia, for flight training but aptitude tests showed him qualified for navigation training. Howie maintained his friendship with Mitchell and both men were reunited at Boise, where Mitch arranged to have Howie assigned to his crew. Howie was elated at this good fortune because he had always admired Mitch because of his cool-headedness, especially while shooting crap. He was most calm when rolling the dice, even though every cent he possessed could be lost on the outcome of the toss. He was generous, flamboyant and gregarious and one of the smoothest talkers Mesnard had ever known. Months later, they arranged a furlough to Chicago over New Year's Eve. After six of the crew had been ridiculed by the desk clerk for even inquiring about getting a room, Mitch, in his charming way, finagled the bridal suite of the Congress Hotel for the whole crew! Mitch, who was born, raised and educated in Roanoke, Virginia, loved to gamble. Several times at Boise and Colorado Springs Mitch had gone bankrupt playing poker at the Officers' Club. He would come back to the barracks and borrow money from Mesnard then return to the game. If he lost he would repay the loan fully the next payday. If he won he absolutely insisted on splitting all his winnings with Mesnard!

Anoxia, if left unchecked, resulted in death. At altitude oxygen mask hoses were prone to ice up simply from breathing. If not monitored, chunks of ice could form and completely block the flow of oxygen. On the mission to Berlin, Charles Clague, who was sitting under the navigator's table in the nose of *Sweater Gal*, trying to keep out of Mesnard's way, recalls:

I loved Howie and thought that he was a great guy until we had to be together in the cramped nose of a B-24! It took a lot of patience in both of us to keep from having some good old-fashioned fisticuffs when someone stepped in or snagged your oxygen hose or happened to yank a wire leading to your throat, mike or heated suit. Howie was standing at the table. Suddenly his legs buckled but he caught himself. I tapped him on the leg and made a gesture to pinch or crunch his oxygen hose, which he did. He gave me the OK sign. About twenty seconds later his knees buckled again and we went through the same routine, except I noticed that the skin around his eyes was a pasty white and he did not look healthy. So I took a deep breath, gave him my mask, took his mask off and disconnected his oxygen hose. He was puzzled and even irritated by my action but a few breaths of good oxygen brought him back to full consciousness. Meanwhile, I crunched his hose again and fortunately noticed that a large block of ice had formed inside the hose where a metal band connecting the hose to the mask prevented the squeezing action from being effective. I quickly cleared the obstruction before I became a victim of hypoxia myself. We each put our own masks back on and were back to normal!²⁶

The 452nd hit a target in Berlin led by their new Commanding Officer, Lieutenant-Colonel Marvin F. Stalder. The Group diarist declared that: 'Our group hit hard and returned safely. This is a world's championship boxing match and the Eighth Air Force has its opponents against the ropes, throwing dangerous punches into his most vital nerve centre. Nothing can save them, not even the final bell. Weather to the target was undercast. When the target was reached, undercast was ⁸/10.'

'I think we did a pretty good job. There were breaks in the clouds and I could see the city through it. I don't think there was a hellava lot left of the target. Hitler must have moved a long time ago to new quarters,' commented S/Sgt Robert A. Lalumiere, ball turret gunner on *Sunrise Serenade*. Flight Officer James B. Williams, bombardier on *Round Tripper*, said that 'We saw the target through a break in the clouds and let our bombs go down. They really hit and we could see black smoke starting to pour up into the sky. They'll hang up the sign, "Out of Order" on the door to the target. That is, if the door is still left standing.' S/Sgt Jimmie C. Campbell, tail gunner on *Round Tripper*, claimed that 'the sky was filled with our fighters. They looked like a flock of blackbirds'. 'We did a terrific amount of damage,' exclaimed 2nd Lieutenant J. A. Kelly, bombardier on *Lady Satan*.

Berlin is a city in flames tonight. Flak over the target was intense but not one of our planes was damaged seriously. Everyone returned safely to base. Enemy fighter opposition was extremely weak, in fact, not one fighter was seen near any of the formations. This is a sure sign that our aerial blows are weakening enemy fighter strength considerably. Fighter escort was excellent, those P-47s, P-51s and P-38s just covered us up like a blanket, from top to bottom.

'I saw two FW 190s try to get into the formation but two P-47s chased them away,' recalled 2nd Lieutenant Frank L. Houston, co-pilot on *Punched Fowl*. 'This was a good mission. Our pilots handled themselves well, and the crew contributed toward the destruction of Berlin. Moderate flak was experienced by the group all the way back from the target.'[27]

Next day, Thursday 23 March, 767 bombers were dispatched to attack airfields in western Germany and aircraft factories in the Brunswick area. Due to unfavourable weather conditions, only sixty-eight bombers bombed Handorf airfield, the primary target, and 205 bombed the secondary target, the city of Brunswick, and 423 others bombed targets of opportunity. For 1st Lieutenant Joe Wroblewski, a pilot in the 351st, it was his first mission as pilot in command. 'We had a mixture of five crews. We were briefed to go to Lippstadt, Germany, getting up at 0230. I didn't get much sleep. I flew *Shady Lady II* on her thirteenth mission without knowing it 'till we got back.'

Twenty-eight aircraft were lost, mostly to fighters. Ignoring what appeared to be certain death, the pilot and co-pilot of *Four Freedoms* in the 452nd refused to bail out of their battered and wrecked B-17. Eight of the crew had bailed out over enemy territory because all hope had been given up for the plane. *Four Freedoms* was torn apart by enemy fighter machine-gun fire and flak hits. The pilot, 1st Lieutenant John J. Pesch, of Mespeth, Long Island, New York, said that just before the target, fighter-producing Brunswick, was reached, thirty Focke Wulfs and Bf 109s swooped down on the formation and singled out his Fortress, among others, in their first attack. Their 20 mm cannon and machine guns blazed away at the Fortress. Two of the four engines were shot out of commission; part of the wings was shot off, the ailerons were wrecked and the control cables were blown apart. The right waist gunner was shot in the head by one of the 20 mm shells. He was slowly dying, blood pouring from his gaping wounds. The crew members put his chute on and dropped him out of the plane so proper medical aid could be given him when captured. That was their only chance of saving his life.

They dropped out of formation and tried to limp back home. They didn't turn back until they had dropped their bombs on the target. They were alone in the enemy-filled skies over Germany. Seven other crew members had now bailed out as all signs pointed that the Fort would never make it home. The co-pilot, 2nd Lieutenant Joyce C. Amley, was told to bail out; he refused. He told the pilot that two were needed to keep the ship in control and he was determined to take the gamble with him. The blown out control cables were the main cause of trouble. 'We flew the plane with our knees locked and braced against the steering control column,' recalled pilot Pesch. 'It was like trying to steer a bucking bronco on the loose,' he said. While flying over the Channel, the Germans opened fire on the ship. She received about 100 hits.' One bullet pierced the co-pilot's window and barely missed his head. The two members crash-landed the *Four Freedoms* at Deopham Green. Neither of the two was injured; the B-17 was a total loss.

At 0045 hours on Friday 24 March, a PFF crew in the 305th took off in their B-17 from Chelveston to fly to Deenethorpe to lead the mission to Schweinfurt when the aircraft stalled at 200 feet and crashed into a barracks site about 1,200 to 1,400 yards from the end of the north–south runway, and then into a cottage at Yielden village in Bedfordshire. Eight members of the 876th Chemical Company inside their billet were killed, as were 1st Lieutenant W. D. Sellers and the crew of the aircraft and the assistant crew chief who was flying with them. The aircraft burst into flames on hitting the cottage and Mr and Mrs W. Phillips were injured and their two children were killed in the blaze.

At around 3 a.m. at Attlebridge, Major Herman A. Laubrich, the 785th Squadron CO, broke into the crew room where Claude V. 'Mac' Meconis, co-pilot on B-24 the *SNAFU SNARK*, was sleeping, to help awaken the crew and give them a ride to the mess hall. It did not take Meconis long to dress because he had spent most of the night before arranging everything, including his personal effects, in preparation for this first mission, the third one for the group. He was in his ODs in a flash, grabbed the letter he had written his wife and bolted out the door after the navigator and the bombardier. The pilot tagged along as usual. That letter Meconis wrote his wife, he mailed at the mess hall, wondering at the time, like most of the fellows, if it were possibly the last his wife would ever receive from him. Just the usual random thoughts a fellow had when he knew that there was a chance, after all, that the first may be the last. Two days' missions before had seen four planes lost, not all through enemy action they knew; nevertheless, it made all of them conscious of the fact that war does have its casualties.

Briefing on the line was like any other briefing they'd had for practice missions, except that an atmosphere of intentness prevailed and Meconis thought he saw the briefing officer's finger quiver as he pointed out flak areas and the route on the large map of Europe in the war room. Their target, as originally briefed, was an advanced German flying school at Essay airfield near Nancy in France, but another order received later directed them to another target and assigned more fighter groups to protect them. It was not until they were almost ready to take off that their original target was reinstated. Navigators were unhappy about all the last-minute changes since it meant a lot of recalculating on their part. Before they broke up briefing to don their flying clothes and go out to their ships, Colonel Arthur J. Pierce, the Group Commander, had a few last words to say to the boys: 'It's a pretty nice mission,' he said, 'and I'd like to go along, but I haven't been able to talk Major Hamel [Roger C., 784th Squadron CO] into letting me take his place. All I can do is wish you luck and give a little advice. You've proved you can fly in formation. All right, now relax and keep up the good work.' Crews rode trucks out to their Liberators in darkness. It was almost dawn. Crews loaded and checked their guns. The bombs, fifty-two incendiaries, were clustered in the bays, ready for the trip over.

1st Lieutenant Albert L. Northrup Jr's crew at Seething had been among those aroused at 0230.

Wallace Patterson, the bombardier, wrote:

We took off in fog and haxe so thick that we couldn't see the end of the runway, after a big delay when one of the ships stuck in the mud on the taxi strip. We had to fly through 5,000 feet of cloud before we broke through and then only caught the formation just before zero hour. We were carrying incendiaries. Just after reaching the French coast we got flak which was intense but not on our position. As there were only two groups of us, the others caught most of the stuff but two of our ships got hit and aborted, bringing back six wounded men to the base. We could see ground then all the way to the target and back to England. We passed close to Paris, which was partly covered with a smoke screen. But the Eiffel Tower stuck up like a sore thumb. We got some flak on the way but none at the target and no bombs were dropped by our group – why, I don't really know. We also tried to run on a secondary target but that failed too. Some of the ships brought their bombs back. We threw ours into the Channel. Some of the crews and our gunners said they saw some green flak. Our closest call was a near series of collisions when we met another formation at about a 45° angle and flew right through them. Planes were dodging all over the place and doing apparently impossible manoeuvres for a B-24. We saw some flak on the way home. Fighter support was very strong and we did not see a single German fighter. Every Jerry airfield we passed seemed plane-less. This mission gave me the Air Medal.

At Attlebridge, the *SNAFU SNARK* was the first Liberator back. Claude Meconis felt good to see all the familiar faces beaming at them and holding their thumbs up as they taxied back to their revetment, where the crew chief and assistant were waiting, grinning from ear to ear with joy over seeing them back. There was nothing quite like the sweet feel of terra firma under foot when he jumped out of the B-24 and knew that they had survived the first one, that they had now seen action – even if it was only light. Coffee and donuts, even oranges, were waiting for them back at the briefing room. Plenty of Scotch too, during interrogation. Everyone was so serious, long faced Meconis could not help breaking out with laughter at his own attempt to act as if – 'Aw, it was nothing at all.'²⁸

On Sunday 26 March, crews were scheduled for a mission to Leipzig but it was scrubbed and nearly 500 B-17s and B-24s bombed V-weapon installations and targets of opportunity in the Pas de Calais and Cherbourg areas. On the mission to Watten, *Omar The Dentmaker* in the 401st, flown by Captain William M. Rumsey Jr of Folson City, California, received a direct flak hit between the No. 3 and No. 4 engines, exploding in the Tokyo tank and breaking off the wing. The aircraft was observed to spin down on fire, the flames spreading back to the waist. Sergeant J. B. Carson the tail gunner was seen to leave the tail position before *Omar The Dentmaker* exploded and crashed at Pouquemaison, just south of Frevent. The bombardier, 1st Lieutenant J. D. Baeffner, was the only other survivor.

Al Saunders wrote:

We were briefed at 0500 on a suicide mission. The target was Zeichen and we were to fly within 30 miles of Berlin to try and get the fighters to come up, then 150 miles south to the target or the secondary, Schweinfurt, then home through Happy Valley. They scrubbed it at 0630 and until eleven we waited for another target. We got a No ball just west of Abbeville, one of the worst flak areas on the so-called invasion coast of France. We were carrying 'G.P.' our puppy. For the first time I rode the whole trip on the flight deck and let Rod do the toggling. Lovell rode the nose turret. The lead navigator did a wonderful job of dodging the flak areas, plus evasive action by the pilots and staff. We caught heavy flak only at Abbeville and then only because we were on the bombing run. We lost no ships and were ourselves unscratched but the lead navigator lost a fingertip and two enlisted men in another ship were wounded. Coming back we flew over the Thames Estuary and had a beautiful view of a big convoy going out through the anti-submarine net, flying balloons. Also there were many warships and invasion barges parked around the harbour and at the dock. The Limeys threw bursts of flak at us and some of these days we'd pay the bastards back, with interest. This was my sixth mission. Bill had twelve now, Rod eight and Hoffman seven. The rest had ten and would get a cluster to their Air Medal. I went to town as soon as we got back and went to a dance. There was whiskey after the mission and at the dance and in my tired condition I was still a bit muzzy.

On Monday 27 March the three divisions dispatched 714 bombers escorted by 960 fighters to hit airfields and air depots in central and southern France. Charlie Herbst in the 466th at Attlebridge flew his third mission, in *Jamaica?*, 'and it was,' he wrote, 'a real long one'.

Going down to the Bay of Biscay near the Spanish border for a visit to a Luftwaffe training base at Biarritz. Seems they have been getting a lot of pilots from this school and we were to interrupt their education. The formation was lousy all the way, for we took off in lousy weather and couldn't get together like we should. Both our wing men never appeared but we found out later they had run together right after taking off. This was the first loss of any of our real close friends. The first quatrains in did a good job, one of them cut us off and we had to make a second run, much to our dislike. Even with this we missed the target completely, for the lead ship's bomb sight screwed up. As we dropped the bombs the ship on our right started something really new by letting its bombs explode before they reached the ground. They got a lot of 'hold' in their bomb bay, but that is about all. The 'girl' got damaged for the first time with a few small holes in her right wing. It wasn't due to enemy action so no Purple Heart this time. As we came up the coast the gunners on the ground figured they needed some practice so they opened up and got plenty close for awhile. The weather was plenty bad when we got back to England (by the way, that is where all these trips are starting), as usual and the formation broke up. We were on our own and the old girl needed gas, so we dropped in at a Limey base for the night, got gas the next morning and headed for home base.

Six bombers were lost and ten of the escort failed to return.
Al Saunders' crew had a rest on 27 March.

Bill made some pretty good fudge out of D-ration chocolate. We found an egg-legger who sold us two dozen at nine shillings a dozen; so we ate them all day. Even the dog ate one. Next day the group was going to hit Ijmuiden in Holland with 2,000-pounders but they were recalled from out in the Channel and nearly had to land at another field. But the weather cleared up in a little while. We were back on the alert list for the 29th and the red light showed that the target was already in. We all went to a show in Norwich in the afternoon. The 29th was another No Ball, very near Watten. We still carried the 2,000-pounders that they didn't drop the day before. It was a Pathfinder mission. With a very low ceiling we experienced the unpleasant job of going up and down through 5,000 feet of clouds and the clouds were full of ice, some pieces so large that we could hear them bang on the ship. The boys saw two planes from another group collide and break up in the air, with only two chutes opening. Another ship from our group dropped a bomb in the Channel or over England by accident. Over the target and on the whole trip, which involved only fifteen minutes in enemy territory, the flak was negligible for us, though some of the ships in the first section got hit. Bombing was very spasmodic. We dropped on our wing ship. Some didn't drop at all or dropped only part of their load. A few minutes after we landed it started raining and continued ever since. For some reason we were alerted again. Bitching about it probably would not do any good but we tried. The doctors said that we should not have to fly more than three days in a row. Thornton came in just after we'd retired and said the target was to be Berlin. All of a sudden I developed a baseball in my stomach and I guessed I was not the only one but oddly enough I was still able to sleep well even when I knew it was going to be a rough one. I had become a trifle more nervous after I got in the ship, until we hit the enemy coast; then it all seemed to go away with the coming of the necessity for alertness.

The roar of bombers overhead was an everyday occurrence in the skies over East Anglia. Americans took the British children to their hearts and many rode their bikes out to the bases in the early morning to watch the planes take off and again when the planes returned. They were genuinely sorry when they saw their aircraft limp back full of holes with wounded aboard. Wednesday 29 March started like any other day did in 1944 for Gordon Reynolds, a young lad cycling with his mate the 3 miles to the Hall gardens, where they both worked as gardeners to the Lord Lieutenant of the County. Given their day's work by the head gardener, both boys then got on with their duties, while above them in the clear morning sky, B-

24s, heavily laden with bombs and fuel, were climbing to get in formation before making their way to their target in France (Watten). Suddenly, above the usual roar of the engines, a ghastly high-pitched noise of engines in trouble broke the air. Looking skyward, Gordon Reynolds saw to his horror two B-24s locked together for a moment and then one of them breaking in half. With that still ghastly noise, both stricken B-24s plunged earthwards, leaving a trail of wreckage in the sky. Gordon feared that both would end up on top of him.

Now above him he heard a new noise. It was of falling bombs, whistling down. He then prayed – he had to, as he was sure his young life would soon be over. The two bombs (each 2,000 lbs) exploded on the parkland near the Earl's Hall. Not a pane of glass remained in any window, thick plate glass littered the lawns and not a leaf remained on the trees that grew in the park. Cattle were charging about the park, terrified of all the noise (it was many a day before the milk yield got back to normal). Earth and bomb fragments were still flying through the air, as the two stricken B-24s crashed into the ground not more than a quarter of a mile apart. The nearest to the lads was no more than a stone's throw away and in one moment both thoughts were for the crew trapped in the wreckage.

Running across the parkland to the crash, the boys suddenly saw the earth and wreckage rise into the air (one 2,000 lb bomb had exploded). They dived into the soft earth as once again earth and steel flew through the air. One fragment of a bomb embedded itself into the earth close by. The blast and fumes took their breath away for a while and when they recovered, a sight laid before them never to be forgotten. A burning mass of metal and flesh was strewn about them. Nothing could be done and with heavy hearts they returned to their work while airmen from the nearby airbase arrived to put out the flames. This was not to be the end of the boys' ordeal. Shortly after returning to their work, there was another terrific explosion as the second 2,000 lb bomb went off in the already wrecked plane. Blast and metal again tore through the air to tear into the ground inches away from the boys, who by now were just about shattered. The head gardener was at his wits' end (all his glass houses were wrecked) and he sent the boys home.

The two B-24s[29] that crashed that fateful morning were from the 93rd at Hardwick. Only two crewmen survived; they were the waist gunners in the aircraft that was sliced in two. Eighteen other crewmen were killed and when the second bomb went off while rescue attempts were being made, another nineteen personnel were killed. Forty-two others, including four civilians, were injured. Nothing now remains to show what happened that morning except to those who were there, a top of a tree missing, a burn mark where bark should be, but most of all quietness now reigns over the spot where so long ago many young American lives were lost and left a scar in the memory of a young lad.[30]

Unteroffizier Albert 'Addi' Böckl was trying to relax and unwind. It was the morning of Saturday 1 April and he and his fellow pilots in the 12th Staffel, JG 26, had just landed back at Laon-Athies airfield in France after combat north-west of Reims with Liberators heading for the chemical works at Ludwigshafen. Thick cloud had grounded the 1st Division and all 192 B-24s of the 3rd Division were forced to abandon the mission over France, leaving fifty-four B-24s to continue to the target while 162 B-24s bombed targets of opportunity at Pforzheim near Karlsruhe and Grafenhausen. The First and Third Gruppen, JG 26, had met II/JG 2 and combined to attack the 20th Combat Wing north-west of Reims. At 1150 hours Böckl singled out a B-24 – it was *Judith Lynn*, flown by Lieutenant Joseph M. Soznoz in the 329th Squadron, 93rd Bomb Group – and claimed it as destroyed although he had to share the Abschuss with two of the JG 2 pilots.[31] The air battle was not all one-sided. The engine of Unteroffizier Kurt Hofer's Focke Wulf 190A-7 in the 3rd Staffel, JG 26, was hit by return fire from the Liberators and he died in the wreckage after trying to force land north of Reims-Pont Faverger.[32] One by one the remaining Focke Wulf 190s, low on fuel and ammunition, landed. Schwarzemenn or 'Black men', as the ground crewmen were called because of their black coveralls, swarmed over the aircraft, feverishly refuelling and rearming them while the pilots ate a hurried lunch and awaited the return of the bombers, which could be expected later in the afternoon.

Stronger-than-forecast tail winds forced the Liberator formations to zigzag in an effort to maintain course and direction. Lieutenant Richard L. Henderson, who was flying in the second element of the first section on Lieutenant Harrison Mellor's left wing, recalls:

The target area was about $8/10$ covered and we stooged around hunting the target for an hour and twenty minutes. That is what made the difference between some of us getting back and some not making it. We finally found a large town and dropped our bombs on a railroad terminal, by this time we were south of where we should have been.

At the target chaos ensued when PFF equipment in the 448th lead ship malfunctioned. Colonel James Thompson, CO of the 448th Bomb Group, who was flying as Command Pilot in the lead aircraft, which was flown by Lieutenant Alan Teague, decided to maintain the lead. During the confusion the 14th and 2nd

Bomb Wings diverged from the 20th Bomb Wing course and flew further to the east. Thompson ordered a 180° turn in order to rejoin the other two wings but they too experienced PFF failure.[33] The 448th picked out a town and twenty-one aircraft released their bombs over what they believed to be Pforzheim but was the Swiss town of Schauffhausen. The excessive manoeuvring consumed more fuel than planned and the stronger than expected tailwinds now became headwinds as Richard L. Henderson recalled.

> There was a terrific wind blowing head-on about 104 mph. We had taken off with 2,300 gallons of gas excepting to be back on the ground at 1245. But at 1245 we were still an hour inside enemy territory. We were supposed to hit the Channel at 1203. We didn't get there until 1346, an hour and 43 minutes late. That was too late for some.

As they turned for home, the crews faced a dangerous trip in enemy skies with very low fuel levels. With only forty gallons of fuel remaining, Lieutenant Harrison Mellor gave the bail out order 50 miles north of Paris. Everyone made it out safely but one of the crew was killed when his parachute failed to open. Mellor made it, just, after he experienced initial problems with his chute. Teague's aircraft was next to fall out of formation. He ordered his crew out over France before preparing to crash-land and then destroy the B-24 on the ground but Colonel Thompson suddenly reappeared on the flight deck and returned to his seat. Then Thompson said he was leaving and he once again left the flight deck. It was the last time anyone saw him alive. He bailed out but was too low and his parachute failed to open. Teague successfully crash-landed the B-24 in an open field and got away from the scene but when he returned to destroy the plane and all its equipment he was captured by a German patrol.[34]

As luck would have it, when the Third Gruppe took off again it found the only unescorted Liberator Group, the 448th, whose aircraft and crews were off course after bombing the target. Leutnant Peter Reischer and Unteroffizier Heinz Gerhke of JG 26 claimed two 448th B-24s in the Reims-St-Pol area, although these had run almost out of fuel and the crews had already decided to bail out. One of these was probably *Crud Wagon*, flown by Lieutenant Charles 'Chick' Knorr, whose crew bailed out after the plane ran out of gas. Richard Henderson, who had seen Mellor run out of fuel and feather the No. 4 before they started down, bailing out as they went, saw Knorr's ship go down in thin cloud beside him. Henderson decided that he must write to Knorr's wife. He also saw *Eastern Queen*, flown by

Lieutenant Kenneth Weaver, go down. Weaver nearly made it because he was still with Henderson almost to the French coast but they had to bail out. Nine of the crew survived but one man died when his parachute failed to open. Weaver and the others were captured immediately.

When the 4th Staffel duty Schwarm was scrambled from Courtrai-Wevelghem, they located a 448th Liberator struggling across the Pas de Calais. It was *Black Widow*, which was being flown by Lieutenant Jack Black. Flak had damaged one of his engines over Roubaix but Black and his crew had elected to try to make England. Over the Pas de Calais another engine failed and they began descending. A third engine quit shortly afterwards. Small arms fire from troops along the coast peppered the plane as they headed out to sea. Oberfeldwebel Erich Schwartz attacked and claimed *Black Widow* as destroyed but the Liberator continued on one engine before Black finally ditched in the Channel at a point 15 miles off the coast of Dunkirk. *Black Widow* struck the cold, choppy sea at 80–90 mph. It was like hitting a brick wall. Black and his co-pilot, Lieutenant Joseph Pomfret, were badly injured in the ditching because 448th B-24s were not fitted with shoulder harnesses. All the crew were seriously injured but the B-24 stayed together long enough for the ten men to get out and climb into the inflatable life rafts, which the radio operator, Sergeant Eugene Dworaczyk, swam inside the half-filled B-24 and worked underwater to free. Dworaczyk later was awarded the Soldier's medal for this action. Pomfret, who in fact had been thrown out of his seat through the cockpit to the outside on impact with the water, could not swim. The navigator, Lieutenant Peter Wermert, held the injured co-pilot until finally, weakened by the cold water, he was forced to release him or go under himself. Pomfret cried frantically for help but drowned before anyone could reach him. Once in the life rafts it soon became apparent that Sergeant Charles Nissen was injured and suffering from shock. Without the necessary medical attention, his fellow crew were unable to save him and he died of his injuries. The ball turret gunner suffered injuries but his broken jaw and collarbone were not life threatening. Favourable winds miraculously blew the dinghies across the Channel to within 5 miles of the English coast and after forty-four hours adrift they were finally rescued in the Straits of Dover by Bert May and his crew of *The Three Brothers* fishing boat from Folkestone.

At Seething, Richard Henderson's B-24 was the fourth one back. He was sweating his gas but thought that he had enough to make it back to the home field, but No. 2 ran out just as he passed over the fighter base at Wattisham, so he throttled back and landed there to refuel. He took right off for home, where they were 'really sweating everyone out'. All except two ships 'had stopped for gas somewhere'. Henderson concludes: 'It was the biggest single loss that the Group had suffered to date. The PFF equipment didn't work and that, combined with poor navigation and the strong wind against us on the way back, was the cause.'

Colonel Jerry Mason, who took command of the 448th two weeks later, arranged for the frustrated fighter pilot[35] to transfer to P-51 Mustangs in May after the twenty-two-year-old pilot had flown his tour of thirty bombing missions. Henderson flew sixty-eight combat sorties in the 352nd Fighter Group at Bodney. Mostly they were escort for the bombers.

The 1 April mission cost the 2nd Division ten B-24s. One of those in the 'Travelling Circus' who made it back was Lieutenant Joseph A. Buland, whose bombardier Charles Clague and the navigator, Howie Mesnard, were from Mitch Mitchell's crew. It turned out to be the roughest mission yet for the two young officers. Mesnard recalls:

For a time, the assembly of a formation was extremely dangerous; several ships collided. Pilots had difficulty visually distinguishing which was the lead aircraft. Eventually, each group resorted to a target ship on which to assemble. This aircraft was garishly painted or marked with huge polka dots, stripes or other markings so it could be readily seen. At Hardwick the first ship off was always the *Ball Of Fire*. This ship had flown over 100 missions and had been patched and rebuilt so many times that it was no longer serviceable for combat. It was equipped with several flare guns and extra turrets to act as a flying beacon to guide ships from our group into formation. The forming procedure for the group normally took approximately forty-five minutes. The *Ball of Fire* would be shooting red-yellow flares every minute so it could be identified from several miles away. We would also often see two or three other groups forming up on other coloured flares. As soon as the group, which consisted normally of three squadrons of twelve to fifteen planes each, was formed, the *Ball of Fire* would return to base. It was then up to the lead crew to make the prescribed rendezvous with the other groups, which made up the 8th Air Force. This timing had to be accurate to within thirty seconds, altitude within 500 feet and direction right on course.

I worked diligently as we crossed the English Channel and I was fortunate in pinpointing our position as we crossed the coast, which enabled me to calculate the wind direction and velocity for the past hour quite accurately. Surprisingly, my new wind was from the north while the weather officer had briefed us for a head wind of 40 knots. Consequently, with this tail wind, our ground speed was 80 knots faster than anticipated. We were flying deputy lead position, so my responsibility was to determine where we had been rather than lead the group to the target. After close to two hours of flying south over $^{10}/_{10}$ cloud cover, we finally saw a hole in the clouds, which the lead ship guided us through. He proceeded to make a 180° turn and, flying north, followed a large river. I was amazed when Charlie Clague called to say the leader had opened his bomb doors, indicating the target was only a few minutes away. My calculation showed we were over Switzerland while apparently the lead ship, using the wrong wind, figured we were several hundred miles further north and were approaching Ludwigshafen. Sure enough, the lead bombardier dropped his load and all others in the group followed, completely devastating an industrial plant on the edge of the town. The lead ship was severely hit by flak and fell behind the formation. Eight chutes were seen to leave seconds before the plane exploded in mid-air. It was then our responsibility to lead the group home. We immediately climbed approximately 4,000 feet to get above the clouds and as we emerged into the sunshine we heard, "Fighters 9 o'clock high," shouted by the engineer from the top gun turret. In a minute fifteen to twenty specks had grown to full size as they swept through our formation.

All machine guns in the group were chattering at the same time. We could see the fire from Luftwaffe gun muzzles and the path of the tracer bullets as they ripped through our formation during the brief encounter. They came so close I felt I could have knocked one down with a baseball bat. This group of about twenty German fighters dove through our group, knocking down three ships on their first pass. When the enemy fighters appeared head-on, machine-gun bullets smashed through the nose of our ship and passed between my legs. Charlie was sitting under the navigation table. He got a glimpse of the fighters and instinctively threw his gloved hands in front of his face and felt shattered pieces of glass hitting his gloves. Both of my pant legs were torn and one was smouldering, probably caused by a tracer bullet. Charlie asked me if I was all right. I was asking the same! We couldn't believe that neither of us had been hit. Two fuel cells exploded and the hydraulic system was shot out. We maintained a tight formation for the next half-hour and had a running battle with them all the way. Our ship was badly damaged and an explosion had produced a bubble at least six feet long and two feet wide where the wing was attached to the fuselage but we did not catch fire.

As we were almost out of fuel, we were given permission to land on the grassy section of the field at Hardwick because other planes with wounded aboard had first priority on the paved landing strip. When Buland tried to lower the landing gear, only the main wheels came down. Quick investigation showed that the linkage on the nose wheel had been smashed during the enemy attack. The nose wheel was pivoted in the rear and folded up and forward so the wind would slap it down into position if this fouled up linkage could be cleared. The engineer took a machine gun barrel from one of the guns and strained desperately to pry it loose. Suddenly it gave way; the strut snapped into position. Buland brought the ship down in a perfect landing on two wheels until our airspeed was no longer sufficient to hold it up. Our damaged nose gear then failed, a wing tip touched the ground. The plane spun around violently and as it stopped, the crew emerged from all available openings. Buland came out of the top hatch and ran along the wing, so concerned with getting away from the burning ship that he fell head-long off the wing tip. We all took cover in a near-by ditch while we watched the firemen hose down the battered plane. At headquarters, I told my story that I thought we had bombed Switzerland rather than the assigned target and of the ensuing fighter attacks.[36]

On 5 April, Charlie Herbst in the 466th flew his fourth mission:

This is another trip into France, for the Jerries seem to be building things in this area that the higher-ups don't like, so we get the job of visiting them to see what we can do to hinder their building program. Today the weather was different with the clear weather over England and all the clouds over the continent. We followed a radar ship in and dropped our bombs through the clouds. Couldn't see the ground at all and were happy about the whole thing. Those guys around that area have had a lot of practice shooting at planes and are plenty good, but with clouds as they were, guess they didn't want to bother too much. The boys at Dunkirk were ambitious, for they shot up quite a bit but we were five miles from there. Later on, from all reports this was one of the first trips against the flying bomb sites.

When bombing northern Germany, Groups were often routed into the Continent over the Zuider Zee, where the North Sea spills into Holland. Bill McCullah recalls:

Due to the presence of a magna cum laude flak gunner who operated a tower on the north shore, flying the Zuider was extremely hazardous. Air Corps' Brass kept sending us through his gauntlet. Their judgment was almost sacrificial! The man could shoot! To say he was 'good' was understatement. 'Great' best describes him! He took out one or more of our planes every time we came within his range but they continued sending us his way. His presence gnawed me, wondering if we would 'get it' the next time around. Many in the 448th felt the same. We simultaneously admired and hated the sonofabitch! Some year's prior, Guy Lombardo the Royal Canadians' bandleader recorded a hit tune titled Down By the Zuider Zee. It was played and sung in a soft, lilting melody. The piece was catchy and popular. When flying the Zuider route, that tune played in the back of my mind. It wouldn't go away, ragging me! My one-line version of the song was, 'I went down by the Zuider Zee!' (An omen?) Returning via the Zuider Zee, one of our planes dropped from formation. With all fans spinning, nothing seemed wrong but we couldn't contact the pilot. Believing him in trouble, we watched his plane descend. Diverted, we stopped watching. A half-hour later we could see the dreaded flak tower. We also saw something else. A B-24 was on the deck, making a straight-line run on the tower. Boring in, straight and level, the bombardier salvoed his bombs into the tower, blowing it to hell and gone! The pilot, a major, knowing we would return via the Zuider, had deliberately held his bombs. It was 'Payback Time!' We laughed and cheered the crazy bastard! He was our kind! Headquarters never mentioned it. We have a saying in the Missouri Ozarks that goes, 'The sun don't shine on the same dog's ass all the time!'

On a mission over southern France, Raymond Giwogna and I switched positions, putting me in the tail with Raymond in the nose. On the bomb run, in light flak, I watched the plane 200 feet behind drop his bombs. We carried clusters, three 100-lb high explosive bombs on each rack. Each cluster was secured by a metal band that fell away when the bombs were dropped and they commenced to separate. When they did, the bombs from one of the clusters bumped together and then went 'BLOOMMM!', blowing up the remaining bombs. The sky behind me exploded 150 feet beneath the dropping aircraft in the biggest explosion I ever saw. The B-24 was blown apart behind the ball turret, cleanly separating the plane into two pieces. The big gaping hole in the aft section revealed the four rear gunners, as they scrambled to get out. The tail section, catching the wind, slowed, almost stopped but maintained straight and level flight. One by one, the gunners stepped over the edge, into space. Losing its forward momentum, the tail section slowly, then faster, began to spin. The front section, all propellers turning, flew on as though nothing had happened. Ever so slowly it began to veer right.

"Get out, get out. Get out of there," I shouted!

Probably two minutes passed before the six airmen cleared the front bomb bay. "Hooray, all made it!" The front section slowly careened to the right and then went into a tight spin. The entire display was accomplished in exasperating slow motion. The bumping bombs should not have exploded. Strong winds inside the open bomb bays could have rotated a propeller driven, bomb arming mechanism, thereby arming one or more of the impact fuses. It could have happened and I say that it did happen! (I saw arming vanes rotate in open bomb bays.)

I again flew the tail position over southern France when a Messerschmitt 109 popped out of nowhere, laying-off and holding 30 feet directly behind *Boomerang*. He was close; close enough that I could clearly see the pilot's face. There he sat, perfectly framed in my gun-sight reticle. All I had to do was depress my right thumb and I would blow him out of the sky! I had him cold turkey! It was a no deflection, straightaway, dead-on shot. I wanted that 109 and wanted it badly but I could not fire because one of our B-24s flew 100 feet directly behind him! I was helpless to do anything but watch. Conversely, had the nose turret gunner in the B-24 behind us fired, he would have taken-out the 109 as well as us! Had the Me 109 taken us out, the nose gunner in the following B-24 would have wasted him! It was a Mexican Stand Off. No one fired. That 109 pilot, knowing our predicament, controlled the deck of cards. He may have planned it that way. Had he fired, all of us were dead ducks! The German pilot may have been sick and tired of the war. Seeing our helpless situation and knowing that he held the face cards, he could have played God! He may have thought, "They know! I'll just give these guys a break!" Who am I to argue with that?

At Seething, Bill McCullah reckoned 448th pilots admired 2nd Lieutenant Kent C. Mosley, saying:

He could fly the crates that the Liberators came in. Mosley was twenty, the youngest first pilot in the Group. Shot-up badly by flak in *Bucket of Bolts*, he limped home from Germany. Crew 11, back on the ground, thought for sure that we had lost him. I watched Mosley right after he was hit. He put his plane through the damnedest diddles one could ever imagine for a heavy bomber. Most unique were three, out-of-control, inside loops. It was just breathtaking! Shortly after he was hit, he went into a steep dive. It seemed he would never recover, going down, down, down, finally bottoming. Appearing to over-control, he brought it up, up, up, climbing, climbing, climbing. The plane rolled onto its back at the top, hanging, almost stopping. Falling off the top, he again went down,

down, down, thousands of feet below. Three times he regained some semblance
of control only to repeat the process again. The long Davis Wing was curved
and bent with the terrible stresses encountered, similar to a fully drawn archer's
bow. (I marvelled that his plane held together.) Following his third loop, near
the ground, he disappeared from view. Mosley rewrote the book on flying the B-
24. Imagine, looping-the-loop, three times, in a Liberator! Why his crew did not
jump and why his wing did not collapse, I will never understand. Mosley's capers
were the talk of the flight line. Flight crews hung around the tower, waiting to
see if Mosley would make it back to Seething. (Nobody thought that he would,
or could!) Forty-five minutes later, there he was, approaching the runway.
Shooting red flares, he barely managed to keep his plane in the air. Missing his
first approach, he went around. Troops clapped, cheered and shouted as Mosley
finally wrestled the plane onto the runway. He shut down engines, leaving it
where it sat, on the runway. It was damaged so badly that a bulldozer pushed
it to the side, leaving it beside the runway, an ignominious end for a gallant
airplane. There, *Bucket of Bolts* remained, just off the runway, until the day I
departed Seething. The plane was a total wreck, containing thousands of holes
throughout. Several holes were over three feet wide, big enough to walk through.
The plane was virtually shot to pieces, front to back. By some miracle, no one
was injured. Pilots and others pounded Mosley on the back, congratulating him.
Mosley did a lot of grinning. For Mosley to have done such a great job of flying
was to no avail. What a pilot he was![37]

CHAPTER 5

The Quick and the Dead

Crew 11 completed fifteen missions with ten remaining when General Jimmy Doolittle of Tokyo bombing fame replaced General Ira Eaker as Commander, 8th Air Force. Doolittle hadn't enough time to hang up his hat when he announced that total mission numbers had been changed from twenty-five to thirty! That was a death sentence! Keep adding numbers and there was no way anyone would get through the war. I took it personally. "Goddam him!" I said, pissed to high heaven. "That sonofabitch is going to get all of us killed!" A few days passed and he changed it to thirty-five! How I did cuss Doolittle again. It was a Judge Roy Bean, 'the law west of the Pecos', sentence. I had been sentenced 'to hang by my neck until I was dead!' The second order was modified. Thirty missions were required of lead crews. Better than thirty-five but still more than we had bargained for. That stuck. That's what we ended up flying but still it was not fair. We were not 'Johnnie Come Latelys!' We had flown the tough missions, without fighter escort. Then along comes this bastard, changing horses in mid-stream. From the first change order, I had no use for Jimmy Doolittle. Fifty years later, I learned that it was 5-star General Henry (Hap) Arnold who issued those orders, not Doolittle. Sorry about that, Boss.

Staff Sergeant Bill McCullah, 448th Bomb Group.

On Saturday 8 April the cloudy conditions abated and allowed the bombers to assemble in force. Thirteen combat wings consisting of 644 bombers in the 1st and 3rd division groups all had airfields and aircraft depots throughout western Germany as their primary targets while 192 Liberators were detailed to bomb an aircraft plant at Brunswick. The escort force was made up of 780 fighters but thirty-four heavies, twenty-three of them Liberators, were shot down. Worst hit was the 466th, which lost ten B-24s. The 445th lead ship, with Lieutenant-Colonel Robert Terrill, the CO, aboard, had two engines knocked out by flak over the target. Despite this, Terrill succeeded in bringing his bomber home on the two remaining engines and was later awarded the DFC by Colonel Ted Timberlake.

Once a bomber became 'theirs', no one liked flying in replacement aircraft, but Elwood Nothstein and the rest of his crew in the 466th at Attlebridge flew their first mission in a strange ship because *Jamaica?* was being test loaded with 2,000-lb bombs. Nothstein said:

> Funny to fly in someone else's ship, but that is the way it goes. The object of the visit was an airfield near Brunswick. Seems they were building parts for a lot of airplanes down there that may someday come up and try to get us. It was a very clear day and gave us our first good look at the 'Fatherland'. After going and wrecking so many of the Fuhrer's airfields he is getting mad at us. Everything went along fine until we got near the target and the outfits ahead of us started to call for help, as the Luftwaffe was up 'in full strength'. We didn't mind this too much, although it had us worried for a while. The flak was plenty heavy as we made our bomb run and had turned for home when they came after us. They had pulled up ahead of us and were in the sun and high. The nose gunner opened up first and they came at the formation in a pack, both Me 109s and Fw 190s. They swept through the formation firing everything they had but not picking on any ship in particular. On the first pass one of our planes went down but for it we got six of them. They swept on down and came around to get at the 'Purple Heart Corner' (last flight of the group or squadron). The boys on our ships did a good job down there but we were more interested in a bunch that was gathering up in front of us again. They came in and made a sweep at the lead squadron. One of them must have been trying to save gas, for he came in slower than the rest. We poured the lead to him and he went out faster than he came in, blowing up right over our ship. The rest of the group was taking a beating but being in the lead flight we got away very easy, as they only made the initial pass at us and then went after the rear flights. We lost five more behind us but took our toll which at final counting was twenty-five. This was a horrible fascination for us. When we got back to the base we found only one hole in our ship, which was damn good luck. The group lost six ships and a lot of those that got back had wounded on board. The trips were starting to lose the interest we had in them at first; guess all the 'glory' has worn off of them and it was now just a 'dirty job'.[1]

Despite the loss of one combat wing and some combat boxes from another, on Easter Sunday, 9 April, ninety-eight B-17s in the 1st Division placed 71 per cent of their bombs within 1,000 feet of the MPI at the Fw 190 plant at Marienburg. Leaving the target, the B-17s received radio orders to join thirty-three B-17s of the 3rd Division, which had bombed the Fw 190 plant at Poznan, for mutual protection but before they could rendezvous the 3rd Division came under heavy fighter attack. The leading 45th Wing bore the brunt of the attacks but stout defending by the Fortress gunners kept losses down to just two aircraft. Meanwhile, a further eighty-six B-17s bombed the Heinkel plant at Warnemünde, while forty B-17s bombed the airfield at Rahmel and forty-six B-17s bombed airfields at Parchim and Rostock.

At Deenthorpe, the 401st was missing two Fortresses from the raid on Marienburg. Fw 190s came in line abreast from 12 o'clock high. They blew the nose off 1st Lieutenant William R. Dawes' B-17, which turned on its back and finally crashed into the sea about 2 miles off the northern German shore. There were no survivors. A second Fortress, flown by 2nd Lieutenant G. C. Byrd Jr, also failed to return. 2nd Lieutenant (later Lieutenant-Colonel) Fred B. Calfee, the co-pilot, recalls:

Due to weather it took approximately one hour longer than planned for the formation to group all the big birds and head out for the target. Everything waft pretty much routine until we started flying over Denmark. We received flak damage to the No. 2 engine and knew that we were losing oil. We figured we would continue on to the target and feather the propeller when the oil pressure started to drop. We made it to the target and just as we dropped our bombs on the Me 109 factory. The oil pressure dropped and we activated the feathering button. Unfortunately it did not feather and we had a runaway prop in flat pitch. This caused extreme vibrations throughout the airplane and we could not hold formation. Two or three enemy fighters started making passes at us so we pushed the three remaining throttles forward and said, "OK, if she comes apart so be it." We managed to get back into a loose formation position and started checking our fuel consumption. Needless to say it was quite high with a runaway prop in flat pitch. We kept hoping it would sever the shaft and fly off, but it never did. We computed the time back to England and figured lie would have to land in the North Sea about 250 miles from home base. Sweden was off to our right at this time and the decision was made to divert to the briefed emergency field at Malmö.

The radio operator, Staff Sergeant Joseph Exnowski, remembers:

> I was throwing everything out of the aircraft to lighten it. I blew up the IFF receiver. I ate the secret code for the day which was made of paper that could be eaten. The rest of the radio books I put in a bag loaded with .50 cal empty casings and threw it overboard into the sea. The only thing we did not throw out were our machine guns and ammunition in case we had to use them before we got to Sweden.

Fred Calfee concludes: 'We landed safely and were interned until the middle of November when we were exchanged on a one for one basis with the Germans. Delbert Patterson, the top turret gunner on the crew, told me he was sent back to Malmö to assist repairing the engine. It was test flown then put into storage until after the war.'[2]

A single 452nd Fortress, *Silver Shed House*, piloted by 1st Lieutenant James C. Reynolds of Coeymans, New York, became a formation of its own and bombed an important airdrome in northern Germany after the major portion of its bombs had been dropped on its original target, another airdrome in Achmer. When over the airdrome, bombs were released by the bombardier, 2nd Lieutenant Charles Moxhay of Rye, New York. All the bombs dropped except four. Perfect hits on the field and hangers were made. The formation started back to its home base. The navigator, 2nd Lieutenant Joseph F. Olson of Chicago, sighted this second airdrome which the plane was to bomb with its other four bombs. Moxhay called through the interphone, 'I'm going to get that field.' He squatted in the nose of the ship, peered out of the Plexiglas nose, made a V with two fingers of his right hand, made a V with two fingers of his left hand, crossed them over each other so they would imitate a sight, waited until the proper moment came and released the four bombs. His aim was perfect. The bombs fell in the heart of the field, starting a huge fire in what appeared to be a gasoline storage section. The right waist gunner, Captain Harold P. Thoreson of San Bernardino, California, observed three hangers aflame and black smoke pouring 4,000 or 5,000 feet into the air. The co-pilot, 2nd Lieutenant Mark C. Liddell of St Davids, Pennsylvania, commented, 'We conducted a mission of our own within a mission. Moxhay hit the jackpot. He deserves a factory full of cigars for that.'

On Monday 10 April, 730 bombers, including thirty Liberator crews in the 467th Bomb Group at Rackheath, which was making its combat debut under the leadership of the CO, Colonel Albert J. Shower, bombed airfield targets in France and the Low Countries. Colonel Shower referred to his green crews, mostly from jobs in industry and the rolling fields of the vast United States, as 'agriculturists' or 'Aggies' and the name stuck. The group, which was based near a large country estate just a few miles from Norwich, became known unofficially as the Rackheath Aggies. Allan Healy recalls:

> The Air Ministry had built our base. Its plan was far different from that of American bases. There were no serried rows of bleak buildings with grass and trees scraped from the ground and everything barren, efficient, and a scar on the landscape. Rackheath had benefited from the necessities of camouflage. Nissen huts were grouped under tall trees at the edge of woods and in and under them. Roads passed under rows of fruit trees. The farm croft and byre were left untouched. One site was far down by the rhododendron drive, another across the Jersey pasture where the ornamental sheep and tame deer grazed. You walked through bluebell carpeted wood in spring from Site One to the Operations Block, and past straw ricks from there to the Briefing Building. A hedgerow lined the land of a civilian-travelled road right through the base, where, on Sundays, the children stood and asked, "Any gum, chum?" We were impressed by England's state of siege. The wrecked homes and buildings of Norwich showed the ruthless hand of the German bombing that we were about to return to them a thousand fold. Every crossroad had its tank barriers and pillboxes ready for use. We saw how grimly the British citizen was prepared to defend his homeland.[3]

Perry Rudd in the 457th formation, whose target was Evre airfield at Brussels, at first thought that the mission was so low key that he even had time to take snaps of the Belgian capital while he waited for 'bombs away'. Then things changed.

> We made three runs over the target despite the heavy flak. I was sitting in the camera well. Just after 'bombs away' sounded a piece of shrapnel, which had come through the radio room wall, hit me in the back about two inches above the bottom of my flak suit. The whole ship was shot up and we later counted more than 100 holes. Number three and four gas tanks leaked and number four supercharger ran away coming home. The left horizontal stabiliser had a hole in it and another through the elevator. When we got back to Glatton the ship was sent to a sub-depot.

Mitch Mitchell's crew in the 'Travelling Circus' flew the 10 April mission in *Flying Wolves*, an old 'D' model B-24, carrying fifty-two M-47 incendiary bombs to bomb the airfield at Bourges. Howie Mesnard recalls:

We had exhausted our ammunition before we arrived at the coast, so we were relieved when the German fighters gave up the attack and headed for home. Our group immediately started descending so we could remove our oxygen equipment. We usually took this off at 15 to 12,000 feet and would proceed to eagerly eat the one candy bar given us before every mission. They were always frozen hard as a rock but gave us a quick shot of energy. As we surveyed our group on the approach to our home base, we could see that we had lost several ships out of thirty-six, which had started the mission. The planes that were seriously damaged, short of fuel, or had wounded aboard were given priority to land first. This was indicated by firing a red-red flare before peeling off the final approach. We fired our flares and were told by the tower we would be the third to land since two other planes were in more serious trouble. As each ship touched the ground, a fire engine and ambulance would race along the runway beside it to give assistance as required. After landing from a mission, if no help were needed, we would proceed to taxi to our designated hardstand in the dispersal area where the ground crew was anxiously watching and eagerly awaiting our return.

For every man in the air there were another three on the ground engaged in support – cooks, clerks, mechanics, armourers and a score of others performing duties, many of them menial but essential to the functioning of the group. No one had to tell the ground crew that it had been a rough day. They immediately got to work, washing the blood out of the waist and started planning how it would be best to patch up the ship. One time our ground crew counted 160 holes in his beloved plane. The 'Ground Pounders', the name applied to all non-flying personnel, many of whom had come to England in 1942, performed a fine job. There was a friendly rivalry between the aircrews and this group and they looked on us as transients. The crewmembers lived on one end of the air base and the ground personnel at the opposite end of the field. We each had our own mess hall and ablutions facilities. We envied them for their personnel comfort in the way of barracks and club facilities, while they envied our liberal allotments of good food and higher pay.

Many of them were very dedicated men who would have given an arm to be a member of an aircrew. The ground mechanics worked in groups of three to five assigned to maintain one plane. They would be waiting anxiously as the group returned from a mission and race across the field to greet us as we taxied to our dispersal area. They would then swarm over the plane to examine the particular damage and immediately endeavour to make her available for a possible mission the next day. Mitch, Tom and Joe Balate, the engineer, would discuss mechanical troubles with Master Sergeant George Aleski, our crew chief, who would work his crew all night in order to have the plane ready for the next mission. On many occasions, these poor devils worked all night in 0 degree weather, patching holes, replacing parts, overhauling and general checking of the plane and equipment. During this time, they had to work by flashlight and were not allowed even the smallest fire for warmth, since we were under constant surveillance by German reconnaissance planes. On several occasions, our base had been bombed or strafed by German planes, so the entire field was operated under complete blackout conditions. All the ground crews took a great deal of pride in their work and on a few occasions when planes aborted due to mechanical failure, the ground crews took it very hard since it was a personal reflection on their abilities as mechanics. When planes would not return at all, I think the ground crews took it harder than the aircrews. This in part might have been due to the thought that perhaps the ship had been lost due to mechanical failure for which they had been responsible.

Without fail, we were met by a truck, which took us back to the briefing room. As we entered, the flight surgeon dispensed 2-ounce shots of whiskey. As it had been almost ten hours since we had breakfast, the booze had quite a stimulating effect. We were then interrogated as a crew by one of the S-2 officers. He was particularly interested in observations anyone had while we were over enemy territory. Shipping in the Channel, train movements, activity on German airfields, when and where our planes had gone down, markings of the German fighter groups, tactics used by the enemy, or anything else of general interest were all recorded. All of us had a great deal of respect for the S-2 officers. Several of them were veterans of the First World War and a very dedicated group. One of my closest friends was Brutus Hamilton, who was affectionately known to everyone as Pop. He had once coached US Olympic teams. While I was with the group, 'Pop' appeared to have aged ten years. For a long time he made it his responsibility to personally know all the aircrews. He would then write long letters home to the parents of each whenever planes were lost on a mission. This often resulted in 100 letters a week to bereaved parents or wives. After debriefing the crew separated into special critiques for the pilots, navigators, bombardiers and gunners.

On Tuesday 11 April it was another early start, with crews being awakened at 0230 hours and briefing at 0400, which meant that the missions would be long. Well in excess of 900 bombers were dispatched to six Junkers and Focke-Wulf assembly plants in eastern Germany and eighty-eight Fortresses in the 1st Division were assigned Cottbus and Sorau, all the way to the Polish frontier. Joe Wroblewski in the 351st viewed the mission philosophically.

The 11th of each month always seemed to be my day for missions. I was picked to fly with a new crew that had just arrived at Polebrook. It was usually standard procedure to take a new pilot and his crew on their first mission. We went to Arniswalde, which was our secondary target near the Polish border. We flew at 15,000 feet, descending to 12,000 feet at the target. That gave the anti-aircraft gunners a field day. They got their share of B-17s over Hannover. Bombers were blowing up, burning and falling out of control all around us. We all got scared as hell when a four-inch piece of flak came right through the nose and cut the oxygen line on the right side. The whooshing sound of the escaping oxygen under pressure made plenty of noise. The new pilot grabbed the controls from me and about pulled us out of formation in panic. I almost had to beat his hands off the yoke. I told him that if we did get out of formation by ourselves the enemy fighters would be on us like a pack of wolves. Some of our crew members had to use portable oxygen bottles after losing half our supply. Enemy fighters did not bother us although we could see other groups under heavy attack.

One of these was the 401st at Deenethorpe. En route to Pölitz while the 401st formation was traversing a flak area, three B-17s in the 614th Squadron were downed by flak. 2nd Lieutenant Frank O. Kuhl peeled off out of formation to the left and turned back to England with gas coming out of his right wing. The aircraft was under control when last seen but it was hit by flak and fighters and crashed at Nordlohne near Lohne. Many of the crew were badly wounded, including Kuhl. Sergeant Ray P. Dziadzia, the ball turret gunner, who was from Milford, Connecticut, was hit in the legs by two 20 mm shells and died in hospital about eight hours later. Kuhl and the rest of the crew survived and were taken prisoner.

Gloria J, flown by 1st Lieutenant Robert O. Stine, was hit by flak near Iserhagen a few kilometres north-east of Hannover and flew along burning for about thirty seconds in formation. It went up steeply, then into a straight dive and a gunner in another aircraft thought that the bomb bay was on fire. 2nd Lieutenant W. F. Empric, the bombardier, one of just two survivors aboard *Gloria J*, recalled:

When we were hit by flak, the formation was approaching Hannover, just north of the city. I turned in my seat and noticed that the oxygen supply under the pilot's seat and co-pilot's seat on fire. I immediately put on my chest pack and tried to call the pilot on the interphone. The line sounded dead so I started to move to the cockpit to notify the other crewmen of the danger. There was evidently damage to the ship since it was not flying a steady course. Just as the ship fell out of control I was alongside the navigator. It fell some distance and then fell apart. I found myself clear of the ship and pulled the ripcord. Due to injuries I was unable to escape and was captured about ten minutes after touching the ground.[4]

Also Ran – Still Running, flown by 1st Lieutenant S. P. Wilson, was hit by flak at Steinhagen near Bielefeld. Wilson pulled out of formation and was seen to salvo his bombs. The inboard engine was feathered and the aircraft was under control when it turned away. All ten men bailed out safely and they were led away to captivity.

Battlin' Betty, flown by Lieutenant Francis L. Shaw, was the third B-17 that was lost when it was hit by flak in the No. 3 engine and left the formation, seeming to be under control. The crew started bailing out just before it was attacked by Bf 109s. Sergeant John L. Hurd, the ball turret gunner, who was flying his eleventh mission this day, recalled:

My squadron was hit hard by flak and we lost four B-17s in this action. There were many flak bursts around our ship. From my position in the ball turret I was able to watch under the wings for fires. Immediately the number three and four engines started smoking and shortly afterwards my ball turret was hit and I was injured in the right butt! Our bombs were salvoed to guard against explosion just as one of our B-17s blew up. *Battlin' Betty* finally came clear of the flak and we slowed down and lost altitude. I was asked to leave the ball turret and have S/Sgt K. A. Terroux the radio operator look at my injury. He was unable to do anything as I had too many clothes on. About this time the pilot gave the order to bail out. I hooked on my chest type parachute and placed my GI shoes inside my 'chute harness. We were over flat country and somewhere east of Hannover. I looked out of the bomb bay and then decided to jump out of the waist door. We were somewhere between 15,000 and 18,000 feet. The two waist gunners and I were waiting to jump when I heard a loud crash. The ship started to rock to the left and knocked us against the left side of the ship. I thought to myself, "It's now or never," so I gave a big push and all three of us went out the door. It was very noisy as I left the ship and shortly after I pulled the rip-cord. The 'chute opened and then the world was quiet.

Hurd landed, injuring his ankle and was captured immediately. So too were the rest of the crew. Hurd finished the war at Stalag Luft 17, Krems, in Austria.

At the target the lead bombardier in the 351st was hit in the arm, which had to be amputated later. Other groups suffered loss in the ferocious flak barrage, as Perry Rudd in the 457th formation, recalls.

> We were knocked out of formation and fell a thousand feet before we recovered. We levelled out just in time to witness a burning B-17 fall off its right wing directly over us. Lieutenant Matterell, the co-pilot, pulled our ship upon the left wing and we fell another 3,000 feet. The burning B-17 missed us by only a few feet. A piece of flak had entered the cockpit before exploding and had set the nose on fire. The flames spread through the open radio hatch of the doomed ship, leaving a trail of smoke as it spiralled down. Two men got out. The tail gunner went through a wing and a pilot banked his plane to let him by. Neither 'chute opened; if indeed either of them had them on. Our bomb doors would not close and we headed back to Belgium alone. We received about twenty flak hits on the homeward run. The right aileron was knocked out of position, the rudder was holed and the right flap was put out of commission. Lieutenant Hovey did a remarkable job of getting us back. We took our crash landing positions but it was a great landing at Glatton despite the damage, although the plane was later declared a sub-depot job.

Most of the crews who returned to England had been in the air for more than eleven hours and tiredness had already begun to take effect during the last stages of the homeward leg. Joe Wroblewski recalls: 'I kept seeing the English coast all the way back across the North Sea. It must have been a mirage. It seemed like we would never get back. I was dead tired when we eventually did get back and I passed out in the sack and slept like a log.'

Lieutenant Bryce S. Moore, pilot of B-17 *Esky* in the 551st or 'Green' Squadron in the 385th Bomb Group, returned from Stettin, his twenty-sixth and next to last mission and longest at ten hours and thirty minutes. He recalls:

> I was terribly distraught that the group lead radioed in the clear that because of weather we would bypass Stettin and bomb an alternate target. I knew the Germans monitored our frequencies and to alert their defences of our eminent arrival seemed sheer stupidity at the moment, though I don't recall actually encountering any enemy fighter attacks or anti-aircraft fire over the

target, whatever its name. On reflection I suspect that Colonel Vandevanter, the Command Pilot as well as Group Commander, was using a code name to mislead the enemy. If so, it worked. We were flying left wing (low) in the second element in the low squadron – not a good position because of the stratus clouds the group was struggling to climb over at about 28,000 or 30,000 feet. Being the lowest ship in the group we were dragged through the tops of several cloud layers made worse by dense contrails from the planes ahead and above us and by other groups ahead of us whose contrails were sometimes at right angles to our heading as they climbed. This created a false sloping horizon and made us feel that we were in a turn when we weren't. Very uncomfortable, near-vertigo intermittently for a few seconds. To avoid running into other planes in the clouds I pulled to the left ten or 15 seconds then continued to climb straight ahead with all aboard keeping a lookout for other aircraft.

Suddenly I noticed a small break in the cloud layer below us to my left and was surprised to see for perhaps two seconds a squadron of six twin-engine German fighter-bombers about 500 feet below heading in the opposite direction. Apparently they were unaware of our presence, though of course I couldn't be certain. I called out their location to the crew and told the co-pilot that if the German squadron should attack our lone airplane we would dodge them by re-entering the cloud layer a few feet below. I then called the navigator and suggested he tune nearby Malmö, Sweden, on the radio compass in case we needed a safe haven from the German fighters since the clouds seemed thickest to our right (north). "It's been tuned for five minutes!" was his quick reply. Happily, the Germans didn't attack and in a few minutes we were between cloud layers, sighted the group a short distance ahead, quickly caught up and proceeded to the new target. The trip home was uneventful till letdown, when we broke up into squadrons and widened our disassembly pattern because of hazy conditions over East Anglia. Suddenly our squadron met another squadron head-on, with no time to manoeuvre. How we missed each other will forever be a mystery.

Lieutenant Edward Michael and Lieutenant Westberg in the 305th brought *Bertie Lee* home to England after it had been devastated by cannon fire and had plummeted into a 3,000-foot dive. Michael crash-landed at a RAF airfield on the South Coast, despite his undercarriage and flap having been put out of operation and the ball turret being stuck in the lowered position with its guns pointing downwards. The airspeed indicator was not working and the bomb bay doors were jammed full open. Fighting off unconsciousness, Michael skilfully brought

Bertie Lee down safely on its belly. His miraculous feat earned the second Medal of Honor awarded to a member of the 305th Bomb Group.

The 92nd, which had been assigned the industrial area at Stettin, also suffered loss. Six aircraft in the low squadron were brought down by vicious and persistent fighter attacks and a concentrated flak barrage. The 13th and 45th Combat Wings in the 3rd Bomb Division force were confronted with bad weather in the Poznan area. They were forced to bomb the secondary target at Rostock. Rocket-firing Me 410s and Ju 88s took advantage of a lapse in fighter cover and wrought havoc among the leading groups. The 'Snetterton Falcons' was worst hit, losing ten of the twenty-five bombers shot down this day.

After a number of missions and a ten day rest period Staff Sergeant Mike Ciano, of Belleville, New Jersey, returned to the 445th at Tibenham on Tuesday 12 April. He found himself assigned to Lieutenant Joseph Pavelka's newly formed crew as left waist gunner on *Sin Ship* for the mission to Zwickau, on the Mulde in eastern Germany:

> The much dreaded sound of the Jeep halting at our Quonset hut; the hut door opened and the driver called out our new pilot's name. Before we knew it, we were eating chow and off to briefing prior to take-off time. After briefing, we made our usual preparations: checking out personal equipment; pre-flight preparations, start engines and taxi out. We took off one at a time and slowly gained altitude. We joined formation in our assigned rear slot spot and we were on our way to Zwickau. As soon as we crossed the Channel[5] and were over Belgium, all hell broke loose. Flak hit our far left engine and black smoke started pouring out of it. A hole the size of a basketball opened up at the feet of our waist gunner. Another direct hit in the waist ripped open the floor. As we gathered our wits and resumed our gun positions we were informed over the intercom that the nose also was badly hit. Bullets began ricocheting around my tail turret; a Me 109 was coming in at eye level. I opened up fire when I felt he was in proper range and was rewarded by the Messerschmitt disintegrating in a ball of fire, almost hitting the tail turret as it exploded.
>
> By now the ship was too crippled and we lost altitude and dropped out of formation, becoming a 'sitting duck' for the rest of the enemy fighters. We tried to keep our guns firing to discourage the fighters from getting in close enough for a clean kill. But the handwriting was on the wall by this time. The intercom ceased to function; then a crew member from up front crawled back to tell us to bail out. Bail out! Those were words we gunners heard in training lectures, saw

demonstrated in training films; but to each of us it was always going to happen to 'the other guy', not to me! I quickly put out the fire (luckily it was superficial) and put on the chute. There were four of us in the rear section by this time; Staff Sergeant Wayne Luce, right waist gunner, badly wounded by our first blast; Staff Sergeant Pete Clark, our tail gunner; 'Chet' [Tech Sergeant Chester B. Hincewicz of Scranton, New Jersey], our top turret gunner; and myself. We got Luce's chute on, carried him to the waist window and released him, pulling his ripcord at the last possible minute. The chute opened clear of the plane and we looked at each other and smiled. The rest of us decided to jump out the camera hatch as our exhausted condition and the urgency made any other exit impossible. I gave a last look down, jumped, pulled the cord and looked up to see the ship moving away. Everything then became a blur until I hit Terra Firma; the stinging pain ran from my ankles up to my head as I buckled over and passed out. I opened my eyes some time later to see German soldiers looking down at me and mumbling and civilians in the background gawking at me.[6]

Elvin O. Cross, a ball turret gunner in the 445th, recalls:

Zwickau was my twentieth mission. We took off loaded with 4,200lb of fragmentation bombs. We entered the coast of France at Dieppe and as we made our way over France we had not encountered any flak or enemy fighters. The weather started closing in and we were ordered by radio to abort the mission and return to base. We made a long swinging turn and dropped to 15,000 feet to get under the cloud formation. Our fighter escort was very high and above the clouds. From nine o'clock several formations of 'planes appeared in 'V' formation. There were five 'V' formations of about twenty 'planes each. They started firing at us and flying through our formation which consisted of nine 'planes only, since we had been separated from the rest of the group when we dropped through the cloud formation. By the time I had been lowered down in the ball turret the 'plane on our left wing was already on fire. I saw the tail turret shot completely off, with the gunner reaching his arm back as if to get his parachute. They lowered the landing gear and the German fighters made no more attacks at them. Those that were able bailed out.

I saw one B-24 blow up just under us. The enemy fighters attacked for about forty-five minutes. By the time it was over we had lost five B-24s. Our tail gunner shot down three Me 109s, one after another, and they blew up right over us. The ball turret got one Me 109 just under us, causing the 'plane to bounce like a ball. The top turret, nose turret and left waist each got one Me 109. The enemy fighters would line up about twenty in a line and fly into us and just keep coming, then another twenty would line up and do the same, over and over. We fired most of the ammunition we had on board our ship. There was a little ammunition left in the right waist and ball turret guns as these guns finally jammed. The tail turret gunner's guns melted and he had no ammunition left. It was the same at the other gun positions. When my ball turret guns jammed I thought we had just about had it, so I opened my turret door, planning on getting my parachute and getting ready to bail out. As I opened my door I could see the rear of the 'plane and the tail gunner must have had the same idea. We hesitated as our eyes met and explained our situation on the intercom to each other. Then he said: "Why don't we try flashing our trouble lights (small lights on the end of our extension cord to help see when making repairs) off and on and maybe the fighters will think it's our guns flashing." It was crazy, but we did it.

Enemy shells were bursting all around us. One 20 mm went up between the right and left waist gunners and exploded in the ceiling. One hit the column on top of the ball turret. One cut our hydraulic lines in two and exploded in our hydraulic reservoir. In general, the ship was full of holes and looked as if someone had used a can opener on it. We were just sitting Colonel, waiting to be shot down as there was nothing more we could do, when out of nowhere came the prettiest P-38s and scattered enemy fighters everywhere. After the P-38s took care of the enemy fighters, they escorted the four of us B-24s left back to our base in England and peeled off and tipped their wings. We had no hydraulic system left and no brakes so we had to crank the landing gear down. We hit the runway at about 100 mph and as many of us that were able ran to the tail end of the ship as far as we could so that the tail would drag on its tail skid and slow us down. We slowed it down some but still ran off the runway. Our ship was full of holes and had to be completely overhauled before it would fly again. We all felt lucky to be back and that for some reason God had been with us on this mission.

On Thursday 13 April, overall command of the Combined Bomber Offensive and the 8th Air Force officially passed to General Dwight D. Eisenhower, the newly appointed Supreme Allied Commander. It was on this day that the 1st Division was sent to the ball-bearing plants at Schweinfurt for the third time. The 3rd Division went to the Messerschmitt plant at Augsburg and the 2nd Division was assigned German aircraft manufacturing installations near Munich. A total of 626 heavies were dispatched, of which only 566 were effective. Colonel (later General)

Maurice 'Mo' Preston, CO of the 379th, flying at the head of the leading 41st Wing, led the 1st Division.

> We encountered strong fighter opposition. In all probability they made a direct head-on approach from a distance of some fifteen to twenty miles. The first we saw of them they were among us and already firing their guns. They made only a single pass and then went on through the lead wing, maintaining an upright position, thus abandoning, for at least this one time, their practice of attacking inverted and then pulling out in an earthward dive. The great majority of attacks were concentrated on the high box (384th) presumably because it was separated some distance from the remaining boxes. I made a determined effort via the radio to induce the element leader to get back into formation, but to no avail. (Whether or not he received my orders is something else.) He and his entire formation paid dearly. Every single aircraft [eight] in that formation was shot down on that single pass made by the German fighters. I never saw such a thing happen before or since. One pass; scratch one entire formation!

Despite the losses, the raid on Schweinfurt was considered a great success, as Colonel Preston recounts.

> It was on this mission that we finally achieved a direct hit on the number one prime building, the elimination of which would do the greatest good. At least one 379th bomb went into that prime building. It probably didn't make a great difference to the war effort, but it's little successes like these that spice things up for the participants.

At Deenthorpe, there was no word from *Command Performance* and 1st Lieutenant A. E. Vokaty's crew on the mission to Schweinfurt. At interrogation three crewmembers of another B-17 told interrogators what had happened. Fighters set the B-17's No. 2 engine on fire and then, ten minutes later, still smoking, Vokaty was hit by a single Bf 109, which started a bad fire in the gas tanks. Eight crewmen bailed out before *Command Performance* went into a dive and exploded. The same three crewmembers related that after fighters had attacked 1st Lieutenant B. Stimson's B-17 and left the wing tip burning, the pilot had pulled out of formation to the right. Four 'chutes (two immediately and two delayed) were definitely seen. The aircraft turned back and seemed under control for about forty seconds and then went into a steep dive and exploded at 16,000 feet. Stimson and seven of his crew survived. Sergeant John C. MacQueen, the right waist gunner, of London, England, was killed in the fighter attack on an early 'pass' and 1st Lieutenant John E. O'Neal, the navigator, of Savannah, Georgia, was killed when his 'chute failed to open.

One of the returning B-24s in the 453rd carried the 2nd Combat Wing Leader, Major James M. Stewart, who on 31 March had joined the Old Buckenham Group as Operations Officer. The 3rd Division was badly mauled by fighters and ten Fortresses were forced to head for Switzerland. Many others were either shot down or badly damaged. When the returning Fortresses in the 447th began landing back at Rattlesden at 1830 hours, men on the base could see that four aircraft were missing. Three had landed in Switzerland but there was no sign of *Blue Hen Chicks*, flown by Lieutenant William H. Johnson, an aircraft commander who put his crew first and whose actions on 30 December saved the life of his left waist gunner. Technical Sergeant Frank J. Hazzard, engineer recalls:

For about twenty minutes after we hit the French coast and were well on our way to Augsburg, everything went along smoothly but then suddenly trouble broke out. A terrific explosion sounded directly beneath my turret. I knew we had been hit badly because I heard the co-pilot, George W. Freas, saying that he was going to feather number four engine and that number three was out also. The power line in my turret was hit, rendering my guns useless. All four officers had been wounded by flak so I proceeded to the cockpit to see if there were anything I could do. The co-pilot had been hit severely in the arm. I cut his sleeve open and bandaged his wrist and arm. The pilot had been hit in the back of the neck but he told me to take care of the navigator, William S. Fancher, first. I then went to the nose and saw that the navigator had been hit in the leg. I slit open his trouser leg. The wound was bleeding badly and he must have been in great pain, but all the time I was working on his leg he stood up and continued to navigate the ship. The bombardier, George H. Ney, had also been hit in the arm but the cut was not bleeding, so I figured that he would be OK. About this time the co-pilot called and asked me to transfer the fuel from the No. 4 to the No. 1 engine. This done, I proceeded to throw all my ammunition and ammunition boxes, flak helmets and other movable equipment out of the plane in order to lighten the load. I went to the nose and did the same thing there. About this time we were hit again and No. 1 engine went out. We were flying on one engine, losing altitude and flying speed all the time. I guess we were in a bad spot but I was too busy running from my turret to the nose to the cockpit and back again to think too much about it.

Down in the nose I put another bandage on the navigator's leg. By this time the leg must have been hurting him horribly but he continued to navigate the ship. He did a wonderful job; in my opinion he deserves a lot of credit for getting us home. When we hit the Channel we were flying at 8,000 feet and when finally we finally reached the coast we were at 1,500 feet and at a speed of about 70 knots. Just as I was thinking that we were going to make it back home in one piece I could feel the ship vibrating something awful. Looking out of my window I could see that she was on fire. Tapping the navigator on the shoulder, I showed him the fire. I then went back to the pilots' compartment. I saw the bombardier on the catwalk of the bomb bay looking for his chute. I remembered that he had left it in my turret position so I immediately went there and got the chute. Since the bombardier, because of his wounded arm, couldn't get the chute on, I snapped it on for him and assisted him in getting out of the plane through the open bomb bay. We were at 800 feet so I figured it was high time for me to get the hell out of the plane. By this time I thought that everyone outside of the pilot and me had left the ship. I looked towards his seat and saw him getting up preparing to jump. I went out through the bomb bay. Later on I found out that the pilot never got out of the plane but had been killed when the plane crashed a half mile from where I jumped. The plane landed near Ham Street, Kent. When I landed, I saw the co-pilot a few feet away. The first thing he said to me was, "Combat's rough, you can get hurt at this sort of thing." It struck me very funny at the moment but I guess there was nothing very humorous about what we went through. If it hadn't been for the courage and skill of our pilot in bringing the ship home on one engine and for the wonderful job done by our navigator even though he was in constant pain and weak through loss of blood, we never could have made it back.

Hazzard in all probability saved the lives of the co-pilot and navigator by rendering first aid to both of them. Bill Johnson was put in for the Medal of Honor, but instead was awarded the Distinguished Service Cross. His body was returned to his home town, Minneapolis, for burial after the war.[7]

In the 94th, *Nine Yanks and a Jerk*, flown by 2nd Lieutenant Gordon R. Wiren, and *Lassie Come Home*, piloted by 2nd Lieutenant W. Gault, headed for Switzerland. Gault's radio operator was Frank J. Bonz, who was on his twenty-fourth mission. He recalls:

We were to bomb at 20,000 feet. Upon arrival at the target, about 100 flak guns fired on our formation. In spite of accurate flak, we dropped our forty-two 100 lb incendiaries. After the bombs went away, we thought the world would end. Our #1 and #2 engines were hit by flak. Three pieces of flak went through my radio room, two going through the radio table, missing me by an inch. We were hit in one of the tanks and we started losing gas. The plane caught fire so we headed for Switzerland. We didn't make it. We bailed out in southern Germany late in the afternoon. We were captured and taken temporarily to a detention camp for elderly Jews. Security was lax because of the advanced age of the other prisoners. I slipped out with another GI and ran toward Switzerland, ten miles away. With dogs tracking us, the two of us leaped across the wire that marked the boundary between Germany and Switzerland. We had jumped into what turned out to be a GI paradise. After interrogation, we were sent to Adelboden. There were no training or formation schedules to attend. The only supervision we received was from an easy-going American captain and a handful of Swiss guards. We had the run of the town, plenty of good food and beer and an opportunity to meet many friendly Swiss women. We had everything except American music but I corrected that by organising a band called the Frankie Bonz, His Drums and His Melody Men. The YMCA Prisoner of War Aid provided the instruments as well as orchestrations and arrangements of the latest hits in the States. It wasn't hard for me because I had played drums for weddings and bar mitzvahs, in taverns, on the radio and even in a Jersey City burlesque theatre. I held auditions for my band. One who signed up was Keith Wall, who had played tenor sax with the Tommy Dorsey Band. The other guys were good too, with high school band experience.

At first we played for our own enjoyment. Then we moved on to more formal shows. Our debut was at the Palace Hotel. The people liked us right off the bat. They stomped and clapped. They wanted more and more. We played until five in the morning. We became celebrities, drinks were on the house. News of our group spread. The American Military Attaché in Berne ordered that we give a show there. The Swiss girls became even friendlier. It was like a dream but it didn't last forever. As the war got tougher for the Germans in late 1944, a company of German soldiers crossed into Switzerland and demanded to be interned. It was rumoured that the Germans wanted them back for Russian Front duty. We heard also that the US Army wanted back some of its men. A deal was made and two Germans were returned for each American released. In February 1945 I said goodbye to my girlfriend and my other friends and headed for home.[8]

April saw the high-water mark of the 8th, the most sustained period of operations yet mounted. It was a record month with the highest expenditure in men and machines; 361 heavy bombers were lost over Europe. Since 11 April the 94th had lost about fourteen crews in combat or rotated home. On Monday 17 April ten B-17s in the 94th and nine in the 385th were shot down. Both combat boxes were alone and without fighter cover. That night Anthony 'Chick' Cecchini's crew, who had arrived at Molesworth to join the 'Hells Angels' in the bitter cold spring of March 1944, were alerted to fly the next day's mission. Ben Smith Jr, the radio-operator-gunner, wrote:

> As I looked up and down the row of bunks, there were many cigarettes glowing in the dark. There was not much sleeping going on. In the early hours of morning, the door flew open; and this cheery soul named 'Fluke' came in, switched on the lights and started calling off the crews who were to fly the day's mission. He yelled, "Cecchini's Crew," and my heart sank within me. I felt like a condemned man.

At the briefing the target was announced and Ben Smith was shocked. 'It was hardly a milk run,' he wrote: 'It was Berlin!'[9]

More than 750 bombers attacked aircraft industries, the 303rd forming part of the attack on Oranienburg in the suburbs of Berlin. They had been told to expect heavy fighter opposition and they did. Cecchini's crew flew in the No. 3 position in the High Squadron and though they made it back they took a savage mauling. Ben Smith, whose life was only saved by his flak vest when a piece of jagged shrapnel hit him in the chest, wrote that their B-17 'was one more lacerated lady. That morning our bomber had been a lovely girl without a blemish. They made her a "hangar queen" and cannibalised parts off her'.

Nineteen bombers failed to return from the day's missions.

On Thursday 20 April crews in the 447th at Rattlesden thought that they were 'living it up'. 'Bankers' hours,' Doyle Shields said. 'Briefing was at 1430 hours. Our targets were Noball sites in the Cherbourg area.' The three divisions put up an armada of 842 heavy bombers, of which only 570 attacked their targets in the Cherbourg and Pas de Calais areas and twenty-four of the thirty-three assigned targets were hit. Nine of the bombers were lost. Shields continues:

> At about mid-morning on Friday 21 April, as we were walking to the briefing room, there was a tremendous explosion out on hardstand 16 adjacent to the hangar on the north side of the field. You just knew there was a loss of life. No details were known at time of briefing, so it went on. Our target was Leipzig.

We were briefed, dressed for the mission and went to our planes. Our heart just wasn't in our work. The mission was scrubbed. After we were dressed, we walked to hardstand 16 to see what had happened. A plane was being loaded with 4,200 lbs of bombs made of a new type of explosive, oxygen and 2,700 gallons of fuel. Electronic equipment was being checked out, no one knows exactly what caused the explosion. Thirteen men lost their lives; one was an air crewman.[10]

Further carnage was about to unfold. During Friday evening at 1700 hours, at Horsham St Faith on the outskirts of Norwich, Bill Griffiths waited for the crew chiefs to come into the 754th Squadron engineering office to make their reports on the status of their Liberators. The evening was no different than any other night in England. Blackout was being observed and an occasional searchlight lit up the sky and in the distance, the krump-krump-krump of the Ack-Ack and bombs could be heard. The reports made, Griffiths settled back to wait the 'poop from group' on the next 458th Bomb Group mission. When it came, there were the usual questions: how many and the numbers of all aircraft available. This time there were seven with two more possible. The ground crews were still working on their Liberators even though it was past 2200 hours. Group advised that it would be a maximum effort. Gas tanks to be topped after marshalling. Gas-up time, take-off time was given. Much the same information went to Pete Blanton, operations clerk. Griffiths relaxed again until time to 'get 'em up,' ground crews, that is, for breakfast and to get them to their hardstands for pre-flight and gas-up. All was well. Armourers were loading guns with ammo, filling bomb bays with the 'goodies' to be delivered that day. Oxygen was delivered, all systems serviced and checked. Aircrew were arriving at the hardstands. Soon marshalling would start and then as scheduled, all marshalled ships had their tank topped. Everybody was ready to go! One by one, they lumbered down the runway, lifted off and began assembly. Griffiths saw them pass as if in review and in the early light, turn towards their targets. 'So far, so good!' he thought, as all the armourers, mechanics, oxygen men and gas trucks straggled in from the hardstand area. Griffiths learned it was to be a long mission, to the marshalling yards at Hamm. Return time would be dusk. A little unusual, but all he could do now was wait.[11]

Among the replacements sent to the 94th in April was Lieutenant Frank Scannell's crew, whose navigator was Abe Dolim, the Hawaiian who three years before had witnessed at first hand the Japanese bombing of Pearl Harbor. When Abe Dolim got assigned to a bomber group, he thought that was a big deal and the B-17 was quite an airplane. He was literally on top of the world but there had been distractions when the love bug got to him and some others on the crew before leaving the States. One had married the 'girl back home' and another remarried his ex-wife, while co-pilot 2nd Lieutenant Harvey Brown married his South Carolina sweetheart. Then it had been Abe's turn when his cousin's wife arranged a blind date for him with the babysitter for their two-year-old son. There was no doubt that he was smitten on meeting Mary Frances Nuzum, a real sloe-eyed brunette beauty. This eighteen-year-old cadet nurse led him a merry chase, but it was fun all the way until she turned him down when he asked her to marry him. She was the only girl he ever considered for marriage, his true soul mate, so he was not about to give up on her. On 12 March he had kissed his ladylove, the unobtainable Mary Frances, good-bye and geared up for the big move to England.

Abe Dolim had to wait only until Saturday 22 April, fifteen days after disembarking from the *Queen Elizabeth* in Scotland, to fly his first combat mission, to the marshalling yards at Hamm. Unfortunately, the weather was to play a large part in shaping the mission and was responsible for its ultimate fate. Crews were apprehensive from the start. They were awakened in the middle of the night because the mission was scheduled for the usual early morning start. It was later postponed for several hours while command waited for the bad weather front over the Continent to clear. After several stop-go decisions, final clearance was given in the afternoon. Crews who had been awake since 0200 had their briefing updated with more recent weather information and began assembling for take-off. One of them was John W. Snider in the 448th, who recalls:

> Our first indication that this was to be a different kind of day came after a rude awakening at 0230 and a briefing, which lasted from 0330 to 0500. The mission was scrubbed just as we were ready to be ferried to the hard stand where our plane was waiting for us. After a second breakfast, we went back to the briefing room to find that the target had been changed from Stuttgart to Hamm, with take-off now scheduled for 1030, leaving time for yet a third breakfast.

Kenneth L. Driscoll's crew in the 'Rackheath Aggies' prepared to fly their third mission in *The Monster*. 'At our afternoon briefing, our instructions were that when it got dark, we were to break formation, turn on our running lights and each crew was on its own to return to base. My crew was flying No. 2 position (deputy lead) in the 788th Squadron formation.'

Joseph Broder in the 'Bungay Buckaroos' recalls:

Within two hours of noon, crews were rounded up from all over the airdrome – mess halls, barracks, flight lines, orderly rooms, officers' and airmen's clubs and wherever else aviators congregate. At exactly 1200 the 446th (including me) was to be briefed for a major mission. When the target, flight altitude and ordnance were announced, there were many gasps and groans. It was a surprise, not unlike the late briefing. Flixton airfield became a beehive of activity. Vehicles brought personnel from briefings to the aircraft, planes were hurriedly bomb-loaded, ground crews hastened to their specialised assignments and tarmacs became busy with equipment handling and testing. Cars and jeeps raced back and forth. *Old Hickory* stood at ready, fully war painted and thoroughly inspected by crewmates Elizer and Whaley. Just a few minutes later the pilot's position cackled: "Thirty minutes delay." We waited. Unfortunately, it was the only delay. It lasted fifty minutes and the mission was not cancelled. At 1440, mid-afternoon, we accepted the green-green Very pistol signal from the tower, rumbled awkwardly ahead, raced down the runway at full throttle, finally picked up enough air speed and barely rose at runway's end. Clearing into a shining sky, we were followed by the rest of the 446th and our adventure began. Only one aircraft in our 707th Squadron, which led on this day, had to feather a prop and it turned home. He was lucky. We cleared to altitude and droned on.

The 2nd Wing, which would lead the 2nd Bomb Division to Hamm, with Lieutenant-Colonel Robert H. Terrill, the 445th CO, as command pilot, began taking off from their Norfolk and Suffolk bases between 1615 and 1630. The Fortresses of the 3rd Division and the 1st Division groups further west followed the Liberators into the sky over East Anglia. At Bury St Edmunds, Lieutenant Frank Scannell's Fortress lifted off from the rubber-stained runway and climbed to altitude. Abe Dolim recalls:

We took off in beautiful CAVU weather topped with high cirrus clouds. Finally, after more than an hour of forming, we took our place at the lead of the 4th Combat Wing and proceeded at 150 mph indicated airspeed. Our fighter escort of P-47s and P-38s picked us up just north of Ijmuiden on the Dutch coast. There were no reports of enemy fighters as we turned at the IP and opened our bomb bay doors for the bomb run. From the IP onward there was absolutely no evasive action. We saw the flak before we spotted the target. The 88 mm explosions looked like double black mushrooms, as though the shell exploded in the middle and worked itself out at both ends vertically. The railroad marshalling yards at

Hamm, the choke point to 'Happy Valley', were 3½ miles long, the largest in Germany, so large that we bombed in combat wing formation – three groups abreast. Flak was not too accurate and we were lucky to be the first over the target. Our bombs blanketed the yard; only a few appeared to go astray. As we turned off to the Rally Point, I looked toward 5 o'clock and saw a sky full of flak with two B-17s in trouble, one in a shallow dive afire and the other exploding after a short vertical dive. I watched several parachutes descend to German soil and then looked for my chest pack – it was not within reach. I made a note to stack it between my position and the emergency hatch, against the bulkhead next to my navigation table.

Kenneth Driscoll meanwhile, had taken off in *The Monster*:

The group got into formation at about 24,000 feet altitude at the assigned radio beacon north of our base, Rackheath. At the designated time, the group turned east and joined other groups flying in formation at the division assembly line. When we crossed the North Sea, our altitude was approximately 27,000 feet. After landfall, we saw some flak bursts in the distance but no enemy fighters. About ten minutes prior to reaching the IP our plane got hit by flak which disabled the No. 2 engine. I dropped back out of formation, lost some air speed but was able to hold altitude. We dropped back about 200 yards from the formation before we had No. 2 prop feathered to reduce drag, mixture controls full rich, propellers in maximum rpm and the throttles full forward. We were too far over enemy territory to turn back. A single B-24, with one engine out, flying alone, would be an inviting and easy target for enemy fighter aircraft. Luckily, I had been able to maintain altitude. With full power on the three good engines, I was able to catch up to and rejoin the formation. Another aircraft had pulled into my vacated position and I pulled into the open spot at the back of the 788th formation. With the extra power on the three engines, I did not have any trouble staying in formation. Within a couple of minutes, we got to the IP and the various flights got in trail position for the bomb run.

After dropping the bombs, the flights turned right off the target and reformed into the normal group formation configuration for the return flight. The flight to the coast was routine with the exception of having to keep extra power on the three good engines to enable us to keep in formation. Just prior to reaching the coast in semi-darkness, enemy anti-aircraft guns shot up some tracer shells at us. They resembled the bright white Roman candles used at 4th of July celebrations.

There were ten or fifteen of them. I saw them passing nearby to the right of us. They were going straight up. Because my field of vision was cut off at the top of the co-pilot's window, I could not follow them up. I had never seen anything like that before. Shortly thereafter, we crossed the coastline and headed back across the North Sea. When we were over the water about fifteen miles, darkness was becoming a reality.

The 'Bungay Buckaroos' had also encountered opposition, as Joe Broder recalls:

When met by Focke-Wulf fighters stationed fifty miles south of Hamm, we were clearly able to see the swastika-painted planes become engaged by our P-47 Thunderbolts, dogfight our escorts almost to a standstill and yet still manage to attack our columns. These Germans were very determined. Bitter battles filled the skies as our turrets turned and fired, friends and foes clashed and two bombers exploded – smoke and debris fluttering earthward. The Fw 190s caught it, too, cannon fire exterminating some of them as our friendlies exacted a degree of revenge. Of the three dozen to forty Luftwaffe interceptors, not less than one-third of them were downed by our snub-nosed, fat-bellied friends. At that time I caught a glimpse of an enemy face as he broke off an engagement with one of our nearby bombers. Turning hard and swiftly to his left from what was a ten o'clock high attacking position and then standing on his wing before deliberately hurling himself nose first towards the below, I spotted a dark-haired, squinty-eyed, pale looking youth who hardly looked Teutonic. He looked like me.

As our B-24 formation lumbered on to its target, an avalanche of ground fire exploded in our midst, the black puffs of smoke downing still another Liberator in the wing directly behind us. It was identified by tail gunner Baker as being from the 458th. There was little let-up. Massive bursts of enemy fire continued, chaff drops proved ineffective and the Ruhr Valley's smoke screen all but obliterated the aiming point and the target. We bombed to unknown results.

In the clear conditions of late evening, the bombers had little difficulty in locating their target – 3½ miles long and nearly a mile wide. Such a large target necessitated bombing in wing formation but despite the tight wing pattern adopted, some bombs fell wide. Strong headwinds and too many short zigzagging legs to the target took parts of the 2nd Wing over the Ruhr Valley, where they were subjected to intense flak and delayed the approach to the primary target. Instead of crossing the target on a 1350 heading as briefed, the bombers came into the target from 260°. The 2nd Wing missed the IP and the 445th and part of the 453rd were prevented from bombing the primary target owing to other, incoming groups. The Liberators therefore continued down the Rhine and bombed marshalling yards at Koblenz.

Colonel Albert J. Shower, the 'Rackheath Aggies' CO, recalls:

After the target the wing lead told us when over the sea to break formation and return to base in individual streams of aircraft, due to our inexperience of night flying. We began to let down over France and some of our gunners began returning ground fire. I told them to cease firing because we could not make out the targets properly and the firing might disclose our position. As we came over the sea I directed a manoeuvre to break out into elements and then into single aircraft from a 360° turn. This, the group performed. It was not a standard operation, as we had never trained for night flying.

Kenneth Driscoll decided to break out of the Aggies' formation a little early because he had been pulling excessive power on *The Monster*'s three good engines while in formation and did not want to risk losing another one at night over the North Sea.

I wasn't sure how far a B-24 would fly on two engines and I did not want to find out. Shortly after dropping back out of formation, we turned on our running lights and started a very slow descent. This allowed me to reduce the power and take the strain off the three good engines. When full darkness came, I started to fly by instruments, which was normal procedure on night flights over water. The navigator, Lieutenant Harold Pantis, kept getting electronic fixes. He kept us all informed, over the intercom, as to when we would make landfall near Great Yarmouth and the ETA over our base at Rackheath. We did not see the lights of other aircraft. The formation had pulled ahead and dispersed in front of us. They were flying faster than we were. Pantis, who was superior at his work, gave me a few small corrections as we kept our slow let down to the English coast. There was radio silence.

'Dusk was barely beginning to settle as we were departing the south central sector of Holland,' continues Joe Broder, 'and were hit by Messerschmitt 109s, perhaps seventy predators in all.'

Luckily, our revolving escort was there. A brilliant defensive effort by an outnumbered group of P-51 Mustangs saved our skins, enabling us to escape with losses of only two bombers in our entire wing ... but three more of the giant warbirds suffered damage. One aircraft had a section of its right tailfin blown out by a 20 mm shell; one had Davis wing damage and was fast losing fuel and altitude and a third ship had two feathered props. These Libs would barely make it back to base or else ditch in the Channel. They might be rescued by the Royal Navy – they might be rescued by German boats – or they might drown and die. Not an inconsiderable number of our bombers had wounded aboard. More bad news: I was right ... Our ETA to Flixton was almost exact and would take place with darkness falling. But even worse news was yet to come.

Kenneth Driscoll says:

Just about when our ETA over the coast was up, Pantis called and said we were then crossing the coastline. The night was very dark and there was a 100 per cent blackout on the ground. We could not see the coastline or anything on land. He gave me the heading to the base and an ETA which was only minutes away. I told the crew to get into their normal positions for landing (ball turret up, tail gunner out, waist guns secured, etc.). The navigator was to stay in place in the front of the aircraft until the base was in sight. When the ETA at the base was up, the navigator called over the intercom and said that the base was directly below us. I banked the aircraft to the left and looked down. I could see absolutely no base lights or runway lights – everything was blacked out. Norwich was about eight miles south-west of the airbase. Barrage balloons were up to protect the city from low flying German bombers. We had to avoid flying over the blacked out city or risk being off course and having a cable from a balloon knock us down; or being fired upon by the anti-aircraft guns protecting the city. While circling around near the base, some other aircraft were also flying around with running lights on. No aircraft had an assigned altitude. We were on our own. Horsham St Faith, another B-24 base in our Wing and Division, was about eight miles to the west of our base. We could not see any lights at that base either. We did not have an alternate airfield assigned during the briefing. There was still radio silence. The control tower did not send out any instructions. I do not remember if I, or any other pilots flying around, broke radio silence. If one of us did, the tower did not respond.

With headings supplied by the navigator, I made about six passes across the blacked out base. The entire countryside was very dark with no lights or landmarks visible. I then told the navigator that we would fly north-east for five minutes and then make a 180° turn and head back to the base. I thought that by flying straight and level for that period of time, the navigator would be able to better reconfirm our exact position in relation to the base. After making the 180° turn, he gave me the heading and ETA back to Rackheath. When the ETA was up, he again stated that the base was below us. I then began to circle to the left again but the base was still not in sight. By this time, I was getting quite concerned. We had been flying for about three hours with an engine out; Norwich, with its barrage balloons and anti-aircraft guns was close by; other aircraft were milling around in the darkness; no alternate airport to go to; no radio contact with the tower and no lights on the ground to indicate our base and runway. The whole countryside was still blacked out. Luckily, fuel was not a problem. We had taken off with a full load of gas and the flight to Hamm was not a long one.

At 10 o'clock that evening Wallace Patterson, Bill Trunnell and Rod Webb, all from 1st Lieutenant Albert L. Northrup Jr's crew, returned to Seething from pass in Norwich with the chaplain in his car. Patterson recalled:

We noticed a lot of excitement in the air and several fires about; so we got out. The air was full of fighters and bombers, many of which were shooting flares, while some were crashing. The British ack-ack was going and so were their searchlights. We got the full story on the base. Jerries picked up our bombers over the Channel when it was nearly dark and followed them in. Our fighters were unable to do much as they were out of gas and falling into the sea. Our crews saw several bombers fall in the Channel. The Huns followed our ships right into the field, shooting them down as they were trying to land. Five of our group piled up one after another on the runway. Skaggs' B-24 caught fire and some of his crew bailed out at 400 feet. Miraculously, no one was hurt, though the ship was still burning this morning. A Fortress exploded in the air and crashed right near where Bill was visiting and sprayed the civilian crowds with 50-calibre bullets. The boys around the base counted at least ten ships going down in our vicinity. We lost two; Pitts and Pulcipher, both replacement crews from the 715th.[12]

Alvin Skaggs, pilot of *Vadie Raye* in the 448th recalls:

The ultimate German plan did not begin to unfold until we started back across the English Channel. It was getting dark and tail gunner Bill Jackson noticed

German fighters taking off from bases along the coast. He alerted the crew and I passed the word along to the command pilot, Captain Blum. He had heard no word over the command radio but listened a while in case any of the commanders ahead of us were reporting this information to Fighter Command in England. After waiting a while he broke radio silence to report this threat and request fighter support.

The Liberators crossed the French coast between Nieuport and Furnes while German fighters were taking off. The 448th began re-crossing the English coast at points from Orford to Southwold and other groups were even further north. The skies over England were fairly clear and although there was no moon the stars were out. Night flying with hundreds of aircraft in the same general area was very hazardous under the best conditions but the lack of adequate signals by which to identify themselves to British anti-aircraft forces served to increase the difficulties of the American crews. The Luftwaffe pilots soon began switching off their lights but the Liberators kept theirs on to facilitate formation flying.

The landing procedure required the Liberators to approach a homing beacon near Great Yarmouth at low altitude, go out to sea at about 1,500 feet, make a 180° turn for positive identification and return inland at this height. However, British coastal batteries began opening up, their fire not only embracing the enemy fighters but also the Liberators. Francis X. Sheehan was in the waist position of the *Vadie Raye*.

> Flak was showering all around us and it hit the ship directly to our rear. It exploded in midair and as I watched this ball of flame fall away I was completely stunned. On board the stricken B-24 had been Lieutenant Cherry Pitts and his crew, among them our closest friends and barrack-mates, including Sergeant Arthur Angelo. It was later discovered that the anti-aircraft gunners were firing at every aircraft that had followed us back across the Channel; later identified as Me 410s [of KG 51] which hit us around 1,000 feet.

Skaggs broke combat formation after seeing two more aircraft go back down in flames and headed in trail formation back to Seething. He says, 'Several 'planes from other formations had remained at altitude and we could see some of them going down in flames with the fighters shooting at them. We could see others exploding and burning on the ground. At Seething some were on fire and others were off the runways.' The runway and marker lamps illuminated Hardwick,

Bungay and Seething. At just after 2130 the 20th Wing split into three groups near Southwold to begin their landing patterns. By now the airfields themselves were being bombed and strafed. Some of the hardest hit were those in the Waveney Valley, home of the 20th Wing, where five Liberators were shot down within minutes.

Joe Ramirez, crew chief of *Witchcraft*, was waiting at dispersal for the 'Rackheath Aggies' to return. It was dusk and he could see the smaller aircraft coming in with the formation. He believed them to be escorting P-51s. Colonel Albert J. Shower was flying in the lead aircraft, piloted by Lieutenant Richard Campbell, which was one of the last to land. Shower recollects:

We were very close to landing when control told us to remain airborne. We made three approaches altogether. At one time we were all set to land when the runway lights were turned out and we were ordered to go around once again. Another time the lights were turned on for an approach on a different runway. Then one of the crew reported that someone was on our tail. I told Campbell to turn off even the inside lights to avoid detection. I was quite impatient at the delay in landing, as it seemed every time we lined up we received two wave-offs or the lights would be extinguished or the runway switched. The aircraft that were shot down were those that turned on then landing lights.

A worried Chaplain, Arthur L. Duhl, met Colonel Shower. As the first few bombers alighted on the runway the German pilots struck, firing their machine guns and dropping bombs. Aircraft veered in all directions and the normally tranquil Rackheath sky was suddenly turned into a tumult. Anti-aircraft batteries opened up while some crews manned their .5 calibre guns and blazed away at the intruders. A Me 410 made a pass over the airfield at 50 feet, firing tracers and dropping two bombs. A Liberator undergoing repairs under floodlights at the southern end of the airfield was hit. Joe Ramirez, standing only one dispersal away, saw Private Daniel F. Miney killed as he cycled across the concrete. Private Michael F. Mahoney, a ground crewman working on the B-24, was wounded in the explosion. The other burst destroyed a cottage in the vicinity.

Allen Welters, a ground crewman who had been working on a B-24 that did not go on the raid, recalls:

Darkness was setting in and as I neared the bomb dump I picked up the sound of what seemed to be a strange aircraft. Something just did not set right and a strange feeling came over me, a feeling that nothing good was about to happen. I stopped and listened more closely, when all of a sudden I saw a twin-engine aircraft approaching over the treetops, as if it were making an approach to the main runway. A creeping feeling went up and down my spine and neck as I thought this might be a German plane! I raised my weapon and sighted in on it as it came towards me and I slowly moved from left to right watching it to see if I could see the marking on the fuselage and to be sure that it was not an English plane. Unfortunately it was too dark to see the marking and anger came over me as I wanted to fire but then I thought it may be English. The nearby gun pit did not fire, so I assumed it must be English. I heard a bomb blast behind me and as I turned around I saw the blast of another bomb go off! Then the gun pit at the south end of the field began firing at an aircraft as it was heading south, the tracers following it! Then a hellish battle occurred, with planes flying in all directions, tracers between the aircraft and anti-aircraft fire. I saw a B-24 flame up and go down behind the woods and then another B-24 burst into flames and went down. Standing there I realised how much those crews were fighting to get out of that hell they were in and to be able to see where to land. "God help them down," I prayed. Just as suddenly the battle ended and one of our planes landed, but it stayed on the south end and then another came in and seemed to be in trouble. Finally all the rest of our B-24s came in. But there was a very strange aura and situation on the field like I had never seen before.[13]

The attack passed by Rackheath, to be continued at other bases. After circling about three more times, Kenneth Driscoll was relieved when, all of a sudden, the runway lights at Rackheath were turned on.

I immediately entered a normal traffic pattern. As usual, landing lights were turned on during the final approach. The tower still maintained radio silence. We landed and rolled to near the end of the runway, turned right on to a taxiway, turned off our landing lights and started to taxi back to our parking area. Periodically, the landing lights were turned on for a very short time to assist me in taxiing the aircraft in. These lights were not designed for full-time ground operation and would burn out quickly with prolonged use. When we got about halfway down to our parking area, military personnel in a jeep flagged us down and I stopped the aircraft. We were then informed that German fighters and fighter bombers were in the area and had hit the base. The German planes had intermingled in the darkness with the 8th Air Force planes coming back across the North Sea and were not detected when crossing the English coast. We shut off all lights, and due to the extreme darkness proceeded slowly to our parking area. Needless to say, after shutting down the three engines, we evacuated the plane in a hurry. We were told later at the debriefing that German aircraft had come across the base, strafed it and dropped two bombs. One enlisted man, who had been visiting friends at the base, was killed, and five aircraft had not yet returned. It was not known at the time if they had been shot down by the intruding German aircraft or had landed at some other base in East Anglia.

Enemy fighters who circled like vultures, waiting for bombers to make the attempt, prevented Liberators from landing at many bases. Crews panicked and many gunners fired thoughtlessly and at random. One Liberator formation dropped flares, which only succeeded in exposing a Fortress formation heading for home. In the chaos *Cee Gee II*, flown by Lieutenant James S. Munsey in the 453rd, which had its formation lights on, was attacked by an intruder aircraft 15 miles from the English coast. Cannon fire knocked Sergeant Ralph McClure out of his tail turret and John McKinney, the left waist gunner, was hit in the chest and head on the same pass. The hydraulic system was shot out and the No. 2 engine erupted in flames. It ignited the wing tanks, which exploded, blowing the living and dying through the waist hatch. Munsey and his co-pilot, Lieutenant Robert Grail, managed to keep the B-24 airborne long enough for the five remaining crew to bail out over land. William C. Grady, the radio operator, was killed when his 'chute failed to open. The body of Grover Conway, the top turret gunner, was never found. *Cee Gee II* crashed in flames in soft coastal marshland near Southwold with Munsey and Grail still in their seats. Munsey was posthumously awarded the DSC for his extraordinary heroism and months later, at a ceremony in America, the medal was pinned to the coat of his three-year-old daughter, Carole Geane Munsey, for whom her father had christened *Cee Gee II*.

Del Wangsvick in the 732nd Squadron in the 453rd formation recalls:

Because of being so far off from flight plan, Captain George Baatz broke radio silence to identify himself to a British 'shore battery'. He got a response (in good English): 'G for George! For identification, turn on your lights.' Captain Baatz did so and his aircraft was immediately riddled with bullets, apparently from an English-speaking Nazi fighter pilot who had been on the shore battery's frequency. Needless to say, Baatz immediately returned to a blackout configuration and found his way back in the dark. At 'Old Buck' Captain Fern Titus was returning from the mission with Lieutenant Colonel Frank 'Smiley' Sullivan, CO of the 732nd Squadron, in the right seat as Command Pilot. Lieutenant DeWitt E. Jones III – a sharp navigator – was navigating. Three times he directed the plane over 'Old Buck'; the darkest place in England! Finally convinced, though, the pilots managed to land in the dark on what they thought to be the runway and fortunately it was! Some of our aircraft were followed and strafed by German fighters as they were landing. One of our last aircraft to land had been unable to release his load, but spilled his 500 lb bombs on the runway. Our trucks cruised around to the hard stands and picked up crews who had landed. Finally, one crew – Lieutenant Witton's – was still not accounted for and presumed lost. The trucks 'shut down'. Eventually, Witton and crew walked into the debriefing. They had landed in the dark, missed the bombs on the runway and walked in before anyone else on 'Old Buck' knew they were back.[14]

Meanwhile, *Vadie Raye* in the 448th was low on fuel but so close to its home base at Seething that Skaggs decided to try for a landing.

'As we approached the downwind leg with the base just off to our left,' he recalls. 'A Me 110 made a pass at us and riddled our mid-section with hard-nose, soft-nose and .30-calibre tracer bullets. His tracers cut some of our fuel lines and started a fire in the bomb-bay section (later the ground defences shot him down).'

Francis Sheehan was struck in the leg and went down on the floor. When he came to, he and the nose gunner, Eugene Gaskins, bailed out. The fire swept from the rear of the bomb bay to the tail section. The rear gunner, Bob Jackson, also bailed out and landed close to the MP station near Bungay (Jackson was later killed over Liège on 5 September 1944 by a small piece of flak). Alvin Skaggs remained to try and bring the blasted Liberator down safely.

Vadie Raye was now too low for any of the crew in the cockpit and forward section to bail out, so my only alternatives were either to reach a safe altitude for baling out or try to reach the field for a landing. All too soon the engines stopped running. I glanced back at the fire in the bomb bay and could see Master Sergeant George Glevanik standing on the catwalk over the bomb bay doors right next to the flaming fuel lines. Seconds later the two outside engines suddenly sprang to life and I was able to climb back to pattern altitude of 1,000 feet. I later learned that George was able to get some fuel to the engines by holding his bare hands very tightly over the breaks in the lines.

Skaggs was able to bring the burning Liberator down on to the runway at Seething. While it was rolling at 70–80 mph, 1st Lieutenant Don Todt, the navigator, and two others went up through the top hatch and rolled out over the wing. Miraculously, they all survived. Skaggs and the others scrambled from the wreckage. Glevanik, the brave engineer, was the last to extricate himself. Sheehan and Gaskins had landed safely and, after some help from women at a Land Army hostel, had been returned to Seething by ambulance.

The burning pyre of the bomber illuminated the entire airfield. It served as a beacon for preying twin-engined German fighters, who swarmed towards it like moths to a candle. They strafed the base from every direction. Ground defences hit back with tracer. One intruder attempting to strafe the runway was foiled when someone extinguished the lights. Liberators making their final approach run were forced to circle again as officers in the control tower screamed over the radio-telephone for them to remain airborne. Crews unable to make contact with traffic control and with fuel getting low decided to land. Inexperience was evident as pilots bringing in their B-24s applied the brakes so strongly that they burned out from under them and flames blinded crews. Warnings were given of obstructions at the end of the runway and when landing lights were momentarily flashed on, pilots were horrified to see three wrecked Liberators in their path. They feverishly cut their throttles but could not prevent their aircraft hurtling towards the wreckage. With collision unavoidable, ignition switches were turned off to lessen the risk of fire. There was a terrific, sickening crash as the bombers hit. Crews scrambled frantically from the upper fuselage, their escape route from underneath blocked because the bombers were embedded in deep mud. Then a fifth and final Liberator hurtled towards the pile and swelled the wreckage.

David Walpole, a young English lad, was walking on Seething airbase with a friend.

Being dark, the aircraft were coming in with their lights on. I thought it strange that one was coming from a different direction to the others and commented on this to my friend. We soon found out this was a German fighter, which had followed the bombers home and was shooting at them as they landed. One B-24 was set on fire and it crashed in the middle of the airfield. All the crew managed to scramble clear without injury. There was a lot of confusion. Paratroopers had reportedly landed in woods near the airfield. The bombers were still trying to land and were running into one another on the airfield. In the morning, we went to have a look at the damage. It looked a sorry sight; the burned out bomber, which crashed on the airfield, had one wing pointing forlornly at the sky. There were three that had crashed in a heap at the end of the runway. One called *Ice Cold Katie* was sitting quite happily on top of another one.[15]

William E. Ruck, radio operator, *Ice Cold Katie*, piloted by James J. Bell, recalls:

We didn't know that Me 410 night fighters had followed us back to England because it was full dark and they were apparently using clouds as cover. However, the English anti-aircraft batteries knew they were there because they showed up on radar. So a situation developed where English AA batteries were firing at the German night fighters who were firing at the American bombers who were firing at the German fighters. It was mass confusion on a grand scale and no one could say who caused damage to which planes. The first plane to attempt to land at Seething was *Peggy Jo* in the 714th Bomb Squadron. Following standard procedure, it turned on its landing lights as it approached Seething, which was the signal for the tower to turn on the runway lights. With its landing lights on the plane made an excellent target and the German fighters simply followed the runway lights and fired at a point between the two landing lights of the plane. The bomber's starboard engine was set afire, forcing the pilot[16] to pull up so the crew could bail out and the bomber crashed at Worlingham, just beyond Seething. The second plane to come in was the *Vadie Raye* and she was on fire. Most of the crew had bailed out but the pilots, Captain Alvin Skaggs and Captain William Blum, brought the plane down on the main runway and then swerved it off and into the field so it wouldn't block the landing of the following planes. The remainder of the crew got out and ran to safety just before the *Vadie Raye* exploded. The explosion and fire produced dense smoke, which blew across and greatly reduced visibility on the main runway.

George Leininger, a gunner in the 700th Squadron in the 445th, who was on his twenty-eighth mission, wrote later,

What a mess. About 500 to 700 aircraft trying to find bases to land low on fuel plus everything was all blacked out. I shot a few bursts to try to keep our tail clear. Then I got out of the tail turret and put on my chute and stood in the right waist. I didn't know how our pilot, Mike Larson, could see anything. Later he told me that as we were about to land he flicked on landing lights and there was the tail of a B-24 landing a few feet ahead of us. Lieutenant Burke's plane didn't have landing lights on. Larson hit the throttle hard and pulled our ship up. From where I was standing in the waist, I saw our right wingtip just miss the runway by a couple of feet. We went around a couple of times and landed safely. When we had landed I jumped out and kissed the ground of good old England. Larson told me later that our squadron commander, Major Fleming, had been in the tower. He told Mike that he had put his hands over his eyes when he saw us nearly crash.

It was getting dark as Lieutenant Baldwin 'Baldy' C. Avery, pilot of *Chumbly*, a pathfinder Liberator in the 564th Squadron in the 389th, approached England. He was 'a little apprehensive of the whole situation', as he had not landed at night since 'way back in Scribner, Nebraska' during his training days. And to make matters worse, the B-24 was riddled with about ninety holes and his navigational equipment had been damaged so they were 'searching' for their home field at Hethel. Avery did not know how his navigator, Ken Dougherty, found the field but he did. Avery made a wide 360° turn and prepared to 'drag' *Chumbly* in.

All around us there were huge white flashes and balls of flame. With all the bombers flying around in the dark, I just supposed that they were running into each other. This made up my mind to get on the ground as soon as possible. I reached down and hit the toggle switch to make certain that the landing lights worked. They did, so I immediately turned them off and concentrated on making a safe landing. At the proper time the lieutenant-colonel from another group who was riding as co-pilot reached down for the switch and then informed me that they did not work although five minutes before they had worked. I was too busy to check it out and with the hits we had sustained I thought perhaps it was a reasonable possibility that they did not work. I sure did not want to have to go around and come in again so I stared out into the darkness looking for the runway. No lights on the plane – only a few smoke pots identifying the edges of the runway – one engine out – and hoping the tyres had not been hit and the brakes worked. They say I greased it in. By that time I was too numb to remember. As we turned off I reached own and hit the toggle switch for the lights – they worked. But the fact that we did not turn them on may have been a blessing for enemy planes were shooting the planes down as they turned on their landing lights.[17]

After evening chow at Horsham St Faith, the ground crews returned to the line to wait the sighting of the returning 458th formation. It was dark enough now that it would be difficult to see them but at last Bill Griffiths and his engineering personnel heard them and had visual contact. He did not recall seeing any red flares. 'So, Ok, let's get 'em down,' he thought. There, the runway lights were on! The lead plane touched down. Wham! Peace and tranquillity was no more! Searchlights were sweeping the skies; the Ack-Ack was booming and was joined by the sound of machine-gun fire! All blended together with the screaming engines, as Liberators took evasive action. Suddenly there was a red ball in the sky; someone was hit! Russell watched for the chutes! See any? He wouldn't know till the next day. Finally, after what seemed forever, the Ack-Ack and machine-gun fire stopped. Searchlights still pierced the night and until all the Liberators were down, Russell held his breath. Poof, the runway lights were off and then one by one, the searchlights blinked out. The 754th had lost two of the 458th's three aircraft on the mission.[18] The B-24 flown by 1st Lt Teague G. Harris Jr and Lieutenant Robert T. 'Jake' Couch crashed at Lakenham on the south-western side of the city of Norwich. Couch and five of the crew were killed. Harris was badly burned and rescuers found him amid the debris of the bomber. His back was broken but he would recover after months of hospitalisation. Like many Americans, Jake had been 'adopted' by a local family, Les and Vi Murton. The Murtons were drinking with friends at the Bull public house when the Liberator piloted by 2nd Lieutenant Charles W. 'Red' Stilson crashed in flames on a playing field behind the pub. Les Murton and a friend leapt over a hedge and ran to the shattered Liberator, where they managed to extricate Stilson, who was stunned but still alive in his seat.[19] Three of the crew were dead.

Russ D. Hayes, who had flown missions with the 'Sky Scorpions' and was now serving as an instructor at Horsham St, Faith, recalls:

The sirens began to blow. As I looked into the sky the huge hulk of a B-24 was skimming the treetops with half the gliding plane aflame. I watched it until it was behind the trees and then heard a terrific explosion. As I scanned the skies once more there seemed to be one visible on every horizon of Norwich and each bomber was trailing fire and smoke. I think the total was seven or more.

The next day personnel on the bases were told that fifteen Me 410s had infiltrated the bomber stream as they crossed the English Channel. At Shipdham, John McClane, a navigator in the 68th Squadron, said: 'They simply lined up their gun sights between the wing lights of a bomber on its approach to land and had a field day, like shooting fish in a barrel.'

Joe Broder concludes:

Boche Me 410 fighter-bombers wrought enormous damage, confusion and casualties. The return from Hamm turned into hell. Intruders struck at almost blacked-out airfields, shot down some B-24s in their landing patterns and caused blazes and bonfires as ships broke up or belly-landed on nearby farms. Pandemonium ruled. Shots were exchanged. One of the 446th's runways was usable; one wasn't. We landed at Seething, a base about a dozen miles away. When the 446th awoke to Hamm's morning after, they hadn't the benefit of the revelling, just the hangover. Runways were potholed from foreign bombs and had to be smooth-surfaced quickly or the field temporarily closed. Wreckage was removed from what twisted metal remained of what was once a Liberator that had just given up ten charred bodies to an already overworked mortuary station. Then another three charburned remains were yielded from a Me 410 that was still embedded in the B-24. It will never be affixed who destroyed whom on those final fatal yards flown by the young aviators.

Early the next morning, Kenneth Driscoll went down to the Squadron Operations Building to get clued in as to what had happened the night before and to find out the status of the five missing planes.

I was told that three had landed safely at other bases and two were shot down close by with no survivors. One was shot down north-west of the base by a German fighter and the other was shot down by anti-aircraft fire near the base. [Lieutenant Stalie C. Reid went down at Barsham and the pilot and six of his crew were killed. Lieutenant James A. Roden crashed at Mendham with no survivors]. Just by chance, both first pilots on each aircraft (Jack Skinner and James Roden) had been close friends of mine from our early days of training at Wendover, Utah. In my opinion Roden was the best formation flying pilot that I had ever known. I felt a great personal loss upon hearing of both of their deaths. I never received an explanation of why the tower did not break radio silence and instruct us to turn off our lights, scatter in a northerly direction and return in a half hour or so. It is possible that the first few returning aircraft were advised of the situation. At that time, I estimated that we were about 8–10 minutes away and 20–25 miles out from the base. With VHF radios, we should have been able to pick up tower transmissions at that distance. The German fighters probably did not try to shoot down any of our aircraft while intermingled with us coming in over the North Sea. That action would have been detected and their surprise attack ruined. Our incoming aircraft would have been alerted and appropriate dispersal information given to us. The ground bases and anti-aircraft gun sites would also have been alerted earlier.[20]

In all, twelve Liberators crashed or crash-landed in east Norfolk on the night of 22 April. Two more were damaged on the ground. Thirty-eight American crewmen were killed and another twenty-three injured. The fires at Seething were not extinguished until 0330 the following morning. All this destruction had been wrought by just six Me 410s.[21]

After a stand down, missions resumed on Monday 24 April when 750 bombers were dispatched to bomb aircraft plants in the Munich area and airfields in southern Germany. Wallace Patterson wrote.

We went on an 8-hour trip to Gablingen, an airfield near Augsburg. The bombing was good; fighter cover more than adequate and we lost only one crew. Lieutenant John McCune and crew of *The Flying Sac* in the 715th were last seen with a smoking engine headed for Switzerland, which was in sight of the target. We had a terrific sweat job, though. Less than a third of the way through the trip the No. 4 engine blew a cylinder and we had to feather it. Al Saunders told me to get rid of the bombs so we could make speed and intercept the others as they turned off the bombing run. There was a train directly ahead of us and as I didn't have time to set up the sight, I bombed over my toe and missed it by about 100 yards. But with ten 50-pounders landing at once it probably shook them up a little. A while later we lost the supercharger on No.1 engine, which rendered the engine practically useless at altitude. We were also sweating out gas and Hun fighters and other bomber formations took care of us. I got my Air Medal awarded by the Colonel after supper. Incidentally, the flak was frequent but very light and inaccurate. We saw three capitals: London, Paris and Brussels.

The 41st Bomb Wing, which bombed the Dornier repair and assembly plant 15 miles south of Munich, bore the brunt of the attacks carried out by an estimated 200 enemy fighters. Of the wing's fifteen losses, the 384th at Grafton Underwood suffered the worst casualties, losing seven aircraft before the Luftwaffe turned its attention on the 40th Combat Wing. *Little Chub* in the 545th Squadron was on its way to Oberpfaffenhofen when it was badly mauled by German fighters over Stuttgart. Most of the crew were on their first mission, including the co-pilot, 2nd

Lieutenant James Burry. The pilot, 1st Lieutenant Everett Bailey, had completed twenty-one missions, while the navigator, 2nd Lieutenant Charles Wallach, was on his fourth mission. The crippled bomber, with dying and injured men on board, entered Swiss airspace and was met by three Swiss Bf 109s near Zumikon. The American crew fired their flares and dipped the wings and then attempted to get the landing gear down. As only one gear could be extended, *Little Chub* circled for a while. Bailey dared not attempt a landing because gasoline and oil had leaked into the bomb bay, creating a potential fire bomb. The aircraft flew south over the airfield as the crew prepared to ditch into the Greifensee, southeast of Dübendorf. Wallach had been seriously wounded and his crewmates had placed him on the floor of the radio room. As Bailey was getting ready to bring the damaged bomber around for the third time, six Swiss fighters attacked. One of the pilots, Wachtmeister Sturzenegger, noticed that the ball turret guns were pointing downward, the crew obviously struggling to keep the damaged B-17 in the air while trying to decide how to land. *Little Chub* caught fire when Swiss tracer bullets ignited the fuel in the bomb bay and the crew began to bail out. Charles Wallach remembers:

The smoke and the burning aluminium made it almost impossible to breathe. I ran up to inform the pilot and co-pilot and help them bail out. They were crawling through the side windows and I handed them their parachutes. Bailey went out the pilot's window head first. The slipstream must have broken his neck. I was standing on my left foot, head out of the window, pulling back as hard as I could on the stick to keep the plane level when it hit the water. I popped out of the window like a cork and landed about 400 feet from the plane. The next thing I remembered was being under water.[22]

In aerial battles the 92nd lost five bombers, including *Lil Brat* flown by Lieutenant James E. King, which exploded over Baltenswil, Switzerland, with the loss of all ten crew.[23] Thirteen B-17s landed in Switzerland on 24 April from the total loss of thirty-nine bombers.

F. C. Leonard, radio operator in 1st Lieutenant Gordon E. Clubb's B-17 in the 325th Squadron, recalls:

It was my second mission. Near the target, a Fort flying in the middle formation was set afire by a Messerschmitt 109. The bomber lost its power and fell behind to a point directly over our position; the lead plane in the low formation. As the bombardier of the stricken craft jettisoned his 500 lb GP bombs, one struck our No. 3 engine while another smashed the right stabiliser only a few feet from my tail gun position. The impact knocked us silly! The resulting centrifugal force created a huge vacuum of nitrogen bubbles outside our plane. One crewmember from the burning bomber above bailed out and dangled over us in his chute, looking like a paper doll. Suddenly, another 109 appeared out of the clouds and started to pursue us at 6 o'clock level. My first encounter with the Luftwaffe! At 700 yards the enemy took dead aim at our Fort.

"You'd better do something!" I screamed to the pilot over the intercom.

He stepped on the brakes and pitched the nose of our bomber up and down in a violent evasive action. We dropped down – almost colliding with the bombers flying behind us – and fell back out of formation. Our bombs sprung loose from their racks and piled up in the bomb bay, one piercing the radio compartment door. The ammunition bounced out of my right ammo box and draped itself over my shoulder. The pilot of the 109 lost aim and pulled up within a foot from our left stabiliser. He looked at us in amazement through his flying goggles as though to ask, "What's going on here?"

I pressed the trigger of my jammed right .50 calibre and wiggled my guns at his head. He flipped the Messerschmitt over on its side and raced downward before I dared fire my left gun at such close range. Shots from the rest of the squadron chased him away. We followed the Group around the target, which was abandoned due to cloud cover. Flak came up and enveloped our struggling B-17 in black smoke. Our pilot again took evasive action by violently rocking the wings. I could hear the fuel sloshing! We cut to the left and barely missed the formation behind us as they headed for home. We limped home alone, landing at an emergency field [Bradwell Bay] on the English coast. The ground crew discovered that the fuse from the bomb, which struck our engine, had lodged itself in the cowling!

The 1st Division lost twenty-seven B-17s and the two other divisions lost thirteen bombers.

On Tuesday 25 April, 554 bombers were dispatched to blast marshalling yards at Mannheim and airfields in north-eastern France. Only 294 were effective and five B-24s and two B-17s were shot down. The next day 589 heavies were dispatched to Brunswick but only 344 B-17s dropped their bombs because thick cloud prevented bombing at primary targets. Nearly fifty more bombed targets of opportunity in the Hildesheim-Hannover areas. Mitch Mitchell's crew in the

'Travelling Circus' went to Paderborn in *Sweater Gal*, carrying 240 fragmentation bombs. Charlie Clague recalls: 'When we had to go through a zone of heavy flak, we used watch every first burst that was close to us and count the others, "One, two, three, four." Experienced crews told us if you could say "four", you were OK. It meant they had missed you again.'

Howie Mesnard, navigator adds:

The flak on the bomb run was terrific. The Germans used radar to determine the altitude and would fire their shells in groups of four, which would burst when they reached our height. They all contained black powder, so when they burst the enemy gunners could correct for inaccuracies. These shells would explode into thousands of pieces, causing severe damage to anything within a radius of several hundred feet. I'll never forget smelling the black powder that day as the shells exploded. We knew they had us zeroed in. The bomb run normally lasted approximately five minutes. During this time, the formation was kept as tight as possible to produce a concentrated bombing pattern. The leading bombardier was actually flying his ship using the gyroscopic controls in the Norden bombsight. Finally he would reach the target and drop his load of destruction. All other bombardiers in that squadron would manually release their bombs at the same time.

After the cry, "Bombs Away!" very rarely there would be one or two that hung up due to mechanical failure. Joe Stupca, flight engineer, left waist gunner Jim County, oldest man on the crew at thirty-two, or Art Rapp, ball gunner, would see this and report. Charlie Clague would then grab the walk-around oxygen bottle and crawl back to the bomb bay to make sure all the bombs had been released and with a screwdriver, Charlie would pry them loose so they would fall out of the plane. As the bomb load left the plane, the reduction in weight would cause the ship to 'bounce' several hundred feet higher in the air. This would be followed by violent evasive action in order to escape the deadly anti-aircraft barrage, which by this time was at our exact altitude. Looking back at the target area, we could see gigantic fires and smoke indicating total destruction of the ball bearing plants, factory, or whatever had been the target. We were often harassed by fighters all the way back to the coast and beyond.

Over the large cities and industrial areas, the German anti-aircraft firing was surprisingly accurate. This was true at night or when the visibility was zero due to complete cloud cover. The Allied scientists determined this accuracy was attributed to radar equipment, which electronically aimed the guns. In early 1944, to counteract this deadly accuracy, each crew was provided with two or three bails of aluminium foil cut in strips approximately 18 feet long and ½-inch wide. The instructions were, as we approached known gun emplacements, the waist gunners should throw this chaff out of the window, a handful at a time. The theory was the foil would reflect the radar signal the same as an airplane would. It worked amazingly well. As the chaff drifted down, you could see the flak shells explode in it as it followed below and behind the squadron of planes. Apparently, the Germans found the chaff on the ground and realised what we were doing. Several months later the chaff no longer had the desired effect, indicating the Germans and counteracted this method. Shortly thereafter, each Air Force crew was assigned an additional special radio operator who, with new equipment, attempted to receive the German radar signal and jammed them with the transmitter installed in the plane. This worked fairly well but was not nearly as effective as when we first started with the chaff.

The crew of *Sweater Gal* brought their bombs back because as soon as they hit the Dutch coast there was $^{10}/_{10}$ undercast. Charlie Clague wrote in his log, 'Complete Washout. Saw Ruhr Valley Flak. Ugh!'

On Wednesday 26 April at 0358 hours Lieutenant Hugh Wilson and crew in the 452nd began their take-off from Deopham Green in *Tangerine* for a mission to Hildesheim. On reaching take-off speed, Wilson eased back on the yoke but nothing happened; the aircraft would not lift off. He pulled back even harder and the plane rose only about twenty feet and settled back just above the green meadow. He then raised the landing gear to keep down all drag possible. At this point No. 3 engine went out for unexplained reasons. The other three propellers began cutting up the turf for a quarter mile before hitting the second of three fences, cutting down a large tree with the left wing, then going through two more fences and hedgerows before coming to a stop more than a half mile from the end of the runway. It was 0400 hours now and all this was taking place in total darkness so one can imagine what was going through the crew's minds. As *Tangerine* came to a halt, the first thought in the crew members' minds was to get out of the plane as quickly as possible as the bombs could explode any moment or the B-17 might catch fire and explode. All crew members abandoned ship except the tail gunner, who had been temporarily trapped in the tail and was yelling for help. Sergeant Ed Moore ran back to the plane to assist him and there found an English 'Bobbie' (policeman) standing on the wing of the plane. The tail gunner, Sergeant George

Rasiarmos, was helped out of the tail and all were safe. It puzzled the men why a 'Bobble' was there at the crash site at 0400 hours in the morning. Well, it is certain that all men of the 452nd will remember the English fellow riding a motorcycle through the base every morning and night, never slowing for anyone or anything. It was learned many years later that the reason for 'Bobbie' being there at 0400 in the morning was to catch that motorcycle rider for speeding; however, he was not nabbed that April morning.

The Liberators that set out for Paderborn did not get far either, as Wallace Patterson recalled.

The weatherman screwed up when he told us Paderborn airfield would be open to visual bombing. It was our first chance to destroy aircraft on the ground with 'Daisy Cutters', a little fragmentation bomb. We had no PFF ship and from Holland in and back there wasn't a single hole in the stuff; so we brought the bombs back. I couldn't see any tulip fields in Holland though we had a good view of Amsterdam and Ijmuiden. I noticed that a lot of the lowlands have been flooded in preparation for the invasion. The 715th lost a man today from Peck's crew in a freak accident. He left the valve open in his turret while he bent forward to make some adjustment and hit the controls with brought the sight bar down on his neck and either broke it or strangled him.

Thursday the 27th April was the first of the 'daily doubles'. The group went out in the morning to France, 17 minutes in enemy territory. Again in the afternoon, the same crews went to the marshalling yard twelve miles beyond Nancy. The Tannoy announced a congratulatory message from the General on the morning's bombing results. Everybody came back but Broxton brought back another wreck, with a badly wounded radio operator (who died the next day). Parker got a bruise on his leg from a piece of spent flak. The thirty-mission furlough was off after three days; so I guessed we'd have to sweat out the thirty. At two a day we might get done faster, if we lasted.

Robert E. Oberschmid, a pilot in the 329th Squadron at Hardwick, recalls:

Messages on the Tannoy (a simple loudspeaker in each hut) had a profound effect on our lives. Its impersonal, unsympathetic message was simply, "Combat crews alerted, breakfast is being served in the mess hall." That was it, no more, no less, but if you were alerted for that day's mission it meant you would see and do things that day that had no parallel in history.

We had been alerted, so it was off and on for us (off our backs and on our feet). After putting on our cold damp clothes, we headed out to a combat crew fresh egg breakfast. Our hut was across a small baseball field from the mess hall and while trudging through the snow in the cold and dark there was little if any of the usual banter between us. Several members of a crew from one of the other huts came alongside of us and I noticed they were all carrying fully packed B-24 bags. Even though it was four in the morning I assumed they were going on pass to London and made a comment to that effect. Several of them said, "No, no plans to London." So I asked the obvious question, "What are the bags for?" And they said, "We are not coming back."

That was the end of the conversation. After the mission to Southern Germany I inquired as to their status and was told that they had reported a variety of problems with their aircraft and had gone to Switzerland. We never heard another word about that crew. One would assume the brass knew what happened, but then again who knows.[24]

That evening, crews sat in their huts on the bases, resting up and reading, wondering what the next day's mission held for them. At Ridgewell Staff Sergeant George B. McLaughlin and his ball turret gunners gathered in quarters that housed spare crew members, known as the 'Leper Colony'. McLaughlin had just flown his twenty-fourth mission. Just one more to go and he was home safe. Home was in Doylestown, Pennsylvania. Thomas W. O'Brien Jr envied 'Little Mac', as he could all fit into the power turret while wearing his parachute. So too could Ken Stone, Ed 'Shortround' Gartland, John M. 'Shorty' Howery and John Woods. If their aircraft was hit, they had only to trip the hatch latches and roll into the slipstream. 'All Legs' O'Brien was 6 feet tall and he felt lucky to get into the turret while wearing a chest pack harness alone. 'Little Mac' had taught O'Brien all he knew. He was already an old man to him. He was twenty-seven when O'Brien came into life but most important he was an educated man and had completed studies at the graduate level. They had many enlightening talks together and on some days O'Brien travelled with him to visit in the University libraries at Cambridge. 'Little Mac' was well versed in the classics and many happy hours were spent in discussion; the hours just flew by. Mac was a deeply religious man and he read silently from his Bible every evening before retiring. He laid the book down and said, 'O'Bie, are you awake?'

'Ya, Mac, what is it compadre?' Mac sat silent for a few moments and then he said, 'O'Bie, I will never go home again.' There was no trace of fear in his voice, no panic; it was just a statement as a matter of fact, with calm acceptance. The gunners knew that a mission was scheduled for the next day. The Liberty Run had been cancelled. Mac would be flying No. 25 with one of the newer crews.

"But Mac, you only have one to go; you are going home to Doylestown and you are going to get that long black limousine. It's going to be so long that you will need an interphone to talk with the driver and it will have to have hinges to negotiate corners. You will wear a big red carnation in your lapel and carry a gold tipped walking cane and all of the good citizens of Doylestown are going to look in wonder and say 'There goes Mr Mac. He was a BTO in the ETO'."

"No, O'Bie. I know it will all end here. Promise me that you will do some things for me."

He gave O'Brien three sealed letters to be mailed and a list of his personal possessions and the names of those he wished to receive them. Then he reached into the side pocket of his B-4 bag and handed him eight bolt studs for the ball turret guns.

They had breakfast together the next morning, picked up their personal equipment and went to the aircraft – loaded and waiting. The heavies were bombing targets chiefly in France. St-Avord, a Luftwaffe airfield south of Paris, should be a 'milk run'. The 381st started engines and taxied on time. Little Mac's aircraft, *Georgia Rebel II*, which was being flown by 1st Lieutenant Harold H. Henslin, was three ahead of O'Brien's B-17 in take off order. It carried the formation commander, Major Osce V. Jones. Another of O'Brien's buddies, Bill Blackmon, was one of the waist gunners. 'Blackie' loved combat and was always eager to be in the heat of the action. He would often get up early and go to breakfast with Tom O'Brien, even on days his crew was not scheduled for a mission. 'Blackie' would put his hands in his pockets, look up to the sky and say, 'God I wish I could fly a mission. I wish they would come in today. I want to get those bastards.'

The tower fired the green flare and the launch was on.[25]

Ed 'Cotton' Appleman, nose gunner on Ross Baker's crew in the 93rd, who were flying their first mission, wrote in his diary:

First mission over Pas de Calais. Target was the rocket site just outside of Calais. Encountered flak over target and on coast just before we started back. We caught about fifteen or twenty bursts around us but the rest of the formation behind us caught the most of it. Flak pierced a fuel cell in our right wing; put a hole right under the navigator and one through the nose wheel door. 3 hours, 30 minutes. Fifty-two 100# bombs.

The Bloody Hundredth were given a No Ball site at Sottevast near Cherbourg, as Sam Laface recalls:

> We usually flew hundreds of miles, but the shortest mission could be just as deadly. Cherbourg should have been a milk run. Colonel Robert H. Kelly our new Group Commander was leading the formation [in Captain Bill Lakin's B-17]. There was cloud cover at the target, so we wheeled around and bombed; it a second time. As we went over again, the German gunners hit us with everything they had. The lead ship took a direct hit and disintegrated. Kelly hadn't been our CO for a week. Every B-17 received hits and was damaged.

A second Fortress, flown by Lieutenant James W. McGuire, had an engine knocked from its mounting. The engine landed back on the wing, setting it on fire. As McGuire dived out of formation the wing snapped off and the B-17 cracked in two, like an egg, at the waist and went down. It was a huge ball of fire and a 'chute popped open in that fire. It burned immediately. Lieutenant John Jones, the bombardier, who was flying as navigator, miraculously managed to bail out and the co-pilot and engineer also got out into the undercast and were taken prisoner. The rest of the crew, who were on their twelfth mission, with the exception of Joseph Eck, the togglier, who was on his second, were killed. McGuire and Eck were buried at Omaha beach. At Thorpe Abbotts, Major 'Bucky' Elton was waiting at his friend and room-mate's hardstand with champagne to celebrate Bill Lakin's last mission and Kelly's first lead since joining the Group just nine days earlier. He also lost his line chief, 'who at forty had begged to fly'. At briefing it was commented that Kelly, who had come to the Group with the idea of 'straightening it out', 'sure picked a sweet milk run for his first mission' but it all turned sour when at interrogation crews were told that he had failed to return. The intelligence interrogators were awed and amazed. One was heard to say, 'Colonel Kelly hasn't even unpacked yet.'[26]

At Ridgewell, no word was received from *Georgia Rebel II*. They had been the only Group loss, taking a direct hit in the No. 2 engine at the target at 14,000 feet while under attack by fighters and flak. Tom O'Brien was so busy at his own guns that he failed to notice three parachutes leave the aircraft from the stricken aircraft, which was seen to dive and break up. Ed Sell, the tail gunner, snagged his parachute on the tailplane and went down with the wreckage. Only two men survived. George B. McLaughlin was not one of them.[27]

On Saturday 29 April, Wallace Patterson noted:

At long last, Berlin – first, second and last resort target, the Friedrichstrasse Station right smack in the centre of town. The Forts were to hit with 1,000 lb GPs and we to follow with incendiaries. Over the Channel we decided that our oxygen wouldn't last and elected to continue to the target and then hit the deck if need be. We caught flak in Holland, over the Dummer Lake area; then for 30 minutes before the IP we ran into the most accurate, intense and long-lasting barrage anyone has ever encountered. Most flak alerts last only a minute or so. We figured we flew over Brunswick, Osnabrück and Hanover, all hotly defended towns. They threw every colour and every type they had at us. We were thirty minutes late at the target and from then on we were without fighter support. We saw plainly the target, the Olympic Stadium and the Tiergarten and most of the city. Their flak was not so intense but was of heavier calibre than on the way in and they also threw a lot of rockets at us. Lovell caught a piece that came through the nose turret and was stopped by the bulletproof glass. The bombing was good, what we could see of it. After leaving, we saw Howard with a feathered engine and Cathey with one smoking. On the way back we left our own group and went as low as possible to save the little oxygen we had left. En route back we caught the same flak area because the goddamn lead navigator apparently didn't know where he was going. Near Holland we saw the first bandits. At first they circled stragglers and then one stood on its nose and dived on a B-17. It twisted around and headed back toward Germany.

Next they went toward a B-24, which was also on the deck. I saw five individual attacks on the ship and clearly saw the 20 mm stuff bursting around it. It disappeared into the clouds. Then Lovell called out fighters at 12 o'clock. I looked and knew form my lessons that from the formations they were flying they must be bandits. There were six of them, all flying abreast and all painted white. Then they lined up stem to stern and came at the 448th formation we had left. One B-24 shot up in the air, turned on its back and dove down toward the ground. Another caught fire and spun in. We saw five chutes open. Another went off, apparently under control but no chutes came out. Then our fighters, whom Al called, showed up and we were okay from then on except for some light flak. We were out of oxygen and nearly out of gas. We landed with 50 gallons of gas in one main tank and the other bone dry. We had started with 2,700 gallons. A

great many ships ditched in the Channel because of lack of gas. We had quite a
lot of holes in the ship. Williams' crew claimed four fighters and Kronheim one.
We were missing Howard and Cathey, two new crews from the 715th. Cathey's
crew were our roommates, three of them married, one with a baby on the way.
Four others were missing from the group, making six in all.[28] The 715th was
now quite short on crews, what with losses and leaves and my next one would be
12B for me. I hoped that it would be a short one.

Perry Rudd in the 457th recalled that:

Germany announced the raid as soon as we hit the IP, 18 minutes at least from
the target. There was little flak going in but plenty over the target. Their aiming
point seemed to be in the lower boxes and we were in the higher box, so we didn't
get touched. The mission was planned for PFF but we could see the target quite
clearly. Plans seemed to change at the last minute and we made a 360° turn near
Berlin and went in 30 minutes late. We dropped three 1,000 lb demolition bombs
and six 500 lb incendiaries and they hit near a river bridge in the centre of the
capital. Each plane dropped three tons right on the target. The place must really
have taken a beating: three divisions of ten wings bombed different sections and I
saw only one plane go down, right over the target. It was in flames and broke up
after a direct flak hit. There must have been 600 planes and even more fighters. I
couldn't see how the city could be standing that night.

In all, 579 bombers hit the Freidrichstrasse Bahnhof, the centre of the mainline
and underground railway system in Berlin. Thirty-eight other heavies attacked
targets of opportunity in the area, including Magdeburg. One fully loaded B-24
crashed into a Volkswagen factory. The bomb groups encountered strong fighter
opposition and sixty-three aircraft were lost. Fw 190s shot down or fatally
damaged seventeen Fortresses in the 4th Combat Wing in 20 minutes. The 385th,
which was flying its 100th mission, lost seven bombers. 'We were flying a tight
formation and all the squadrons seemed to be in their right positions when the
German fighters attacked,' recalls T/Sgt Clarence L. Mossman, left waist gunner in
the *Worry Bird*, flown by Lieutenant Richard A. Spencer, a twenty-eight-year-old
pilot from Cleveland, Ohio, in the 549th Squadron.

We did evasive action to help us from head-on attacks. We first spotted about
200 fighters about 12 o'clock high and in a few minutes they attacked us head-

on, coming down out of the sun in waves of forty and sixty at a time, and doing barrel rolls right through the formations. They made three passes. Our left and also our right wingman went down. I think we lost about eleven B-17s out of one squadron. We had a lot of flak damage on our aircraft and also damage to our wing from 20 mm shells fired by Me 109 fighter planes that came down through our formation. All of the crew came through the mission with being wounded or killed.

'The sky was filled with so much confusion – exploding planes, flying debris, parachutes, bursting flak and exploding shells. It was all fantastic but horribly real to us up there,' said Spencer when interviewed by the press, appearing in the *St Louis Globe Democrat*.

Worse, the 447th lost ten in encounters with fighters and an eleventh B-17 was lost when it was ditched in the North Sea. Lieutenant Flemming's crew were rescued. Two of the missing crews were on their first mission. One tail gunner in the 710th Squadron that returned to Rattlesden lost both hands. The losses brought the Group's monthly total to twenty-one aircraft lost. The 94th and 'Snetterton Falcons' losses for April 1944 were also twenty-one bombers apiece; the 8th's heaviest of the war.

Richard Walsh, top turret gunner on *Section Eight* in the 452nd, piloted by 2nd Lieutenant George A. Haskenson, recalls:

As we hit our IP we could see up ahead, the great big wall of flak. I looked down on this country where so much trouble came from. From five miles up it looked like any other place in the world but you can't mistake the winding Rhine River that passes through the heart of Germany. To the right I could see the big park that we were briefed to help locate the target.

"Bomb bay doors coming open," the bombardier said.

I checked the doors and relay. "Doors open and all clear below."

"Roger," says he.

Then it happened.

We weren't getting any flak until then, that is, direct flak, but now they were on us and we were hit, or should I say, blasted out of position and the No. 1 and 3 engines were out. No. 1 feathered OK but No. 3 did not. None of the crew was hit but the ship was a sieve. We had a hole big enough to drive a jeep through in the left wing. The fuel transfer pump worked overtime 'till the last. By now we had lost 8,000 feet and were completely alone. Our speed was approximately

120 mph; dangerously close to stalling speed, if the ship was not flown perfectly. Several things happened that required fast action and skill and through all this not one of us was panicky but we were scared. All guns and ammo were thrown overboard, also all of the armour we could loosen. The ball turret was dropped. That in itself was a great help because of its weight and wind resistance.

Well up to now things weren't too bad. We were alive anyhow. We then had a new worry: gas! The gunners and bombardier stripped the ship expertly because of some past experience. Now it was just a matter of time. The radioman was in contact with ASR and we were fixed. With a few parting bursts of flak we left the Dutch coast and started across the Channel. Altitude about 5,000. We passed B-26s of the 9th Air Force going in and two P-47s saluted us and hung around for a while. We were in constant touch with the horizon when I looked at the gas gauge, which read '30 gallons' for each engine. Then I remembered what the books said a long way back, "Don't use all the gas and then crash land. Do it while the engines are turning."

This was it. We had to prepare to ditch. The pilots pulled their safety belts on and the rest of the crew took their places for the ditching procedure. We started down to the smooth green water (it looked like it anyhow). At about 500 feet the two remaining engines 'conked out' so we had to dead-stick on the water. She skipped twice before mushing in completely underwater and then she bobbed to the surface like a cork. We scrambled out and counted heads. All present with no casualties. Both dinghies inflated OK and we got in and pushed away.

The 2nd Bomb Division, flying 30 minutes behind schedule, brought up the rear of the bomber stream and was met in strength by the Luftwaffe. After leaving Celle airspace, the only protection afforded the B-24s was a solitary Mustang group, which was forced to retire just after the Liberators completed their bombing run. At the IP *Play Boy*, piloted by Frank Cotner from Columbus, Ohio, in the 466th, received a direct hit from an 88, which knocked out the No. 3 engine. Cotner completed the bomb run but *Play Boy* was attacked by fighters after the target and went down over Holland. Twenty-year-old Sergeant Robert J. Falk, flying his first mission with the crew as waist gunner, was killed instantly by a shot through the head. Two of the crew evaded capture for the rest of the war but Cotner was sent to Stalag Luft III.[29]

'Mitch' Mitchell's crew in the 'Travelling Circus' flying *Sweater Gal* was among the crews that headed for Berlin. Charlie Clague, who was flying his seventeenth mission, recalls what happened.

We were in flak from the time we hit Berlin until 30 minutes later without cessation. It was a long, cold mission and we ran into several fighters on the way home. A few minutes after leaving the target, our airplane was really rocked by a nearby burst of flak. The plane was pitched up violently and over on one wing, then it nosed down and swung wildly back the other way. Sitting under the navigator's table and looking past Howie out the nose window, I could feel intense G forces and see the horizon veer into some very bizarre attitudes. The bail out alarm bell rang loudly and Mitch's insistent voice came over the Intercom, "Bail Out! Bail Out!" The violent aircraft contortions may have lasted 5 or 10 seconds – it certainly seemed much longer! While it lasted there was little chance that any crewmember could have successfully exited the craft. From my seated position, I had only to lean back and pull the red handle that would jettison the nose doors. I reached, may have even touched the handle but at that moment the plane seemed to calmly slide back to straight and normal flight.

Meanwhile, Howie was crowding me, crouched down and exhorting me with hand and arm gestures to get out quick. I held up a hand with index finger extended, indicating 'just a minute' and Howie quickly assessed the return to normalcy. About that time, Mitchell or Jennings keyed a mike and said, "Report!" Tom Jennings, our boyishly handsome co-pilot, was generally quiet and often kept to himself. We were supposed to be fighting a war and we didn't expect to see any women but he was the choice of the ladies. Beginning in Boise, then in Colorado Springs and even in England, Tom had a string of girls following him in each town. When we moved on they would all write love letters, which he often didn't bother to open. As for Mitch, he led very naturally. I don't think that the rest of us ever thought much about it. We all made our input at every crossroad or opportunity and always felt the crew and its welfare was ours. When a decision was needed, usually we had already given Mitch the answer. Sometimes we didn't have time to discuss things and dawgonnit, Mitch would make the decision and then tell us. I don't remember any of us finding fault with him or his reasoning.

Very calmly, Frank Palumbo, tail gunner, reported, "Tail Gunner OK."

Jim County, Arthur Rapp, Joe Stupca and Joe Balate all answered in order with their OKs.

Howie or I completed the crew check in with an OK from the nose. I am sure Mitchell and Jennings had had all they could handle and more for a few seconds but all miraculously turned out well. Joe Stupca said later that he had refused to jump right away because he didn't want some German fighter pilot to kill him while he was dangling from a parachute. He said that if he was going to die, he was going to die going down in the plane. He added later that the rest of the crew agreed with him. As for me, I had never wanted to bail out. I had sometimes wondered what it would be like. In that frenzied moment, a split second before the plane levelled out, I was more than ready to go. It was a very close call.[30]

Theirs was not the only one. Dale R. Van Blair, the twenty-two-year-old tail turret gunner, who was born in Quincy, Illinois, in 1st Lieutenant Alfred H. Locke's PFF crew in the 'Sky Scorpions' at Hethel who were leading the 466th to Berlin recalls:

As a PFF crew, we had just been assigned two extra navigators and 1st Lieutenants Kenneth Reed and John Bloznelis were flying with us for the first time as instrument navigator and dead reckoning navigator respectively. Because we had a sick engineer and radio operator, T/Sgt Harold Freeman, engineer, and Wallace had been called on to fill in. We were one of several crews which, after special training on a PFF Liberator, had been attached to the 564th Squadron of the 389th Bomb Group. As a PFF crew our assignment was to fly as the lead or deputy lead plane of a formation and for this mission we were to lead the 20th Combat Wing, with Colonel Ralph Bryant going with us as Command Pilot. The target was railroad yards in the heart of Berlin. It was my eighteenth mission, fifth on PFF.

Shortly after we took off, two generators went out, but because the deputy lead had not left the ground because of mechanical problems, Colonel Bryant decided that we would have to lead the mission. After getting the formation assembled, we crossed the North Sea and Holland and flew on across France. Aside from moderately heavy flak, the flight was without incident until shortly before we crossed the German border. At that time our formation was attacked by several Fw 190s that were quickly driven off by our fighter escort. About twenty minutes later we were again hit by Fw 190s, but again our escort of P-51s drove them off quickly, destroying at least one that I saw go down. As we approached Berlin, 1st Lieutenant Arthur Delclisur, the bombardier, reported that not enough power was being generated to operate the bombsight properly and that we would have to bomb by radar, even though there was no undercast to interfere with visual bombing. Immediately upon entering our bomb run, we ran into intense and accurate flak and in the few minutes we were over Berlin, our plane was hit several times. Locke had to feather #3 engine. Also, the main tank in the right wing was punctured and seeping gas. Then, just after Delclisur released the flare that signalled the other planes to drop their bombs, our remaining two generators went out, leaving us no power for gun turrets, radio, interphone, etc.

Shortly after turning away from the target to begin the return flight, our formation was again attacked by a group of Fw 190s plus a few Me 109s. Since we were now without fighter escort, the Germans were free to concentrate on us. Frequently they did not break off their passes until they were extremely close. One flew by so close to me that I thought I might recognise him if we ever met face to face in the future. I quickly learned that operating my tail turret by the emergency had cranks and foot firing pedals was a frustrating experience. I could not begin to keep up with an enemy fighter by using the hand cranks unless he came almost straight at me and none was foolish enough to do that.

After our #2 engine was hit and had to be feathered, Locke dropped to the rear of the formation. The loss of the interphone and my limited view from my tail turret kept me from being aware of the loss of the two engines and the leaking gas tank; however, I figured we must have problems besides the loss of electrical power when I realised that we had dropped back. I watched German fighters gang up on and down four Libs that had been hit and were unable to keep up with the formation, *That's us if we can't keep up*, I thought, and kept an eye on the nearest Lib to see if we were dropping behind. A few minutes later I was relieved to note that we were maintaining our position. Finally, a few P-47s picked us up and the enemy fighters left. When I at last saw the North Sea below us, I breathed a sigh of relief, for I thought we had it made. We had not gone far, however, before I felt a tap on my back. It was Hank Boisclair. "We're going to ditch," he shouted. "We don't have enough fuel to get back." I went back to the waist and helped throw all removable equipment out the waist windows. Because the loss of the generators left us with no power for the radio, we could not send an SOS. We fired up flares calling for fighter support, and soon two P-47s flew over to us. By hand signals we managed to convey to them that we had to ditch and that our radio was out. They signalled that they understood and flew along with us until the time came to hit the water.

When Locke dragged the tail of the plane in the water to slow it prior to setting it down, the escape hatch flew open and icy water sprayed us. It was unbelievably cold. Someone jumped up from where we were sitting on the floor between the two waist windows and tried unsuccessfully to slam the hatch shut with his foot. Then, as Locke attempted to set the plane down, a large wave caught the nose. It was like slamming into a concrete wall. The plane broke just behind the rear bomb bay, and the bottom skin of the waist section was ripped off. There was not even time to take a deep breath before we plunged into the water.

As I fought to get back to the surface, something banged hard against my forehead. Just as I thought I could not hold my breath another second, my head broke above the surface and I found myself still inside the waist section, which had not broken completely free of the forward section. Seeing that the right waist window was completely blocked, I turned to the other window, but Pete was struggling to get through the half of it that was not covered by wreckage. Fearing the waist section would break loose any second and sink, I looked for a way out. After what seemed like an eternity but could only have been a few seconds, I saw a small opening in the side of the fuselage. As I was about to exit through it, someone screamed for help. I turned around but could not see anyone; I swam back a few feet. Still not finding anyone and not hearing another call for help, I went through the tear in the fuselage, inflated my Mae West, and began paddling away from the wreckage. I spotted four men in the water, but the only one close enough to recognise was Delclisur. He had a large gash over one eye. I tried to swim to him, but the waves merely washed me further away and I lost sight of everything but the plane wreckage.

A B-24 flew over very low with its bomb bays open, and I thought it was going to drop a life raft; however, it circled twice and flew off. Why didn't they do something? I wondered. I continued to paddle around, finding it more and more difficult to hold my head up out of the water. I was exhausted. Finally I turned over on my back and discovered that the Mae West held my head above the water and rode up over each wave with no effort on my part. Someone should have told us about that during our training, I thought. Then, off in the distance, I saw a boat approaching, which had probably been contacted by the P-47s. As it came closer, I waved and saw someone wave back. After watching the boat pick up two of our crew, I neither saw nor felt anything except for a vague sensation of someone trying to pour something down my throat. When I next opened my eyes, I found myself lying in a bunk on the boat with Locke looking at me from the bunk above. He told me that he was all right and that we were docked at Yarmouth and would be taken to a hospital in a few minutes. I had been in the water about forty-five minutes and was the last one to be picked up. My recollection of someone trying to pour something down my throat was the result of their trying to get me to drink some Scotch after picking me up.

Of our twelve-man crew, seven survived the ditching. Bryant and Delclisur died of injuries and shock shortly after being picked up. Reed was seen by 1st

Lieutenant John Hortenstine, the Mickey navigator, with his head hanging into the water. John tried to hold onto him but soon became exhausted. Kenneth slipped away from him and was not seen again. Bloznelis and Freeman apparently were killed in the ditching and were never sighted. What made Harold Freeman's death especially tragic was that he had completed his missions and was waiting for orders to return to the States when he was ordered to fill in on our crew. 1st Lieutenant Errol A. Selfe, our co-pilot, suffered a broken back and chipped shoulder bone. He later received the Soldier's Medal for freeing the assistant engineer, S/Sgt Pete Paez, who had got caught on wreckage while trying to get through the waist window. It was probably Paez I heard calling for help. Selfe had come up outside the waist window and immediately pulled Pete loose after the one call for help. I received a minor skull fracture from the blow on the forehead, then three weeks later developed spinal meningitis caused by pneumonia germs and lost the hearing in my right ear. The other surviving men escaped with only minor cuts and bruises. Lieutenant Locke later received the DFC for holding the plane up in the formation with only two engines and bringing it back as far as he did.[31]

Notes

1. The Day Before Christmas 1943

1. Captain Larson and crew were shot down on 12 May 1944 (10 PoW).
2. Doyle Shields and Men of the 447th, *History of the 447th Bomb Group* (1996).
3. *Ibid.*
4. *Ibid.*
5. Only two men survived from Foster's B-24. Altogether, twenty-three bombers and twelve American fighters were lost on the raid and twenty-three German fighters were claimed destroyed.
6. All of Gelling's crew survived and were taken prisoner. Seven of Lt Kittredge's crew bailed out but Lt Edward Fox, co-pilot, and Sgt Kenneth De Soto, radio operator, elected to stay and help the pilot. All three men died when the B-24 crashed at Cul-des-Sarts near Chimay in Belgium. See Jeffrey E. Brett, *The 448th Bomb Group (H): Liberators over Germany in WWII* (Schiffer 2002).
7. Shields, *History of the 447th Bomb Group*.
8. The bucket was the No. 4 plane of a four-plane element.
9. *Harmful Lil Armful* and Lt Phillip Chase's crew went down first, followed by *Cold Turkey* and Lt Max Jordan's crew. Chase's crew bailed out before the B-24 crashed 15 miles east of Cognac. Both waist gunners were killed. Chase and three others were captured. Two more evaded and returned to Seething later. No chutes were seen from Jordan's ship. There were no survivors. See *448th Bomb Group (H)*.

10. 2nd Lt William O. Trunnell, co-pilot.

11. Sgt William A. Munson, the waist gunner, was killed on the way down. Patton, Jack McGough (the bombardier), and Glen Johnson all landed safely and were eventually returned to England via the Bonaparte evasion lines. Ralph Hall, the engineer, returned in August after crossing the Pyrenees into Spain and coming home via Gibraltar.

12. Their Liberator went down in the North Sea and all the crew perished.

13. The 5 January missions were the last under the auspices of VIII Bomber Command. It was decided to embrace both the 8th and 15th in a new HQ called US Strategic Air Forces, Europe, at Bushey Hall, Teddington, Middlesex, which had previously been HQ, 8th Air Force. 'Tooey' Spaatz returned to England to command the new organisation. Lt-General Ira C. Eaker was posted to the Mediterranean theatre and replaced at the 8th Air Force (whose HQ moved to High Wycombe) by General Jimmy Doolittle, the famed Tokyo leader and former air racing pilot.

14. When the French found him, Sweatt was unconscious and seriously ill from wounds and fever. The French hid him in a secret medical facility for several weeks until he recovered. While he was in hospital his watch, which had been attached to his steel helmet when he bailed out, was found, still running, and returned to him. The rest of the crew was never found. Bob Sweatt was later transferred to Paris, sent along the French Bonaparte underground line and ultimately reached England on 23 March 1944.

15. Shields, *History of the 447th Bomb Group*.

16. The Mustang was still a well-kept secret and the 354th Fighter Group in the 9th Air Force was the pioneer Mustang group in the ETO. Major James H. Howard, an ex-Flying Tigers P-40 pilot in China and now CO of 356th Fighter Squadron, displayed 'conspicuous gallantry and intrepidity above and beyond the call of duty' in action with the enemy near Oschersleben. Howard was flying his usual P-51B, *Ding Hao!* (Chinese for 'very good'). As the P-51s met the bombers in the target area, numerous rocket-firing Bf 110 *Zerstorer* fighters attacked the bomber force. The 354th engaged and Howard destroyed one of the 110s but in the fight lost contact with the rest of his group. He immediately returned to the level of the bomber formation and saw that the 401st Bomb Group was being heavily attacked by German fighters and that no 'little friends' were on hand. Howard dived into the formation of more than thirty enemy fighters and for 30 minutes single-handedly pressed home a series of determined attacks. He shot down two more

fighters and probably destroyed another and damaged one other. Toward the end of his action, Howard continued to fight on with one remaining machine gun and his fuel supply dangerously low. Major Howard's brave single-handed action undoubtedly saved the formation. He was awarded the Medal of Honor, the only one ever awarded to a fighter pilot flying from England.

17. 42-31082 (two KIA, eight PoW).

18. 42-31107 (eight KIA, two PoW).

19. Shields, *History of the 447th Bomb Group*.

20. Of the 174 B-17s dispatched to Oschersleben, thirty-four were shot down, while two wings assigned the plant at nearby Halberstadt came through practically unscathed. The 303rd lost ten bombers and a 482nd BG aircraft flying the lead with the 303rd BG was also lost. 2nd Lt J. W. Watson, pilot of *Meat Hound*, bailed his crew out over the Continent and landed alone at Metfield with two engines out. The 351st and the 94th groups both lost seven bombers. Sixty bombers were lost on the three raids, eighty-three B-17s were damaged, nine men KIA, eleven wounded and 349 men MIA. The 94th received its second Presidential Unit Citation. In August 1944, all of the 1st BD groups that took part in the raid were similarly awarded.

21. Eleven of the B-24s dropped their bombs through broken clouds on Meppen, Germany, and others hit a T/O at Zundberg, on the border with Holland.

22. All eleven men on Captain Merle R. Hungerford Jr's crew were taken into captivity.

23. Meg Cole Smith, '1996 Reflections of a 1944 Gold Star Widow', in *2nd AD Journal*. In 1949 Meg met Tom Smith, who was associated with Lockheed Aircraft in the Second World War, photographing top secret material used in the building of that company's products. They met through their friend, Jane Russell, whose notorious discoverer, Howard Hughes, bought RKO during the late 1940s so that he could release her first film, *The Outlaw*, in RKO's Orpheum Theatres, which had been denied him when he made the film eleven years earlier. Meg was also able to work with Jimmy Stewart on *It's A Wonderful Life* but never knew of his career in the 8th Air Force. 'He never talked about his time in the service and I was too young and shy to ask, anyhow,' Meg says.

24. Henry Weiser and Robert Agar were taken prisoner.

2. All the Fine Young Men

1. US. The British term is Shanks' Pony.
2. Adapted from E. Warren Bruce, 'B-24 Versus Fw-109 – Scratch One Fw', in Ed Castens, *The 446th Revisted* (For the 446th BG (H) Association).
3. 'B-24 Versus Fw-109'. Sgt Leslie Jones was awarded the Silver Star, the first such award in the group. Warren Bruce received the DFC and Tom Pretty was awarded the Air Medal for downing the enemy fighter.
4. Two men on Van Syckle's crew were KIA (eight PoW). Nicklawsky's B-17 was shot down by a rocket fired by a Bf 110 about 30 miles south of Frankfurt. He and eight of his crew survived and they were taken prisoner.
5. Five men on *Little Boots* were KIA. Beers and the four others were taken prisoner.
6. 'Debriefing', *8th Air Force News,* March 2008.
7. William McGinley, 'Over The Rainbow', in *2nd AD Journal.* McGinley and five other men on the crew evaded (three PoW).

   'The resistance members in Holland, Belgium and France were truly heroic people and took tremendous risks. Jane, a courageous young woman after whom I subsequently named my daughter, had been caught and beaten once by the Gestapo, but hadn't cracked under extreme interrogation and was subsequently released after managing to convince them of her innocence. I well remember the Belgian count who was also a member of the resistance organisation. He spoke fluent German and, with forged ID documents, would go to an airfield wearing a Gestapo officer's uniform, complete with skull and cross bones insignia, and dine at the officers' mess. Louie, the count's chauffeur/handyman, would wander around the airfield wearing the uniform of a German private and pour sugar in the fuel tanks of their airplanes. Anne Brusselmans played a leading part in looking after the evaders and arranging their moves to different locations. On one occasion the Gestapo managed to infiltrate the resistance network and caught one of her friends harboring downed American airmen. The father of the family was shot and the rest went into concentration camps. I had given my service number to the underground to notify the International Red Cross, not realising that Europeans use a small cross mark on the number seven and subsequently, all the figure sevens in my number were thought to be figure ones, so the Red Cross reported me as dead. My mother at home in Mabelvale, near Little Rock, Arkansas, refused to accept that I'd been killed. After months of hiding at various locations I sat in a Belgian café and witnessed the German Army in full retreat following the Allied invasion of France. It was really something to see. Thousands of German troops with their equipment (some of the trucks and staff cars were being hauled by horses due to the lack of gasoline) jammed the road, barely moving, all heading towards Germany. I felt sorry for the plainly undernourished horses, but had not the slightest sympathy for the soldiers. I was flown back to England in September 1944. Thousands of bomb and shell craters marked the Allied advance from the Normandy beaches and extended back inland as far as the eye could see. As the south coast of England came into view, I saw one of the biggest and most beautiful rainbows ever created.'

8. B-24 42-99949 GO-I *Naughty Nan* in the 328th BS was lost on 21 September 1944 when it was involved in a mid-air collision with 42-94989 over Belgium. Five of Lt Everett E. Johnson's crew were KIA and four returned.

9. *YANK, The Army Weekly*, 12 March 1944.

10. Leutnant Waldemar 'Waldi' Radener claimed a B-24 destroyed 10 km south-east of Albert. His victim was 42-7542 *Black Widow* in the 707th BS, 446th BG, that ditched in the English Channel with Lt Marvin W. Garber's crew. Oberfeldwebel Erich Scheyda claimed a B-17 3 km north-east of Brussels. Leutnant 'Charlie' Willius, 2 Staffel CO, claimed a B-17 1 km east of Cousoire. Oberfeldwebel Alfred 'Fred' Heckmann, 3 Staffel CO, shot down 42-31292 in the 569th BS, 390th BG. All ten of Lt Clarence B. Strait's crew survived and were taken prisoner. A claim by Feldwebel Gerhard Wiegand for a B-17 south of Toureui was not upheld. See Donald Caldwell, *The JG 26 War Diary Vol. 2* (Grub Street, London 1998).

11. Christensen's B-17 (42-97496) was landed at Bulltofta, Sweden, on 9 April 1944 by 2nd Lt G. C. Byrd Jr and all ten crew were interned.

12. Commanded by Lt-Colonel Herbert Wangeman and Colonel Joe Miller respectively.

13. At Melun, Leutnant Charlie Willius, CO 2/JG26, shot down 42-38015 in the 338th BS, 96th Bomb Group, which was in the low squadron in the 45th CBW formation. Willius hit the gas tank, the bomber exploded and the wing came off as the B-17 fell into the undercast to crash at Pisseleux. Eight of 2nd

Lt Jake 'Jacob' Kurftzberg's crew were found dead in the wreckage, which fell at Villers-Cotterets. A ninth crewmember was taken from the wrecked B-17 by the Germans and sent to a Paris hospital, where he died later. S/Sgt Jose Pino, the right waist gunner, from El Paso, Texas, survived to become a PoW.

14. In all, thirteen Fortresses were lost.

15. Also, *Hell's Belle* iced up and only two men got out alive before it crashed to earth.

16. 2nd Lt Douglas T. Leeper was killed also.

17. The co-pilot remained with the aircraft and was killed but the rest of the crew bailed out and were taken prisoner. *Barbara*, Lieutenant Jerry B. Payne's B-17, was also hit and all except the tail gunner died when an emergency landing was attempted in enemy territory.

18. In *Big Week!* by Glenn Infield, it is said that 'after a conference, during which every crew member had an opportunity to suggest a name for the B-17 it was decided to name it 'Mizpah'. In a letter to her son, Nelson's mother had mentioned the word 'Mizpah', remarking that it was a biblical term meaning "The Lord watch between me and thee while we are absent from one another."'

19. Five of the missing bombers were claimed destroyed by II./JG 1, three of them by Heinz Bär to take his score to 185 kills. Two of the B-17s lost were from the 95th BG, which succumbed to fighters of JG 26. 42-30634 *Liberty Belle*, piloted by Lt John P. McGuigan, in the 412th BS crashed into the Zuider Zee with the loss of six crew. The rest were captured after baling out. 42-3462 *San Antonio Rose*, piloted by 2nd Lt Morris R. Marks, in the 336th BS crashed into these waters with the loss of eight of the crew. Two men were captured and made PoW. Oberfeldwebel Addi Glunz, 5 Staffel CO and Unteroffizier Gerhard Loschinksi of 7./JG 26 shot down these two B-17s. Three days later, Loschinksi was shot down and killed in combat with a 357th Fighter Group Mustang.

20. Two 92nd BG B-17s collided in cloud during the diversionary raid, Denmark.

21. Arneson, Schmidt and six others were taken prisoner. The bombardier and the left waist gunner were KIA.

22. At Schweinfurt, 238 B-17s dropped 574.3 tons of HE and incendiaries on the target area, resulting in major damage to three of the four ball-bearing plants.

23. The average percentage of bombs dropped by the 2nd BD that fell within 2,000 feet on visual missions under good to fair visibility in February 1944 was only 49 per cent. (In comparison, the 1st BD achieved 76 per cent and the 3rd 77 per cent.)

24. Including Major Evans, the 702nd CO, and most of the operations staff. Captain Waldher, Operations Officer of the 700th BS, was also lost. Both the 445th and 392nd BGs were later awarded Presidential Unit Citations for their part in the raid. Altogether, the 2nd BD lost thirty-three Liberators, the 1st BD eleven B-17s and the 15th AF seventeen bombers. 236 B-17s in the 3rd BD attacked their secondary target at Rostock after overcast had ruled out the primary objectives at Roman, Tutow and Krzesiny.

25. Three of Lt Robert A. Safranek's crew on *Rigor Mortis* were KIA (seven PoW). Four men in Lt Theodore S. Czarnecki's crew were KIA (six PoW).

26. 'Panda-monium' by Allan E. Johnson, writing in the 452nd BG history compiled by Marvin E. Barnes (The Delmar Publishing Co. 1980).

27. Other crew members participating in this aerial saga were S/Sgt Curtis E. Meinelt, S/Sgt Roy E. Ness, 2nd Lt Ralph D. Mckown and 2nd Lt William J. Campbell.

28. John N. Smith, *Airfield Focus 37: Deenethorpe* (GMS 1999). *Bonnie Donnie* and Lt George E. West's crew FTR on 28 May 1944 (three KIA, seven PoW).

3. The Bloody Hundredth and 'Big-B'

1. One wing, composed of two squadrons in the 95th BG and one in the Bloody Hundredth, did not receive the call signal and continued to the capital alone. Fortunately the Mustang escorts were still with the wayward bombers and they provided support in the target area. The return journey was nothing short of a nightmare and was mostly flown through solid layers of clouds, as the formation was forced to descend due to diminishing oxygen supplies. Fourteen minutes from the capital, German fighters attacked. They shot down four B-17s in the 95th and *Seaton's Sad Sack* in the 100th. Stanley M. Seaton and his co pilot, William Clayton, were taken prisoner with seven of the crew. Crews claimed to have dropped the first American bombs on Berlin. They were partly right – thirty-one B-17s bombed the Kleinmachnow area south-west of the capital. On landing, the

exhausted airmen were given a rapturous welcome by the ground crews, who were anxiously 'sweating them out'. Within minutes, both officers and enlisted men were enveloped by the triumphant ground staff and toasted with 'a general issue of double Scotches'. The 95th was awarded its third Presidential Unit Citation and the Bloody Hundredth was similarly awarded later. Eleven bombers were lost in total; seventy-nine heavies hit targets of opportunity, including the port of Wilhelmshaven. Seven fighters were lost. Altogether, the 8th dropped 4,800 tons of high explosive on Berlin in five raids during March 1944.

2. Shields, *History of the 447th Bomb Group.*

3. Ibid. Captain Doyle Shields completed fifty missions, the last on 8 March 1945.

4. Actually, the Luftwaffe airfield at Bergerac in the French Dordogne, just east of Bordeaux.

5. Lt Robert Martin crash-landed the B-24 in a field of green wheat north-east of Cognac. Seven of the crew evaded. Lt Lawson Campbell, the co-pilot, made it to within half a mile of the Spanish border in the Pyrenees when he was captured by a German patrol. See Brett, *The 448th Bomb Group (H).*

6. McCune flew the seriously damaged *Maid of Orleans* to Seething, where the B-24 required a new tail section, bomb bay doors, flaps, two propellers and control cables while numerous patches were applied to the holes in the skin. Three of Lt William Ross's crew evaded (one KIA and six PoW). In all, 219 B-24s were dispatched to bomb airfields in France but bad cloud conditions forced a target change and multiple aborts. See Brett, *The 448th Bomb Group (H).*

7. Richard Le Strange, *Century Bombers: The Story of the Bloody Hundredth* (100th BG Memorial Museum 1989).

8. *Hello Natural*, piloted by 2nd Lt C. C. York.

9. Shields, *History of the 447th Bomb Group.*

10. Hart, who was from Garden City, Kansas, was shot down flying 42-110025 on 8 May 1944 when his Liberator FTR. Seven men were KIA. Hart and two other crewmen were taken prisoner.

11. All ten men in 2nd Lt Eugene H. Whalen's crew were killed. Nine men in Graves' crew were killed and one was taken prisoner.

12. Morgan was captured and sent to Stalag Luft III.

13. Le Strange, *Century Bombers.*

14. *Ibid.*

15. *Ibid.*

16. Five crew perished when B-24 4264457 in the 733rd BS was ditched. Crockett and four of his crew were rescued. (On 25 April 1944, Elmer Crockett was flying B-24 42-95019 when he and his new crew were shot down over France. One evaded and nine crew, including Crockett, were taken prisoner). In the 735th BS, 2nd Lt Henry J. Meek of Los Angeles, California, also ditched in the sea on the 6 March mission.

17. The crew completed their missions on 23 March 1944 and Tedford was transferred from the 93rd BG to the 448th BG as Group Training Officer. He flew one more mission, on D-Day, 6 June 1944, with the *All-American* crew made up of members of many bomb groups and was promoted to captain a few days later. See Walter W. Tedford, *Tedford and the Reddy Teddy*, Bomber Legends Vol. 2 (2005).

18. Thurman Spiva, writing in Castens, *The 446th Revisited.*

19. B-24 42-64460 *Shack Rabbit* in the 733rd BS went down and crashed and exploded at Plantlünne, Germany, with the loss of six crew. Four men survived and were taken prisoner.

20. On 8 March, five 388th Group B-17s failed to return from another raid on Berlin. Most came from the 563rd Squadron. Keirsted's decision to fly all possible missions had paid off for the crew of *The Worry Wart.* Dopko and the crew of *Little Willie* went down on 9 March. All ten crew were taken prisoner.

21. US fighters claimed eighty-one enemy fighters shot down and the bomber gunners claimed ninety-seven destroyed; the Luftwaffe actually lost sixty-two fighters destroyed, two damaged beyond repair and thirteen damaged. This was a loss rate of 12.5 per cent of those committed to action. Altogether, the Luftwaffe lost forty-four aircrew and twenty-three wounded. NJG5 lost ten of the fourteen Bf 110s dispatched and ZG26 lost eleven out of eighteen Bf 110s and Me 410s it sent up.

22. Bill McCullah recalls, 'Kenneth Dyer was listed as MIA and his mother was officially notified. His mother called my mother in Missouri, telling her that Crew 11 was MIA. This created an uproar, which took several weeks to untangle. Since Kenneth and I were assigned to the same crew, it was a reasonable assumption that Crew 11 was indeed missing.' Kenneth Dyer later took a job in a shipyard and he married a Swedish girl before returning to the States after the war.

23. *A Good Ship & Happy Ship* was later converted to a civil airliner (SE-BAM). On 4 December 1945 it crashed at Mariefred, killing six on board. See Bo Widfeldt and Rolp Wegmann, *Making For Sweden ... Part 2 – The USAAF* (ARP 1998).

24. Adapted from the story by Lt Hubert Cripe in 1944, written while a PoW on a book of blank paper furnished to the PoWs by the YMCA. (Also killed were staff sergeants Gerald B. Yoder, ball turret gunner, and John H. McGue, tail gunner). When Cripe's story was printed in the spring 1988 *2nd Air Division Journal* ('The Rough Edges' by Ken Stevens) the ink by then 'was a little faded and the paper beginning to yellow'. But Hubert Cripe's memory was as vivid 'as it was when he touched his pen to the paper'.

25. Margaret Hawkes Lindsley, '21 Forever', in *2nd Air Division Journal*.

4. Death or Glory?

1. The 392nd suffered its heaviest single mission loss, losing fifteen Liberators and crews and nine other B-24s damaged by fighters and flak, all totalling 154 casualties. Strickler, who became a PoW, was the only survivor on Books' crew. He died aged eighty-five.

2. *Shif'lus Skonk!* crashed at Hanover. Six of Bohnet's crew, including Charles F. Zimmer, who like Bohner was from Brooklyn, New York, and Robert E. Gilbreath of Fort Payne, Alabama, were KIA. Four men, including Herschel H. Carter of Blythevle, Arizona, were taken prisoner.

3. All ten men on Lt James A. Merriman's crew were KIA.

4. In the defence against daylight high-altitude attacks, the co-operation of flak and fighters and the operation of the *Grossbatterien* proved successful. In spite of the continual loss of young personnel to the fronts, Germany found it possible to double the numbers of personnel, principally by decreasing the personnel per battery and using the *Reichsarbeitsdienst* and approximately 75,000 *Luftwaffenhelfer* (schoolboys) from higher schools. All schoolboys in Germany at age sixteen had to enter the flak school in their neighbourhood. This decision had been taken after the German disaster at Stalingrad, when thousands of soldiers within the borders of the Fatherland were needed for frontline duties. In addition, approximately 15,000 women and girls, 45,000 volunteer Russian PoWs and 12,000

Croatian soldiers were drafted in to the air defence of the Reich. 'On the one hand the *Luftwaffenhelfer* had the same duties as soldiers; on the other hand our teachers had to continue our education as well as possible.'

5. Lt Norman Chapman and his crew, who had been hit earlier by fighters but had stayed in formation and dropped their bombs on Berlin, left the formation after the target and all the crew bailed out. They were taken prisoner.

6. *The Hard Way* and Lt Joseph C. Thomas' crew were lost on 15 May 1944 (four KIA, six PoW). *Lucky Lady* and Lt Richard F. Noble's crew FTR on 12 May 1944. *Dog Breath* and Lt Clark G. Graham's crew were interned in Spain on 19 June 1944.

7. *Mon Tete Rouge II* and 2nd Lt Lawrence Downy Jr's crew were lost on 4 December 1944 (three KIA, six PoW).

8. A year later, the 100th was awarded a second Presidential Unit Citation for its Berlin actions on 4, 6 and 8 March.

9. Shields, *History of the 447th Bomb Group.*

10. Six of the crew were captured but the other four evaded.

11. Kenneth Jewell was awarded the DSC. He was fitted out with an artificial leg and he resumed flying duties in February 1945. He retired as a much-decorated major in 1946 and he went on to become a judge in his home state of Pennsylvania and the father of four children.

12. After his recuperation, Burt Joseph was sent to Stalag Luft III, near Sagan in what is now Poland. There followed the usual PoW camp experiences of starvation, forced march evacuations, liberation, and eventual return home to a successful civilian career. The Alabama Chapter, *Propwash/8th Air Force News*, December 2007.

13. Shields, *History of the 447th Bomb Group.* In all, 679 bombers were detailed to hit factory and airfield targets in Germany.

14. (Two Evd; two KIA, six PoW).

15. Shields, *History of the 447th Bomb Group.*

16. Jean-Pierre Wilhelm and Roy Thomas, 'Fishing for Fortresses', in *Flypast* magazine.

17. Nine men in Dalton's crew were KIA and one evaded. In Anderson's crew, seven were KIA and three were taken prisoner.

18. Altogether, forty-three bombers and thirteen escorting fighters were lost on the 18 March raids. The 2nd BD lost twenty-eight of these, the 1st and 3rd eight and seven respectively, and thirteen fighters FTR.

19. All of the crew except Colonel Miller, who landed in a French field and was soon in the hands of the French Resistance, were taken prisoner. Miller, disguised as a priest, made his way across France to Perpignan. He was captured wearing civilian clothing by a German border patrol as he waited to cross into Spain and handed over to the Gestapo. While in his cell, Miller thought back to 1938 when three German officers were attempting to set a new record flying from Berlin to Tokyo. Over the South China Sea, their Heinkel developed engine trouble and they were forced to land in the Philippines. The AAC in Manila had already picked up their distress calls and a rescue mission led by Colonel Miller found them. Miller told his Gestapo interrogators of the incident. The Gestapo chief of the Paris region, T. T. Schmidt, conferred with Major Junge, the deputy commander at Oberusel, who, as luck would have it, was the pilot of the record attempt from Berlin to Tokyo. Junge recounted the rescue and Schmidt casually remarked that he was holding an American colonel by the name of Joe Miller in Paris. Junge was convinced it was the man who had rescued him in 1938. He made a positive identification and Miller was sent to Luft III.

20. In 1945 Bill Rose returned to the 92nd BG and flew part of a second tour.

21. 'Our trails didn't cross again until 1951, in Roswell, New Mexico. I was overjoyed to see the Chief again. Even though our get together was short lived, he took me to his home in Mountainview, Oklahoma where I met his wonderful wife Maggie, his now growing family and a son named for me, Stuart Barr Wahnee. He took me to an Indian Pow-Wow while we were there and explained all the Indian traditions taking place. The Chief was a very real person in my life and he, among all the others I've met, had a greater philosophical influence on my continued existence than anyone since I had left my parents. I would often think of him and I will always be proud to have known him and to have gained his respect.' Stuart K. Barr, 'The Comanche; The Double American – The Chief', in *2nd Air Division Journal*.

22. Mastronardi was recommended for the DFC and it was only on 21 October 1987, forty-three years after the event, that he returned to England to receive his award at RAF Alconbury with his three friends – T. J. Krol, W. R. Rusch and J. Katsaros – by his side.

23. Twelve bombers failed to return.

24. The Attlebridge group lost two B-24s in a mid-air collision. Two days later, the weather was responsible for the loss of two more 466th ships, which were involved in a second mid-air collision near Osterburg. On 27 March two more collided, shortly after take-off from Attlebridge.

25. 2nd Lt Eldred F. Wipple's crew failed to reach Sweden. Harry Hawkins was among the survivors. Their B-17 crashed at Pfarlhausen with the loss of five men killed. Five survived to be taken prisoner. Two days later, Harry Cornell's crew were shot down on the raid to Frankfurt. Leo Hartman was killed on the mission. T/Sgt Gidel had his foot shot off. He was repatriated and sent back to the USA. Sgt Logan was never caught. A Belgian family hid him until the Allies liberated Belgium. Cornell, Eddy and Mayer were all interned at Stalag Luft III. Sergeants Sage and Martinson, Wolak and John Kettman were interned in Stalag Luft IV. All four were on the enforced march for eighty-seven days from Stalag Luft IV to central Germany from February to April 1945. Postwar, Eddy was killed while flying in the Berlin Airlift. Cornell was killed in a flying accident in the USA.

26. Charles E. Clague Jr, *Climbing High with Sweater Girl, Miss Stardust and Others* (July 2002).

27. *Sunrise Serenade* and Lt Francis C. Smedley's crew FTR on 1 May 1944 (one KIA, nine PoW). *Round Tripper* and 2nd Lt Frank W. Brogan's crew FTR on 29 May 1944 (six Evd, four PoW). *Lady Satan* was lost with Lt James L. Bayless' crew on 6 February 1945 (one KIA, eight PoW). *Punched Fowl* was lost with Lt Edwin V. Arey's crew on 4 August 1944 (one KIA, eight PoW).

28. Adapted from the diary of Mac Meconis' missions, first published in the 466th history, *Attlebridge Diaries*.

29. 41-28590 and 42-110033.

30. Gordon K. Reynolds, *A Lasting Scar*.

31. *Judith Lynn* crashed at Bougemeron. All nine crew were KIA.

32. See Caldwell, *The JG 26 War Diary Vol. 2.*

33. En route to Ludwigshafen, the 44th and 392nd BGs veered off course when the command pilot in the PFF lead ship, whose Mickey set had malfunctioned as the formations departed the English coast, decided to carry on to the target. Without visual reference to the terrain, Captain C. H. Koch, the 392nd lead navigator, had to rely solely upon pre-briefed estimates of winds aloft to carry out his dead-reckoning type of navigation.

There must have been quite a change in both the direction and velocity of the winds aloft because the formations were blown 120 miles to the right of course and 50 miles further in distance. Twenty-six B-24s in the 392nd had dropped 1,184 100 lb bombs on a forested area 3 miles south-east of the Swiss town of Schauffhausen, over 120 miles from Ludwigshafen. The mistake led to America paying the Swiss thousands of dollars in reparations. Koch was rebuked and never again allowed to perform the function of lead navigator.

34. They also captured the PFF set intact but its importance was overlooked and it was left in the aircraft, which was guarded by two soldiers. Two days later, three of the B-24 crew who were in the care of the French underground returned to the crash site and overpowered the guards and destroyed the equipment. 41-28763 was from the 564th Squadron, 389th BG, at Hethel.

35. Marc Hamel, writing in *Air Classics*, says: 'Henderson had progressed through flight school showing the skill and inclination of a fighter pilot and so was sent to single-engine training. Achieving the third highest score in gunnery and being chosen to lead the graduation ceremony formation certainly had him primed to fly fighters. Upon graduation however, he was inexplicably diverted intro multi-engine and thus was posted as a co-pilot to the 713th BS, 448th BG. Cater Lee, bombardier in Henderson's first crew when he was a co-pilot, recalls that Henderson was "incensed".'

36. Buland and his crew were lost a week later, on 8 April, when his Liberator took a hit in the bomb bay. Three of Buland's crew were KIA and six survived to be taken prisoner. Howie Mesnard and Charlie Clague were not flying with the crew this day.

37. On 9 April, when 104 Liberators took off from East Anglia for a raid on the aircraft assembly plant at Tutow, Mosley and the crew of *Carol Marie* failed to return. They made it to Sweden and were interned.

5. The Quick and the Dead

1. Elwood Nothstein, writing in the *2nd AD Journal*.
2. One of the waist gunners, Sergeant Larry Muscarella, stayed and married a Swedish girl. He also attended the University in Stockholm for a while before returning to the United States. Widfeldt and Wegmann, *Making For Sweden ... Part 2*.

3. Allan Healy, *The 467th BG September 1943 – June 1945* (Privately Published 1947.)

4. S/Sgt G. Prager, the tail gunner, was the only other survivor.

5. The 2nd Bomb Division penetrated the German border before turning back and the 3rd turned back shortly after the French coast. The 1st turned back before the French coast.

6. 'Mission To Zwickau', as told to Dave Patterson by Mike Ciano, *2nd Air Division Journal*. Pavelka, of Colueland, Ohio, and Pete Clark and one other member of the crew evaded. Mike Ciano, Luce and the four others on the crew were taken prisoner. In all, the 445th BG lost five B-24s, including *Nine Yanks And A Jerk* and *Tennessee Dottie*.

7. Shields, *History of the 447th Bomb Group*.

8. *Nostalgic Notes* (the 94th BG Newsletter), September 1982, and *Sacramento Bee*, 14 November 1982.

9. Ben Smith Jr, *Chick's Crew: A tale of the Eighth Air Force* (Privately Published 1978, 1983, 2006).

10. Shields, *History of the 447th Bomb Group*.

11. Bill Griffiths, 'April 21, 1944: 1700 Hours', in *2nd Air Division Journal*, Winter 1987–88.

12. Lt Eugene Pulcipher and crew, flying *Repluser*, crashed in marshland near Kessingland at 2220 hours. All the crew perished. Lt Cherry Pitts and crew were killed when 42-529608 exploded and fell into the sea.

13. Allen Welters, 'Another Slice of Hamm – From the Ground Up!', in the *2nd Air Division Journal*.

14. Del Wangsvick, 'Bandits In Our Formation', in the *2nd Air Division Journal*.

15. David was also taken up on air tests and some training flights in *Fat Stuff* and *Hello Natural*. Dick Wickham, *The War At My Door*.

16. 1st Lieutenant Melvin L. Alspaugh.

17. *2nd Air Division Journal*, spring 1988. Avery went to the flight line the next morning and the crew chief counted about ninety holes in *Chumbly*. 'Baldy' Avery's crew FTR on 7 May 1945. All thirteen men survived and they were taken prisoner.

18. *Flak Magnet* in the 753rd Squadron was shot down on the raid.

19. See Ian McLachlan, *Night of the Intruders* (PSL 1994).

20. Major Kenneth L. Driscoll (USAF, Ret.), '"Surprise" Attack on Hamm, Germany, 22 April 1944', in the *2nd Air Division Journal*. In 1944 Kenneth Driscoll flew five daylight B-24 bombing missions with the 467th BG and

thirty secret night missions with the 801st/492nd BG – The Carpetbaggers – dropping spies and supplies to support the French underground forces. See Martin W. Bowman, *The Bedford Triangle: US Undercover Operations from England in World War 2* (PSL 1988).

21. See McLachlan, *Night of the Intruders.*

22. Wallach was held at a Swiss hospital for several months, during which time a bullet from one of the Swiss fighters was removed from his side. He escaped from Switzerland and, in November 1944, returned to the United States. Wilhelm and Thomas, 'Fishing for Fortresses'.

23. A funeral service was held in Berne on 27 April before the bodies were interned at Munsingen, where some time before US military authorities had acquired a cemetery. All ten crewmembers on 42-21529, flown by 2nd Lt Earl Howard Jr, were taken prisoner after their B-17 was shot down by fighters and crashed at Weissback, Germany. The B-17 flown by 2nd Lt Richard P. Anthony also fell victim to fighters. All the crew survived, eight being taken prisoner and two evading capture. *Butch*, piloted by 2nd Lt Bernard Rosenfeld, and 42-97203, flown by Lt William W. Parramore, were the two other 92nd BG B-17s that failed to return.

24. Robert E. Oberschmid, writing in 'Three Brief Glimpses of the Air War', in the *2nd Air Division Journal.*

25. Tom O'Brien, writing in Dave Osborne, 'The Reunion 1942–1992' and 'Stars & Bars: They Meet Again,' in *Flypast* magazine.

26. Correspondence with John A. Miller, right waist gunner in Lt Larry Townsend's crew. See Martin W. Bowman, *Castles In The Air* (PSL 1984).

27. Major Osce Jones and William B. Blackmon Jr were the only survivors and they were taken into captivity.

28. Lt Orland Howard, flying *Big Bad Wolf*, left the formation over Berlin after flak knocked out three engines and disabled the nose turret on the bomb run. The crew reached Denmark and bailed out over Bornholm in the Baltic Sea. One man died after his parachute failed to open. Two crew were captured and the rest were picked up by the Danish Resistance, who got them to Sweden. Lt John Cathey's crew bailed out. Sgt Jack Arluck perished in the crash but the rest of the crew bailed out safely. German guards shot and killed the bombardier, Flight Officer Carl Carlson, when he refused to pack his parachute. The other B-24s in the Group that FTR were *Sad Sack* (six KIA, three PoW), *Miss Happ* (one KIA, nine PoW), *Sweet Sioux II* (crew

interned in Sweden) and *Chubby Champ* (five PoW, five KIA). See Brett, *The 448th Bomb Group (H)*.

29. It was not until the Liberators reached the Dummer Lake on the homeward journey that P-47 fighter escorts reappeared. German ground controllers, however, seized upon the time lapse and directed over 100 fighters to the Hannover area to intercept. Lt William Moore's B-24 in the 467th BG, which carried Major Robert Salzarulo, CO of the 788th BS, was shot down over Holland. He and the crew were later reported to be prisoners. Lt John L. Low, the Group Bombardier, evaded capture for 296 days in enemy-occupied Holland and was liberated on 29 April 1945.

30. Twenty-five Liberators were lost, including a 458th BG B-24, which was forced to land in Sweden.

31. Dale R. Van Blair, 'Target: Berlin', in the *2nd Air Division Journal*.